Park Prisoners

Park Prisoners

*The Untold Story of Western Canada's
National Parks, 1915–1946*

BILL WAISER

SASKATOON
& CALGARY

FIFTH
HOUSE
PUBLISHERS

Front cover photographs courtesy John Luckhurst
and Glenbow-Alberta Institute/NA-1870-6
Back cover photograph courtesy Western Canada Pictorial Index/442-14220
Cover design by John Luckhurst/GDL
Maps by George Duff

The publisher gratefully acknowledges the support received from
The Canada Council, Heritage Canada, Multiculturalism and Citizenship
Canada, and the Saskatchewan Arts Board.

Printed and bound in Canada by Friesens, Altona, MB
95 96 97 98 99 / 5 4 3 2 1

CANADIAN CATALOGUING IN PUBLICATION DATA
Waiser, W.A.

   Park prisoners

   Includes bibliographical references and index.
   ISBN 1-895618-65-7 (bound)
   ISBN 1-895618-74-6 (pbk.)

1. Canada - History - 1914– * 2. National parks
and reserves - Canada, Western - History. 3. World
War, 1914-1918 - Conscript labor - Canada.
4. World War, 1939-1945 - Conscript labor - Canada.
5. Forced labor - Canada - History. I. Title.

FC540.W35 1995   971.06   C95-920150-5
F1034.W35 1995

FIFTH HOUSE LTD.
620 Duchess Street
Saskatoon, SK, Canada
S7K 0R1

#9 - 6125 - 11 St. S.E.
Calgary, AB, Canada
T2H 2L6

Contents

For Dad
Hope Relief Project, 1933

PREFACE AND ACKNOWLEDGEMENTS

*P*ARK PRISONERS *HAD ITS BEGINNINGS IN THE LATE SPRING OF 1989* when a small group of friends spent a day in Prince Albert National Park trying to locate former relief-camp sites in the bush. That evening, over dinner, the conversation revolved around the camps and the men who had spent time there, and how many other parks had served as a temporary home or prison for Canada's "unwanted." I decided to look into the question in greater detail, and the idea for the book followed from there. Several people, agencies, and institutions have helped along the way, and without their kind assistance, the story would be far from complete.

Funding for *Park Prisoners* was generously provided by the Multicultural-ism Sector, Department of the Secretary of State; the Prairie and Northern Regional Office of the Canadian Parks Service; and the University of Saskatche-wan (President's Publication Fund, President's SSHRCC Fund; Messer Fund for Canadian Studies). During my many field and research trips to national parks, archival institutions, and government offices, I received assistance and advice from a number of individuals, in particular Susan Buggey, Candace Loewen, Gabrielle Blais, Patrick Burden, Susan Kooyman, Don Bourden, John Parry, Ken Kaiser, Bill Yeo, Celes Davar, Ken Green, Gordon Rutherford, Ann Landry, and John Turnbull. I would also like to thank Rick Stuart, who arranged for my access to former national park records–this included being fingerprinted by the RCMP and screened by CSIS. Merv Syroteuk often took time from his hectic schedule to tramp around in the woods and help me try to find some of the former camp sites. Walter Hildebrandt valiantly offered to carry me out of the bush the day that I slipped and broke my ankle. And Cal Sime and Helen Elder helped me back on my bike when the front wheel came flying off while speeding along a trail towards Camp Otter.

Several students–Laura Zink, Joan Champ, Regan Muir, Bill Martin, John Bonnett, and Bruce Shelvey–diligently combed through newspapers, parlia-mentary debates, annual reports, and secondary literature for any information about the men and the camps. Steve Hewitt provided copies of a number of federal documents related to his own research on the RCMP in the interwar period. The project also greatly benefitted from the many friends and colleagues who read and reacted to all or part of the book in its various stages: Jim English, Graham MacDonald, Jim Miller, Ted Regehr, Pat Roy, Jim Taylor, and Alex Zellermeyer. George Duff drew the maps, while Jean Horosko and Shirley Thiessen helped with the preparation of the photographs.

I have three special thank-yous. First, I am greatly indebted to the many informants who talked openly about their lives, shared their feelings and stories, and provided generous doses of encouragement and inspiration. Their contribution to Canada's special places should never be forgotten. I also wish to thank my family, who heard parts of the book, especially during our many holiday trips to the parks, and probably wondered at times whether I was a prisoner to my computer. Finally, I owe a special debt of gratitude to Fifth House Publishers, which patiently waited for the completion of the book—and to editor Nora Russell, who kept asking during the editorial phase, "Who *are* these guys, Bill?" I hope I've answered her question.

*I*T WAS THE SECOND TRIP HE HAD MADE TO THE PARK IN AS MANY years, and he was not going to be disappointed again—even if it meant crossing a picket line for the lifelong trade unionist. Clutching a handful of yellowing photographs, Joe Gabski of Chico, California, was allowed past striking public service employees at Riding Mountain National Park on 11 September 1991 and entered the administration building. Here, he was briefly introduced to the superintendent before being turned over to the chief park interpreter. He spent the morning going over the pictures with his incredulous host and then cycled several miles along an old road to the site of the former German prisoner-of-war camp on Whitewater Lake. He had finally returned—keeping the pledge that he had made to himself almost fifty years earlier.

Gabski was not the first German soldier to come back to Riding Mountain. Thirteen years earlier, in July 1978, George Foerster, an egg producer from Ullstadt, West Germany, attended one of the evening interpretation programmes and revealed afterwards that he had spent almost two years during the war cutting fuelwood in the heart of the park. There are other men with similar pasts. Frank Goble of Cardston, Alberta, served as a cook in the Waterton Lakes relief camps and gladly shows interested park visitors where every one of the camps was located along the Akamina and Big Chief Highways while he regales them with stories of the men, the work, and the times. Abe Dick of Winnipeg, who performed alternate service work in both Banff and Jasper National Parks during the Second World War, remembers being shuttled from one park to the other along the Banff-Jasper highway in the back of an open truck in the dead of winter, and trying to thaw out during a break at the Columbia Icefields. When he visited the site of one of his former camps near the Maligne Canyon bridge a few years ago, he broke down and wept. A former Japanese resident of the Fraser Valley, however, will never go back. Ordered from British Columbia in February 1942, he and his father were separated from their family and sent to work on the Jasper section of the Yellowhead–Blue River highway. "It has been a very hard experience at that time of my youth," he wrote from Toronto, "and a bitter pill to swallow."

These men, and several thousand others, were sent to Canada's mountain and prairie national parks between 1915 and 1946 as part of a general government effort to remove them from Canadian society. They were Canada's unwanted—unskilled foreign workers, the jobless and the homeless, pacifists, possible subversives and enemies of the state, and prisoners of war. They were men who, because of war or depression, found themselves viewed with unease or mistrust, sometimes even fear and hatred. Their crime was who they were—not necessarily what they did—and they were seen as a genuine threat to public order and a potential source of civil unrest. The Canadian government consequently wanted to find a place to put them, as well as keep them busy. It was not enough to round them up and essentially intern them in remote areas until circumstances changed or conditions improved; they were expected to perform labour-intensive tasks that would keep them occupied and at the same time contribute to the country in some small way.

Western Canada's national parks needed and coveted this kind of labour. The parks system was not only undergoing a period of expansion, but also wanted to take advantage of the coming of the automobile to attract a wider public. Parks were actively promoted at the time as a promising source of tourist dollars, as well as a natural antidote for the ills of modern life. But to fulfil this role as national playgrounds, they had to be developed and made more accessible; they needed visitor facilities and roads. It was not enough simply to set aside special natural areas to be forever untouched in their wilderness state. National parks were like any other natural resource and existed to be utilized for their scenery and recreation. Otherwise, their true value to Canadian society and the economy would never be realized.

Park Prisoners is the untold story of the national park labour camps. It explains why various groups were sent to work in western Canada's national parks, when and where they were placed, and how they were housed and treated. It also documents how the park internees were employed and the conditions under which they toiled, as well as describing the various projects they tackled. Finally, it demonstrates how the men made a significant contribution to the development and maintenance of Canada's so-called special places during the troubled years of war and depression—what they created through their labour for future generations of Canadians to enjoy.

CHAPTER ONE

Aliens

O N THE MORNING OF FRIDAY, 12 MARCH 1915, MAJOR-GENERAL SIR
William Otter and J.B. Harkin met briefly at the Banff railway
station.[1] Otter was a distinguished career soldier, a virtual living
legend, who had helped repulse the Fenians in 1866, led a misguided
attack against the Cree chief Poundmaker during the 1885 North-West Rebellion, and commanded the second Canadian battalion during the South African
War. The day before the start of the First World War, he had offered to serve in
any capacity—even though he had been retired since 1912—and was appointed
by the Borden government two months later as director of Canadian Internment Operations. James Bernard Harkin, on the other hand, had been a
parliamentary journalist and then private secretary to the Liberal ministers of
the Interior, Clifford Sifton and Frank Oliver, before being named to the new
position of dominion parks commissioner in 1911. Nicknamed "Bunny," he was
a tireless promoter of the recuperative value of outdoor activity and an early
advocate of wildlife conservation.

That Otter and Harkin would be meeting in Banff seven months into the war
might seem somewhat unusual. But the men needed each other. When Canada
went to war against Germany, Austria-Hungary, Turkey, and Bulgaria in August
1914, there were over half a million people living in Canada linked in some way
to the enemy countries.[2] At first, the Conservative administration of Robert
Borden counselled restraint and toleration, but as public fears about possible
enemy subversion escalated, there was intense pressure to limit and control the
activities of the alien population, especially the approximately eighty thousand
who were still unnaturalized.[3] The government responded in late October with
an order-in-council, proclaimed under the provisions of the new War Measures
Act and modelled after similar British legislation,[4] which established a national
system of civilian registration centres in Canadian cities. Enemy aliens living
within twenty miles of the offices were required by law to register and report

monthly. Failure to report, or any other breach of the regulations, resulted in internment. Those caught trying to leave Canada without permission or otherwise considered a security threat were also imprisoned.[5] Within weeks of the cabinet order, several hundred men had been detained by local registrars or rounded up by the police; eventually over eight thousand individuals would be held in some two dozen stations and camps across the country.[6]

As director of Internment Operations, General Otter was responsible for the care, maintenance, and employment of all prisoners of war. This last duty—finding work—was one of his most vexing problems in the early months of the war, particularly as the numbers under his care continued to climb.[7] The Canadian public was not simply content to see enemy aliens interned; they had to be put to work and not allowed to laze about at government expense while Canadian soldiers lost their lives on the battlefields of Europe. Arranging suitable employment, however, was not an easy task, given the anti-alien hysteria that gripped the country, and Otter initially concentrated his energies on establishing work camps in northern Ontario and Quebec—at Petawawa, Kapuskasing, and Spirit Lake—well away from major centres. That still left western Canada, which had received the bulk of the new immigration in the early twentieth century. And it was to confer about possible Internment labour projects with government officials such as Harkin that Otter headed west in March 1915.

J.B. Harkin was confronted with exactly the opposite problem. The new dominion parks commissioner regarded parks as a kind of tonic for the everyday ills of city life and believed that Canadians would be a better people—physically, mentally, and morally—by imbibing the recreational benefits of these national playgrounds. He also foresaw parks playing a leading role in the underrated Canadian tourist industry, especially if they were made more accessible to automobile traffic.[8] Harkin was consequently preoccupied with road building during his first few years in office, and contemplated a number of possible park road projects while seeking the latest expert advice on construction techniques.[9] These plans were jeopardized, however, when war was declared and the Borden government sliced the annual Parks appropriation in half. Not overly discouraged by this turn of events, Harkin simply changed tactics, arguing that national parks would help heal the national soul once hostilities were over. In the interim, though, as the war degenerated into a prolonged, bloody stalemate, few park development projects would get beyond the planning stages without money and manpower. It was not surprising, then, that Harkin and Otter reached a tentative agreement at their Banff meeting to begin using Internment labour in the mountain national parks that coming summer.

·   ·   ·

The men who were to be made available to the national parks service were technically prisoners of war. In reality, however, the majority of the internees were unemployed or destitute Ukrainians from Galicia and Bukovyna in the

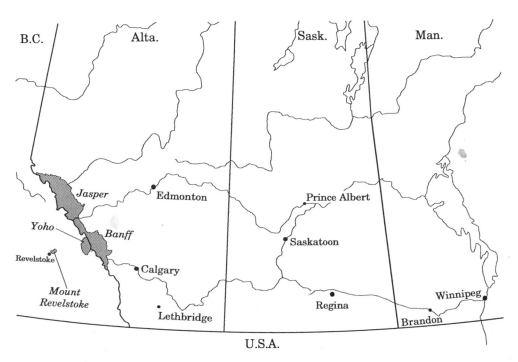

National Park Enemy Alien Camps, First World War.

Austro-Hungarian Empire.[10] These people had been brought to Canada in increasingly large numbers in the years immediately prior to the outbreak of the war to serve as a temporary, industrial workforce. In fact, it is one of the great myths of Canadian history that only immigrant farmers entered Canada during the boom years of the early twentieth century. The enormous development projects of this period, in particular the construction of two new transcontinental railways, required a vast pool of unskilled labour, which would work not only cheaply but also under adverse conditions in isolated regions of the country. And the people who were deliberately sought by Canadian business to fill this "guest worker" role were mainly unattached males from continental Europe who would labour at various jobs for a few years and then return home.[11]

This migrant labour force initially generated little public interest or concern, especially since the men lived in relative isolation on the margins of Canadian society. But as the boom years gave way to a recession in 1912 and the economy hobbled into war, thousands of unskilled foreign workers began to drift into western Canadian cities in search of employment and, more importantly, relief. Here they were received coolly—if not with revulsion—and forced to eke out a miserable existence in crowded, filthy, urban ghettos.[12] They were Canada's "pauper immigrants"—"ignorant foreigners" at the best of times, the "scum of Europe" at the worst. And Canadians were afraid not only that this imported proletariat could not be assimilated, but also that it would drag down western society and destroy forever the British character of the country.[13]

The coming of war compounded the men's plight and also caused their numbers to swell. Immigrants from Austria-Hungary—already scorned for their language, religion, and habits—now faced the added stigma of being enemy aliens and were dismissed from their jobs in large numbers for "patriotic" reasons. Many had been in the country for only a few months. It was an ironic twist of fate that almost half the record four hundred thousand immigrants who had entered Canada the year before the war were from central and southern Europe.[14]

With the outbreak of war, the Canadian public grew increasingly alarmed about the presence of these men in their midst. Any peacetime toleration of these immigrants was now overridden by concerns about their nationality and loyalty. And it is easy to see why they were feared. Since these migrant workers had no intention of remaining in Canada, most had not bothered to become naturalized and hence were still citizens of their home countries.[15] Many were still classified as reservists in the Austro-Hungarian army. In their search for work, these men also travelled to and from the United States, an unfortunate pattern since it was widely believed at the beginning of the war that American-based subversives posed the greatest security threat to Canada.[16] As a result, Austro-Hungarian workers became objects of suspicion and paranoia, and the federal government was inundated with demands to do something about them, along with other persons of enemy nationality. Close surveillance revealed, however, that Canadians had absolutely nothing to fear from these people. Colonel A.B. Perry, commissioner of the Royal Northwest Mounted Police, said as much when he advised Ottawa in late February 1915 that he had discharged all but one of "our high-priced Secret Service Agents," including the man disguised as a barber in Edmonton, who had been hired by the force at the beginning of the war to infiltrate the immigrant community. "The closest investigation," Perry reported from Regina, "has not revealed the slightest trace of any organization or concerted movement amongst the alien enemies."[17] As far as the commissioner was concerned, public fears about these people seemed to be groundless; his men had yet to discover a single case of sabotage. This assessment of the situation in western Canada was echoed in the House of Commons one year later by William Martin, a Saskatchewan MP and future premier of the province, who calmly observed in response to heated calls for increased vigilance, "I am . . . inclined to look upon these people . . . as being entitled to a certain amount of consideration."[18]

Such sentiments, however, were an exception, and as the war called for higher levels of sacrifice, westerners demanded increasingly repressive measures against enemy aliens, including the suppression of their newspapers, the closure of their schools, and the elimination of their vote. M. Donaldson, the

Winnipeg-based general manager of the Grand Trunk Pacific Railway, for example, was greatly worried that "the foreign element" might rise up along the rail line in eastcentral Saskatchewan, and urged the imposition of martial law before it was too late.[19] The Edmonton *Journal* went a step further, suggesting that even naturalized citizens from enemy countries were a potential menace and should be interned "where there is at all a reasonable doubt."[20] These immigrants, whatever their contributions to western development, had never really been welcome in Canada, and the war provided nativists with an unparalleled opportunity to strike a blow for all things British. As the Swift Current *Sun* smugly observed, "This has been brewing for a long time, but the war has brought it to a head, and Anglo-Saxons to their senses."[21]

The Borden government initially resisted implementing any restrictive measures. It was fully aware of the Mounted Police surveillance reports on enemy alien activity, for it approved the massive discharge of three hundred men from the force one year after the beginning of the war. It had also been advised by the British Foreign Office as early as 1915 that Ukrainian labourers from Austria-Hungary did not constitute a threat.[22] What evidently troubled the Conservative government during the opening months of the war, however, was not that these unemployed workers were potential saboteurs, but that they were massing in the thousands in major urban centres. And the problem

The Castle Mountain camp, Canada's first internment facility in a national park.
Glenbow Archives, Millican Collection, NA–1870–18

seemed about to get worse; in October 1914, Prime Minister Robert Borden warned the British government that up to one hundred thousand enemy aliens could be released from their jobs that coming winter.[23] When these men joined those already sidelined by the prewar recession, Ottawa could have a major crisis on its hands, especially when civic and provincial governments had no intention or desire to provide relief to destitute migrant labourers, let alone enemy aliens. The Borden government got a glimpse of what might lie ahead in late May 1914, when two thousand immigrants, mainly unemployed Ukrainians, had marched through the streets of downtown Winnipeg, waving shovels aloft and shouting WORK OR BREAD! Twenty armed policemen were needed to disperse the protest rally, but only after a constable had been beaten for trying to arrest one of the group's leaders.[24] It was certainly not the kind of public event that authorities wanted to see enlarged and repeated, especially during the war. Hungry impoverished men might not stop at demonstrations. It was clear, then, that something had to be done to defuse the growing unemployment crisis among immigrant ranks, or the government could very well face a serious outbreak of civil unrest.[25]

The question of what should be done about displaced workers also troubled business leaders—ironically, many of the same men who had used their influence to override government concerns about allowing this migrant workforce into Canada. During the first month of the war, Thomas Shaughnessy, president of the Canadian Pacific Railway, privately recommended the establishment of voluntary, government camps. This idea had its detractors, such as federal Solicitor General Arthur Meighen, who believed that detention camps might be mistaken for a "lazy man's haven" and that destitute immigrants should be given forty acres and left to fend for themselves.[26] The proposal, however, was doubly attractive to other members of the Borden cabinet because it was not only a way of removing these men from urban centres, but it would also help ease public concerns about internal security. At the same time, Ottawa was not prepared to intern all unemployed labourers or create separate camps for them—the costs of such a policy were much too prohibitive. Nor did it want detention to be voluntary, or the problem in the cities would likely persist.[27] These objectives and concerns were reflected in the government's enemy alien registration and internment policy, which was proclaimed 28 October 1914. Under the terms of the privy council order, only aliens living in urban centres and their immediate vicinity were required to appear before a local registrar; those in rural areas were deliberately excluded because they were not regarded as a problem—real or potential. Aliens who lacked "the means to remain in Canada" were to be interned as prisoners of war and "to do and perform such work as may be . . . prescribed."[28] In other words, Canadian authorities were given the power to detain unemployed or destitute workers from Austria-Hungary and then send them to distant work camps.

Some of the Castle Mountain "enemy aliens." *Glenbow Archives, Carothers Collection, NA-3959-1*

This policy, one of the first acts of a new interventionist state, would be justified later by politicians and officials alike as a generous gesture on the part of the federal government. C.J. Doherty, the federal minister of Justice, explained during a heated debate on enemy alien policy in April 1918 that the unemployed workers had been interned "largely under the inspiration of the sentiment of compassion . . . [rather] than because of hostility."[29] The men were starving because of the glutted labour market, remarked Doherty, and the camps provided temporary asylum. General Otter, for his part, regularly observed during his tenure as director of Internment Operations that municipalities were shirking their responsibility for the unemployed labourers and that Ottawa had stepped into the breach. He even went so far as to suggest in a 1915 interview that internment was "a treat to them [aliens]" and that "they were in no hurry for the war to close."[30]

There was some truth to these comments. In Winnipeg, for example, there had been cases of indigent Ukrainians being gaoled as vagrants for rummaging through garbage cans in search of food; others had asked to be taken into custody to avoid starvation. There had also been more hunger marches in the city, culminating in a trek to the United States in May 1915 by two large groups of unemployed immigrants in search of jobs. When the men who reached the border were stopped and detained by the Mounted Police, a few of them expressed relief at the prospect of regular meals.[31] The real reason behind internment, however, had nothing to do with charity or relief. The Canadian government had never done anything to protect migrant workers from abusive employers before the war, and there was no reason why the government would start to do anything special for them now. The simple truth of the matter is that Ottawa was haunted by the spectre of public disorder and was determined to control the number of unemployed immigrants pouring into urban centres. Meighen, one of the Borden government's most able ministers and a future prime minister, gave this reason for internment shortly after the war had ended. Always forthright, Meighen bluntly told the House that the aliens "were out of work and in that state were a menace to the community."[32]

Curiously, Ottawa's apparent benevolence towards the unemployed aliens did not extend to work. Under the rules of the 1907 Hague Convention, Canada could put prisoners of war—except officers—to work at various tasks, as long as the projects had no connection to the war effort, the labour was not excessive, and the men were paid at a rate equivalent to that of soldiers. In dealing with the workers from Austria-Hungary, however, the Borden government looked upon their internment as an opportunity to use their labour to the fullest; it had no intention of allowing them to attend to duties simply associated with their upkeep. These men had done heavy, manual work under primitive, at times appalling, conditions for resource industries and the railways before the war. And it made perfect sense, from the federal government's point of view, to call upon them to perform the same kind of demanding work during their detention. Justice Minister Doherty, in his typical sanctimonious fashion, attributed noble intentions to this policy. "Handling the matter in this way," he claimed, "we are doing . . . an ultimate benefit to the country generally."[33] W.J. Roche, the federal minister of the Interior, was much more candid during an exchange with Frank Oliver, his Liberal predecessor, in February 1916. Oliver had no qualms about the internment of the men, but was greatly disturbed that they had not committed any crime against the state and yet had to do compulsory labour. Roche replied, "It was thought that it would be better for the men to be doing some work rather than eating their heads off."[34] General Otter subscribed to these same views—as did most of the Canadian public—and he made a clear distinction between enemy nationals from Germany and Austria-Hungary in devising Internment policy during the early months of the war.[35] He regarded

German nationals as a genuine security threat and tried to ensure that they were closely and separately confined. Austro-Hungarians, on the other hand, were considered a sturdy though simple-minded labouring class, and Otter saw it as his duty to find them employment in isolated regions of the country. Canada's mountain national parks would do nicely.

The exact details of this arrangement were worked out between various government departments in the early spring of 1915, and it was not until 19 May that Commissioner Harkin finally learned that the employment of prisoners of war in national parks had been approved.[36] Under the terms of the agreement, the Militia Department would supply the Internment guard, while the Parks Branch would house the men and select the work projects, providing all the necessary equipment, materials, and supervisory personnel; otherwise, the overall operation of the camps and welfare of the prisoners, including any remuneration, remained the responsibility of the Internment Operations Branch and the Department of Justice. The men were expected to work a six-day week at the rate of 25¢ per day. This daily wage was far short—in some cases by as much as $1.00—of what the workers had secured during the prewar boom years, even for the most distasteful jobs.[37] It also compared less favourably with the pay of enlisted men; soldiers received a basic rate of $1.25 per day,

By mid-July 1915, almost two hundred internees had been transferred to their new home—a 120-by-240-foot stockade, with 10-foot barbed wire fence, at the base of Castle Mountain in Banff. *Glenbow Archives, Millican Collection, NA-1870-6*

earning an extra 25¢ for any special work beyond their regular duties. The internees could spend a maximum of $3.00 per month at the canteen for such items as fruit, tobacco, and candy. The balance of their earnings, along with any money, valuables, and other personal items they had in their possession at the time of their internment, were held in trust in the event it was decided at the end of the war to apply these assets against the costs of their maintenance. One can only wonder what the federal Custodian of Enemy Property would have secured for this odd assortment of confiscated material, ranging from passports and personal papers, razors and pocket knives, watches and keys, to a mandolin, pillow, wig, and opera glasses.[38]

Commissioner Harkin would probably have preferred a freer hand and less financial commitment, but the prospect of free labour was extremely attractive and he called upon Parks Engineer J.M. Wardle to draw up an outline of possible highway construction work for the coming summer. He devoutly believed that "the twentieth century [was] to be the century of the automobile as the nineteenth century was the century of railways," and that park roads would "attract touring autoists in the tens of thousands."[39] Once Harkin learned officially that he would have Internment labour at his disposal, he also consulted with Senator Sir James Lougheed and R.B. Bennett, Calgary law partners and members of the Borden government, about his intention to use alien prisoners to work in Rocky Mountain National Park (renamed Banff) on various projects. Lougheed had no qualms about the idea, whereas Bennett, whose Calgary West riding included the park, attached certain reservations to his blessing. He was quite adamant that "these men . . . must be employed in remote portions of the Park where they will not come in contact with the population of this province." He also lectured Harkin that to "give them work and supply them with food and clothing much better than that which can be obtained by our own people would be monstrous."[40] These concerns aside, Lougheed and Bennett used their political muscle to secure ministerial approval for Harkin's plan, and by early June 1915, it was agreed that Canada's first national park would soon become the site of Canada's first internment camp in such a setting.

• • •

The official announcement was made on 19 June by Banff Superintendent S.J. Clarke, who had personally served as Harkin's go-between with Lougheed and Bennett over the past few weeks.[41] Close to two hundred aliens were to be transferred from the Lethbridge internment station to work on the Banff-Laggan (now Lake Louise) highway, which had been completed as far as Castle Mountain; it was expected that the camp would eventually number four hundred men. This announcement ended days of local speculation and rumour. On 10 June, for example, the Calgary *Daily Herald* had reported that a "considerable number of alien enemies will . . . work on a motor road through

Roll call at the Castle Mountain camp. *Glenbow Archives, Millican Collection, NA–1870–5*

the Rocky Mountains."[42] The Banff newspaper, the *Crag and Canyon*, was also rife with stories about the proposed internment camp and endorsed the plan—not only was the labour needed to make up for the reduced park appropriation, but local businesses also stood to benefit from provisioning the camp. At the same time, the paper reminded the public that these men were "enemies of our country" and that camp authorities should "make them work good and hard, with long hours, and guard them well."[43] Ironically, several of the Lethbridge internees were actually local, unemployed immigrants who had been released from their mining jobs only that spring.[44] And their guards, detailed from the 103rd Regiment, Calgary Rifles, were also to be recruited from the local unemployed—the only difference being their nationality.

The Banff internment camp was expected to be in full operation by early July. The site that Superintendent Clarke had selected at the base of Castle Mountain, however, was considered too wet by military authorities, and the camp had to be relocated farther west near Mile 102 on the Canadian Pacific Railway main line. It was therefore not until the middle of the month that the first shipment of 60 prisoners, herded like cattle, arrived by train from Lethbridge; two other consignments over the next few days brought the total number of men to 191 by 19 July.[45]

According to a contemporary report in the *Canadian Annual Review*, the Borden government was "generous" in its treatment of enemy aliens and was reluctant to send anyone to an internment camp "for anything but the most obvious offenses."[46] The personal stories of men, however, suggest a different assessment.[47] Most individuals at the time of their arrest were unnaturalized aliens without work; such was the case of twenty-three-year-old Keyron Kushnu, who had just served two months in the Winnipeg gaol for vagrancy. Many others, like Fred Nykorick and Wasyl Borszcz, were rounded up for failing to register or report. A large number of aliens—for example, brothers John and Philip Marchuk of Bienfait, Saskatchewan—were also interned for attempting to cross into the United States without an exit permit, even though the Royal Northwest Mounted Police commissioner readily admitted that he could not "say that these [men] are a menace to the state."[48] Still others were held under a July 1915 government order that gave authorities the power to apprehend and intern alien workers who had been released from their jobs because of wartime hysteria; the wording of this new law suggested that the action was taken in the interests of protecting the fired men.[49] A few, such as John Dykun, John Letwyn, and Mike Koma, were sent to the camps for falsely enlisting in the Canadian Expeditionary Force, despite their status as enemy aliens. There were also a small number of immigrants, including Iwan Milan of Melville, Saskatchewan, who were hauled before local magistrates for using seditious language or uttering threats, and made prisoners of war for their intemperate behaviour. In most of these instances the men had clearly broken the law—something that they themselves recognized. But what many could not understand was why they were effectively being imprisoned as traitors.[50] This feeling was best expressed by Jacob Kondro of Dalmuir, Alberta, who wrote to military authorities in February 1916 to complain about the internment of his seventeen-year-old son John. A resident of Canada for eight years and a naturalized citizen, the elder Kondro pleaded, "I do not think that Canada would take her own people and put them in an Internment Camp . . . Please let him go."[51]

The Banff internees' new home was a large canvas camp within a 120-by-240-foot stockade surrounded by a 10-foot barbed wire fence in a clearing that had been covered by fire-damaged timber only a few weeks earlier. The castlelike mountain backdrop, combined with the almost constant rain the week of their arrival,[52] probably created an initial sense of unreality. But the men had little time to get their bearings. No sooner had they arrived and been assigned new prisoner numbers than they were put to work on the highway. It was the Parks authorities' plan to have the interned aliens complete the motor road from Banff to Lake Louise (now the Bow Valley Parkway) and, if possible, construct a new road around the lake to the base of the glacier over the next year or so.[53] It was reasoned that if the park was made more accessible by automobile—and not just by the railway—then tourism would grow.

By the end of August 1915, the aliens had cleared and grubbed four miles of new road, grading almost one-quarter of this distance as well. Although Parks Engineer J.M. Wardle found the work satisfactory, he complained to Harkin about the slow pace and the almost constant supervision that the men required; he also expressed the hope that the rate of construction would quicken once the aliens became more familiar with the nature of the job.[54] One wonders, however, what more the men could have accomplished since they were using only picks, shovels, and wheelbarrows.

Using hand tools, the internees worked on a new motor road from Banff to Lake Louise (now the Bow Valley Parkway). *Glenbow Archives, Millican Collection, NA-1870-77*

They were also an unhappy lot. Not only did they resent their captivity—many did not believe that their supposed crime deserved such a punishment—but they also recoiled at the way they were being treated as little more than chattel, and passively resisted in whatever ways they could. In addition, they were the victims of conflicting objectives: the Parks Department wanted them to labour long hours at demanding work, while the Department of Internment Operations was equally determined to reduce the costs of maintenance, especially rations. This situation was perhaps best illustrated on 17 August, when a work gang returned to camp too early and was denied its midday meal, prompting a general hunger strike by the rest of the internees. When one of the prisoners collapsed the next afternoon at the jobsite and the supervising park foreman ordered the suspension of the work programme, camp authorities relented and served the men supper.[55] Adequate nourishment continued to be a problem, however, as evidenced by a despondent letter from Nick Olinyk to his wife: "The conditions here are very poor, so that we cannot go on much longer, we are not getting enough to eat—we are hungry as dogs."[56]

Given these conditions, it was not surprising that the men would try to escape. And run they did. The first successful escape took place only a week after the prisoners had arrived at the camp, when Joseph Jelinick went missing while collecting firewood. Eight others slipped away in one week alone in mid-August: four from a bridge construction site, three during a severe night-

Men leaving the stockade at the Castle Mountain camp, 1915. *Glenbow Archives, Carothers Collection, NA-3959-2*

time thunderstorm, and one in the swirl of smoke from burning garbage.[57] The desperation of the prisoners was underscored by the fact that even so-called "trusties"—men who worked for the troops and usually enjoyed special privileges—ran away at the first opportunity. Not even the threat of being shot by the guards deterred them. Major Duncan Stuart, the commander of the camp, blamed the rash of escapes on the lack of sufficient guards and the location and nature of the work.[58] But it quickly became apparent, as the *Crag and Canyon* noted in a colossal understatement, "that conditions are not just what they should be at the camp."[59] General Otter discovered this for himself during an official inspection of the Castle camp on 24 August, noting in his private diary that the guards lacked experience, the prisoners were being punished by being hung by the wrists, and the commandant was "apparently at odds with everyone, prisoners, troops & civilians."[60]

· · ·

Despite these troubles at Castle, a second national park camp opened in early September 1915 at Mount Revelstoke. This park had been established just one year earlier, essentially to take advantage of the tourist potential of the view from the summit of the nearby mountain. Construction had no sooner got underway, however, than the war brought the work to a standstill with little

The internment facilities at Mount Revelstoke National Park were built into the side of the mountain. *National Archives of Canada, C38296*

more than half the fifteen-mile road completed. The residents of Revelstoke, who had been the driving force behind the creation of the park, were not easily discouraged. Already hurting because of a reduction in railway traffic and forestry activity, they believed that the summit road and the tourism it would generate were the only foreseeable way of lifting the region out of its economic doldrums. So they decided to follow Banff's example and try to complete the road to the top of Mount Revelstoke with interned aliens. As one member of the community remarked at a public meeting on 15 July 1915 to discuss the proposal, "They would be a nice bunch to have in Revelstoke."[61] Getting an internment camp for the park was no easy matter, though, given the number of detention centres already in British Columbia, and it took several weeks of persistent lobbying by the seasoned Conservative MP for the region, R.F. Green, before the idea was endorsed by the government.[62]

Parks Commissioner Harkin visited Mount Revelstoke on 29 July 1915, selecting a site for the camp on the side of the mountain at the point where road construction had been halted. He also took time to remind local citizens in a newspaper interview that "war prisoners are not criminals . . . but are entitled to certain consideration."[63] Because of prisoner complaints about the cold at Banff and the need to keep park expenses to a minimum, it was decided to house the internees in log buildings. These structures, reasoned Harkin, would be warmer and cheaper. They were also quick to put up; construction of the 225-man camp took less than two weeks. General Otter visited Mount Revelstoke on 20 August, just prior to his Castle inspection, and found the campsite to be "cramped for room" and "a difficult place for work."[64] These problems were not considered serious, however, since it was assumed that the aliens would be able to complete the road up the mountain that season.

The Mount Revelstoke camp received its first consignment of prisoners—some 50 Austrians—from the Vernon detention centre on 6 September 1915; an additional 50 followed two days later. The population doubled again when another 100 arrived from Brandon on 18 September.[65] They had a formidable task ahead of them; the road right-of-way had to be cleared and grubbed, several thousand cubic yards of earth and rock dynamited and excavated, and cribbing and culverts installed to keep the new roadbed from sliding away. Even more daunting was the fact that the men were not only expected to do most of the clearing and removal by hand, but they were also trying to beat the first snowfall. The work proceeded without incident in September but was plagued by a number of delays the following month as the prisoners began to protest their forced labour. At first, the alien blacksmiths refused to dress the tools for the road crews. Then, the men decided not to turn out for work for a number of days.[66] Parks authorities tended to blame the camp commandant for not making the men work—he was described as indifferent and lacking energy—and complained to General Otter that the results were not in keeping with the expenditures on the camp.[67] They seem to have forgotten, however, Harkin's own warning to the people of Revelstoke that the internees were not slaves. Nor did they seem to realize that completion of the summit road that fall was nothing short of impossible given the working conditions and the nature of the job itself. Besides, the days of the Mount Revelstoke camp were numbered. Less than a month after the first batch of men arrived, it was determined that the

General Otter, director of Internment Operations, visited the new Mount Revelstoke camp in August 1915. He found the campsite "cramped for room" and "a difficult place to work." *National Archives of Canada, C38295*

camp water supply could not be used during cold weather and the search began immediately for an alternate campsite for the prisoners.[68]

. . .

The Castle camp was also on the move. With the impending approach of winter, military and Parks officials decided to relocate the camp temporarily to the Cave and Basin pool in the Banff townsite, and house the men in two large bunkhouses that had previously been used by construction crews. The transfer of the prisoners and their guards was made by train on 9 November 1915, and within a week, alien work gangs were busily engaged in a number of improvement projects in and around the townsite: brushing the buffalo paddock, clearing the recreation grounds, working at the woodpile and rock crusher, cutting new roads, and building a bridge over the Spray River. Banff residents were naturally pleased and looked forward to the rumoured arrival of several hundred more men from nearby camps that were supposed to be closing down operations over the winter months.[69] Supplying and provisioning the aliens and their captors were expected to be a great boon to local businesses.

The relocation of the Castle camp, in the meantime, did nothing to improve morale. Although the men were now out of their cold, unheated tents, their clothing and footwear were badly in need of replacement—a situation made worse by the arrival of cold weather and snow. Repeated requests by the commandant for a new clothing issue, however, had been greeted with silence throughout the fall. On 1 November 1915, Major Stuart sent his third telegram to Otter seeking authority to purchase some overalls and boots. He followed

During the winters, the Banff internees were temporarily housed near the Cave and Basin pool. *Glenbow Archives, Gushul Collection, NC-54-4336*

The internees lived in large bunkhouses at the Cave and Basin camp on the outskirts of Banff. *Whyte Museum of the Canadian Rockies, Byron Harmon Collection, NA-71-3571*

this request three days later with an impassioned letter to the commander of the local military district, in which he argued that some of the men "preferred to take the chance of being shot while escaping than live under the conditions."[70] The situation was nothing short of horrific. "Some prisoners have boots with their soles half off . . . and nearly half of them are in rags," Stuart told his superior. "I am ashamed to meet them." Within a week the prisoners were finally issued new overalls and woollen mittens. The distribution of the clothing, however, probably had more to do with the upcoming inspection of the camp than with Stuart's pleading.

It is doubtful whether the Canadian public knew, let alone cared, what was going on at Banff and other internment facilities across the country. As the war degenerated into a bloody, prolonged stalemate and the death toll mounted, English-Canadian hostility towards foreign minority groups grew more virulent and strained. Word of camp conditions did nonetheless reach the immigrant community through censored letters to family members or published firsthand accounts in the Ukrainian Social Democratic newspaper, *Robochyi narod* (Working People). In the 28 October 1915 issue, for example, Banff inmate Dmytro Tkachyk described in shocking detail how the men were "mercilessly driven" at bayonet point and often chained and fed bread and water for insubordination.[71] This harsh treatment was confirmed when a representative of the United States Consul office in Calgary, in response to a letter that had been smuggled out of the camp, inspected the new Banff quarters on 14 November. Accompanied by the local military district commander, S.C. Reat heard complaints about the crowded and poorly lit huts, empty palliasses, worn-out shoes, and no change of underwear. A number of prisoners also spoke candidly about incidents with their gaolers. Prisoner Chiskolok related how he had been "forced to work when he was sick and on refusing the guard struck him with his rifle butt and called him a son of a bitch."[72] Another prisoner, J. Hawrysynyzn, explained that he had once tried to avoid work because of the pathetic condition of his clothes and boots by taking refuge in the latrine, and that one of the guards had flushed him out by firing his gun. J. Bilak also tried to skip work one day and was driven from his hiding place at rifle point. Two other men expressed concern about support for their wives. These complaints were dutifully forwarded to General Otter, along with a brief statement of the corrective measures to be taken. Internment officials, however, were not prepared to restrain or reprimand the Banff garrison; although Otter found the brutish behaviour of the guards regrettable, it was apparently in keeping with practices at other internment facilities.[73]

Unfortunately, such incidents would only get worse and more frequent as the guards now went on drinking sprees in Banff saloons. Several were found drunk on duty shortly after the camp had been relocated to the townsite and had to be discharged. Two privates, J. Lee and J. McLeod, were court-martialled for giving liquor to a work party of prisoners they were supposed to be supervising. The most serious trouble occurred, however, when the two senior noncommissioned officers of the guard trashed the camp orderly room in a drunken fit and then tried to blame the vandalism on some fictitious, late-night intruders from one of the nearby immigrant communities.[74] It eventually reached the point, as Otter discovered to his dismay during his second visit to Banff in late November, where the situation was "out of hand,"[75] and he had to ask shortly thereafter for the resignation of the camp commandant because of his "inability to cope with the situation."[76] It was only then, just before Christmas 1915, that an additional two hundred Austrians were shipped from Brandon to Banff.

· · ·

The Mount Revelstoke internees were headed elsewhere. In mid-August 1915, the superintendent of Yoho National Park had suggested that a large group of aliens could be kept busy for several months clearing an area of fire-killed timber almost seven miles from Field, near the junction of the Otterhead and Kicking Horse Rivers.[77] Little was done about the idea—apart from an inspection of the proposed site—until early October, when it became clear that the Mount Revelstoke prisoners had to be relocated. Yoho, Canada's second-oldest national park, was a logical new home for the men, since it was only about a hundred miles east on the Canadian Pacific main line, and thus allowed for an

The new Yoho camp was located some seven miles from Field near the junction of the Otterhead and Kicking Horse Rivers. *National Archives of Canada, C81380*

easy transfer of the prisoners and camp equipment. It also made sense, in the interests of economy and time, to have the internees construct their own prison, especially with winter only a few weeks away. Twenty-five Mount Revelstoke prisoners were consequently dispatched to Yoho on 21 October, only a week after the new camp had received official authorization. Once the stockade had been erected, another twenty-five men arrived at the temporary tent camp to assist with the construction of the buildings.[78] To facilitate this work and the future operation of the camp, the Parks Department made arrangements with the Canadian Pacific Railway for a special spur track near the Otterhead to avoid hauling supplies from Field.

While construction of Camp Otter—named in honour of the director of Internment Operations[79]—continued apace at Yoho, a heavy snowfall effectively ended work on the Mount Revelstoke summit road. The prisoners' primary concern then became one of simple survival as they divided their time, while forlornly awaiting relocation, between shovelling snow by the wheelbarrow out of the compound and felling any nearby trees for firewood. It was as if the world was collapsing in on them—a feeling driven home by the death of one of their own, Anton Marcela.[80] Military and Parks officials tried to accelerate construction of the new Yoho camp by transferring an additional fifty Mount Revelstoke men the second week of November. It was not until 20 December, however, with four feet of snow on the ground and the roofs of the buildings braced to keep them from caving in, that the last group of prisoners was literally rescued and removed to Yoho.[81]

This delay was caused in part by a last-minute change in the design of the buildings. It was originally intended, in the blind hurry to get the camp ready as soon as possible, that all the structures would have earthen floors. The site

Camp Otter was still under construction when the Mount Revelstoke internees were transferred to Yoho. *National Archives of Canada, C81375*

on which Camp Otter was located, however, was extremely wet and prone to flooding—an omen of things to come—and it was decided that the bunkhouses, mess hall, and hospital would have to be floored in order to avoid a potentially serious health hazard.[82] Military officials were also probably reluctant to transfer the remainder of the Mount Revelstoke men to Yoho before the camp was operational because of the discovery in early December that the construction crew was evidently planning to overpower their guards and seek refuge in the surrounding hills. The guards had twigged to the scheme because of a "general surliness" on the part of the work party and upon investigating, concluded that a nearby immigrant settler might be involved in providing assistance. This escape plot made the guards extremely wary of their charges and for several nights thereafter they slept with their weapons.[83]

While Camp Otter was taking shape, there was some debate about the nature of the work to be performed by the internees. The park superintendent reiterated his desire that the men be put to work clearing timber for the commercial market; "by this means these prisoners, instead of being a burden on the government, could be made to pay for their own keep."[84] He regarded road work as a wasteful exercise, especially given the severe winter conditions and the short working days, and argued that any such activity would best be undertaken in the summer months. Commissioner Harkin felt otherwise. Although the Mount Revelstoke internees had opened up only one and a half miles of new road—a far cry from what had been expected—Harkin was eager to take advantage of this road-building experience at Yoho and have the men build part of a proposed loop highway outside Field. There was no telling when the Dominion Parks Branch might have so many submissive hands at its disposal again. For the better part of November, then, the national parks engineering service surveyed and staked the route for a new scenic motorway from the Otterhead River northeast along the Kicking Horse canyon to the Natural Bridge, a rock formation on the Kicking Horse River.[85] The Yoho internees started clearing this right-of-way the last week of December.

The Yoho internees cleared the right-of-way for a new road along the Kicking Horse canyon. *National Archives of Canada C81374*

. . .

Once Camp Otter was finally occupied and the Banff internees settled into their new quarters, work started on yet another national park internment camp in early 1916–this time at Jasper. The plans for this camp had been developed several months earlier when General Otter evidently told Commissioner Harkin that he could have as many aliens as he could possibly use.[86] The establishment of the Mount Revelstoke and Yoho camps, however, took priority that fall, and it was not until the early new year when a site between the Athabasca River and the Jasper railway station was finally decided upon. Construction of the fourteen-building encampment got underway immediately and by early February, 200 prisoners–again, all Austrians–were transferred from Brandon. The guards and various military personnel brought the total camp population to 268.

Jasper was desperate to secure this labour. Created in 1907 to complement railway construction through the Yellowhead Valley,[87] the park had been forced by wartime cutbacks to put a number of ambitious improvement plans on hold, and the superintendent's role, as a result, seemed reduced to that of a kind of glorified caretaker.[88] The arrival of the aliens promised to lift this gloom.

There were even suggestions that park development would reach unprecedented heights. "Life at the camp is not one continuous round of sightseeing for the prisoners," the Edmonton *Journal* assured its readers about western Canada's newest internment station. "The amount of work to be accomplished is only limited by the duration of the war."[89]

What Jasper had in mind for the men, as in the case of the other national parks, was primarily road work. Because of the depth of snow that winter, however, the prisoners spent most of February cutting an amazing fifty-five hundred fence posts for nearby Wainwright Park, and hacking a ditch out of the frozen ground for a water main in the townsite. They were also kept busy shoring up the compound against an expected flood. Commandant Hopkins was worried that the low-lying campsite—in retrospect, a stupid location—would be claimed by the Athabasca in the spring.

In 1916, a new fourteen-building internment camp was established in Jasper National Park on a parcel of low-lying ground between the railway station and the Athabasca River. *Provincial Archives of Alberta, A2926*

There were more immediate concerns as well. Several of the guards recruited in Edmonton, especially the returned veterans, were found medically unfit for duty. Major Hopkins reported instances of one man whose "nerves are completely broken down" and another who "does not seem to be quite right in his mind";[90] the sorriest case was that of the shell-shocked private, C.H. Royal, taken on as camp bugler, who could not learn to blow his horn and yet was incapable of doing anything else. "I am sorry this has happened, but I am doing my best for the returned soldiers," Hopkins commented in trying to explain the release of the men. "I find the duties for the men here rather hard." There was also a minor uproar when the Edmonton *Journal* flaunted censorship regulations and carried a photograph of the Jasper camp on its front page on 19 February; an embarrassed commandant disavowed any responsibility for the publication of the picture and promised his superiors that it would not happen again.[91]

The new Banff commander, Captain P.M. Spence, was under similar scrutiny. Upon assuming his duties in late December 1915, he was warned that the prisoners under his care had certain basic rights and that the garrison was to be closely supervised, especially in light of earlier discipline problems. He was also told that the Dominion Parks Service expected more labour from the prisoners—as if they were not doing enough already—and that he was to "co-operate heartily" with park officers.[92] Getting more work out of the men proved difficult, however, because of a bout of extremely cold weather in January. There were several consecutive days during the month when the prisoners did little more than cut wood to try to keep warm. When they did turn out for park projects, moreover, the working conditions were far from favourable. During an official inspection of the Banff facilities by the commander of the local military district in late February 1916, it was learned that the prisoners and their guards put in exceptionally long days walking to and from the project sites. In some cases they marched from four to six miles each way; according to the inspection report, this amounted "practically to a day's work in itself,"[93] especially given the snow conditions that winter. To make matters worse, the distance from the camp precluded a warm midday meal and the men had to choke down frozen food. The situation was little better back at camp at

A group of internees marching from the Cave and Basin camp to their worksite. *Whyte Museum of the Canadian Rockies, Anderson-Wilson Collection, V20/PA228–20*

night. Here, the 420 internees shared a single washhouse and bedded down, exhausted, in one of four crowded 25-by-80-foot bunkhouses; if there was one consolation, it was the availability of the old Cave and Basin pool for bathing. General Otter, in consultation with the district commander, made a number of minor recommendations to correct some of the worst problems, but hesitated to do much more since the camp was to be moved back to Castle in the late spring. These changes were apparently enough, though, for when the American consular representative made a second visit to the camp three months later, he found conditions "very satisfactory"—hardly a surprising conclusion given that the men were "all of the labouring class."[94]

The Banff internees at work on a new bridge over the Spray River, April 1916. *Provincial Archives of Alberta, acc. no. 69.218/1316, box 14, f. B64–10, v. 1*

Despite the desire of Internment authorities to correct past shortcomings at Banff, then, the camp remained a troubled one—in large part because of the conditions under which the men existed. The prisoners saw nothing but an empty future—endless days of heavy toil and long marches. They had no idea how long they would be held. Nor did they know what was happening beyond the barbed wire fence. It was as if time had stood still[95] and the world that they once knew had ceased to exist. "The past was dead," wrote a German civilian internee about his experience; "the future, if there should be a future, was a blank, there was nothing left but the present, and my present was the life as a prisoner."[96] Day after day after day was the same for the men—without family, friends, and, most of all, women. It really did not matter how they were treated by their keepers; internment was internment, and the unnatural, stagnant conditions of camp life had a demoralizing influence on the men's mental well-being. A few succumbed to the bleakness and were shipped to the provincial insane asylum at Ponoka, Alberta. Others quietly waited for the right moment, and as the weather moderated, the number of escape attempts escalated. On 22 March, for example, five men slipped away from two separate worksites; just over two weeks later, another seven fled from the Spray road project. The date of this second escape could not have come at a worse time, for General Otter arrived the next day to inspect the camp. While search parties were sent out to suspected hiding places and nearby immigrant communities, one of the senior camp officers sat hidden in the bush for forty-eight hours and surprised two of the escapees as they made their break for freedom during the night.[97] This extraordinary action underscored the frustration of the garrison, and the commandant tried to provide some relief by recruiting more guards to augment escort parties. But the rash of escapes continued unabated through the spring—more than sixty men absconded during the first eleven months—prompting an exasperated Otter to demand an explanation for the camp's sorry record and threaten possible dismissals.[98]

The Banff garrison was equally demoralized. The guards not only put in extremely long days themselves—it was estimated they worked an average eighty-five hours per week—but their quarters were even more congested than those of the prisoners and they lacked a canteen and recreation room.[99] They were also held personally accountable for the prisoners at the various worksites and were grilled before a special board of officers whenever an escape occurred and disciplined accordingly. In a sense, they were captives themselves, who came to resent the work and the demands placed upon them. This stressful existence probably accounted for the fact that almost one-quarter of the guards volunteered for overseas service when a recruiting officer visited Banff in late February 1916. It also took a personal toll. On 10 February, John Grindlay, a thirty-one-year-old private, died of complications brought on by influenza; he had lain delirious in his bunk for a week before being taken in an open ambulance to the local hospital. Then, on 19 May, Private J.H. Brearly, who had been ill for several months, calmly walked into the bush a short distance from his home and sliced open his throat with a razor; his body was discovered after his wife reported him missing.[100] The death of the two men cast a pall over the detachment and probably further strained relations with the internees. It certainly made the guards jittery. Late one night at the end of June, Private Henri Martin accidentally shot Park Warden W.G. Fyfe near the Bow River bridge. When Martin ordered a suspicious-looking Fyfe to stop and identify himself, the warden drew his revolver instead, causing the nervous guard to discharge his rifle. Both men were out looking for an escaped prisoner at the time.[101] The *Crag and Canyon* took great delight in poking fun at the incident. "This is the first time one of the guards has shot a man since the interns were stationed at Banff," the paper sarcastically observed, "and it is the irony of fate that a white man should be chosen as the target."[102]

Tim Hotchkiss and Ben Short, internment camp guards, Banff National Park, 1916.
Whyte Museum of the Canadian Rockies, Dan McCowan Collection, NA86–21

For General Otter, the solution to the camp's woes was to place the internees in two smaller camps outside Banff as soon as the weather permitted. There was even the possibility that some of the men would do tree planting in Calgary.[103] But this proposal to close the Cave and Basin camp did not sit well with Banff residents. The prisoners were performing valuable improvement work in and around the townsite—whether it be building a new bridge, cutting new roads, or clearing the recreation grounds—and the townspeople were anxious to see the work continue. Their federal representative, R.B. Bennett, felt much the same way and had suggested to park authorities in mid-March that the aliens be put to work upgrading the Lake Minnewanka and Tunnel Mountain roads for automobile traffic.[104] Commissioner Harkin politely turned down the idea, noting that it was too far to march the internees and that it was inadvisable to have the men working so close to the coal-mining community of Bankhead, where there was a large foreign population that might be tempted to help the prisoners should they run away.[105] Bennett was not easily dissuaded and sent Harkin a local petition in favour of the road projects, as well as another missive imploring him to undertake the work without delay. In response, Harkin argued that the internees had to be kept away from park visitors during the summer months—something that Bennett himself had been adamant about when the Banff camp was first proposed—and that the completion of the Banff–Lake Louise road was a greater priority. To appease Bennett, however, he promised that he would try to have the new Hot Springs road ready for the tourist season, as well as make some improvements to the Lake Minnewanka road.[106] This work was done by prisoner work gangs in May and June, along with some clearing on the Sundance Canyon road. It was therefore not until the last day of June 1916 that the internees returned to their summer quarters at Castle Mountain. Not all of them, though, made the trip back. Five men successfully made a dash into the thick bush along the Sundance Canyon right-of-way, despite the best efforts of their guards to wound, if not kill them. Another four wandered off when their guard slipped behind a tree to relieve himself; they were recaptured over the next few days.[107]

· · ·

The Yoho and Jasper camps also had their share of problems. At Camp Otter, Superintendent Russell tried to cultivate a good working relationship with his new charges by granting a prisoner request for the observance of Ukrainian Christmas (7 January) as a holiday. As he told Commissioner Harkin, "We can get far better results out of these men if they are contented, but if sulky it is pretty hard to do much with them."[108] The spirit of Russell's gesture was effectively negated, however, by the miserable working conditions during January and early February. From the very day—27 December—that work started on the right-of-way for the new Ottertail–Natural Bridge automobile road, the prisoners had to brave unseasonably low temperatures and high winds. A blizzard in the second week of January brought work to a standstill, and for much of the next month, the men could do little more than retrieve firewood out of the bush and haul snow out of the compound; it was as if the Mount Revelstoke nightmare were repeating itself. Indeed, the foul weather probably seemed like a second punishment to the men, and their spirits sank even lower. Conditions were so severe, according to J.N. Stinson, the Dominion Parks engineer assigned to the road project, that the prisoners were able to work on the right-of-way for only three days during a four-week period.[109] To make matters worse, an ice jam in the Otterhead River threatened to flood the camp. Although the danger was averted by digging a channel to carry away the water, the incident served to remind them of the vulnerability of the campsite and the fragility of their situation.[110]

The guardroom outside the prisoners' compound at Camp Otter. *National Archives of Canada, C81362*

The weather continued stormy through February into March but it was not as cold, and the prisoners were pushed hard to try to make up for lost work days. A large gang slashed and burned the right-of-way for the new road, while smaller groups cut logs in the bush for bridge work and culverts, or began excavating foundations for the piers. Local project officials, in the meantime, took steps to reduce the walking distance to the bridge site over the Kicking Horse River by cutting a more direct trail from the camp; this shorter route—

reduced from six to four miles—had nothing to do with prisoner welfare but was meant to increase the actual working time of the men.[111] It was also decided to take advantage of the longer daylight hours and request an increase in the internee work day from seven to eight hours. The aliens passively resisted these changes by deliberately slowing down their activities, and Superintendent Russell was soon complaining that the men should be made to walk faster and labour longer. The camp commandant, on the other hand, seemed to recognize that little more could be humanly expected of the prisoners, given their worn-out footwear and the extremely wet conditions under which they worked, whether it be on the road or the bridges; most of them worked with cold, soaked feet.[112] His understanding of the men's situation, however, had its limits. When Camp Otter experienced what was probably its second escape attempt in late May, the prisoner was recaptured after an intensive three-day search that kept one of the work gangs confined to the compound while the guards scoured the local terrain. "Our friend now shows on the daily requisitions," the superintendent gleefully reported, "as, in cell."[113]

Park authorities believed that many of the camp problems would be resolved once the men had been relocated to a temporary summer base at the junction of the Kicking Horse River and Boulder Creek, near Emerald on the CPR line. This move was designed to bring the prisoners closer to the road and bridge work in the area and thereby end the need for long, tiring marches. It was also necessitated by the growing fear that Camp Otter would probably be marooned, if not partially submerged, by the spring run-off.[114] In the end, it really did not matter where the camp was located. The transfer was no sooner completed on 10 June than a spell of hot temperatures combined with heavy rains turned the Kicking Horse River into a raging torrent, which carried away many of the bridges in its path and briefly threatened to inundate Field. At the new Boulder Creek camp, the prisoners and guards were swamped by the flood and had to scramble up the valley with their waterlogged equipment and belongings and pitch their salvaged tents along the new road right-of-way. Life in the makeshift camp over the next few weeks was nothing short of miserable, as captured in a plaintive note from one of the project foremen. Tired of spending his days in wet clothes, he begged the superintendent to send out some lengths of stove pipe "or I will be through with the job forever."[115] It was an omen of things to come.

The situation at Jasper was little better. The Brandon internees had been sent to the park to provide the muscle for several possible road projects.[116] But by the spring of 1916, when this work was finally to get underway, the prisoners and their keepers were locked in a war of wills. At first, the men complained about the food and staged a hunger strike. This protest was apparently not taken too seriously—by either side—for the guards allowed two young Jasper girls to slip some of the fasting men a plate of doughnuts.[117] The men then

The main entrance to the Jasper internment facility. *Jasper Yellowhead Historical Society,* *PA18/56*

changed tactics and refused to work. This was the first time that a national park camp had been hit by a strike, and Parks authorities did not like it. In response to similar work stoppages elsewhere, however, General Otter had cautioned that civilian prisoners could not be compelled to work or punished for not doing so; all Internment officials could do was reduce the men's daily rations and encourage them to take up their tools.[118] The Jasper commandant could do little except try to convince the striking men that the work was for their own good health. It was a spurious argument given the circumstances, and the prisoners were not won over. Neither were the Parks people impressed. They wanted work out of the men and began to blame Major Hopkins for the camp problems; there was even a suggestion that the commandant should be replaced.[119]

The stalemate at Jasper was finally broken when twenty-seven prisoners were persuaded to help build a new summer camp at the Maligne Canyon; this camp was to serve as the base for a new road along the Maligne River to Medicine Lake. Major Hopkins was worried about the security of the site and had originally planned to select men who could be trusted until the wire enclosure was in place. With a strike underway, though, he had to take whatever men volunteered, particularly since the park was anxious to see the new camp established and the road construction proceed.[120] It was a decision he probably regretted. The work gang had no sooner settled into its temporary quarters than three of the prisoners–Joe Wala, Tony Pyziak, and Lorenz

Maki—under the pretext of visiting the latrine, stole away into the bush late one Sunday afternoon without being noticed. The escape caused panic in nearby Jasper, and martial law was declared. Within forty-eight hours, however, two of the men were captured walking along the railway tracks. Maki was cornered by park wardens later that same day and forced back to Jasper, where he surrendered to waiting authorities.[121]

The trouble was not over, though, for the remaining prisoners at the new campsite now refused to work. At this point, patience and prodding gave way to intimidation and compulsion. An additional ten men were sent out to the Maligne Canyon site and together with the striking prisoners, set to work on the new compound. Once the tents were in place, they were joined by another batch of prisoners in early June—bringing the total camp population to about fifty souls. For the next two months they toiled away at the Maligne–Medicine Lake road, completing two miles, including bridges and culverts, as well as doing the initial clearing on another mile of right-of-way. It was no easy feat, especially since the prisoners, in the words of one of the supervising officers, would not work "without actual force . . . and did everything under protest."[122]

These continuing tensions at Jasper did not sit well with General Otter, and it was decided in early August 1916 to shut down the Jasper operations and transfer most of the men to jobs with the railways or resource industries, a process already well underway at a number of other internment camps and stations. By early 1916, Canadian military commitments had translated into a serious manpower shortage at home—exactly the opposite situation from that at the beginning of the war. Several companies, including many that had dismissed immigrant workers for patriotic reasons only two years earlier, now approached Internment Operations about the possible use of enemy alien labour. Otter was receptive to the idea. He was worried that the incidence of camp strikes and escape attempts would only escalate as the war dragged on, and reasoned that the interned aliens might as well be released to fill wartime vacancies. Beginning in April 1916, then, prisoners began to be discharged to various companies on the understanding that there were no other available labourers and that the prevailing rates of pay would apply.[123] Before being paroled, however, the internees not only had to accept their job placement for a minimum period of time, but also promise to remain within Canada, faithfully observe the laws of the country, and report regularly to the local police office. Those individuals, moreover, who had been labelled troublemakers or were otherwise still regarded as security threats were not released. In most instances, these men had either broken registration provisions, such as failing to report, or had run afoul of camp authorities during their period of internment. Once again, one wonders whether the continued confinement fit the crime.

General Otter also took steps to have chronically ill prisoners discharged from the camps and sent back to the communities that had recommended their

The Jasper internees being marched out from camp to their worksite. *Provincial Archives of Alberta, acc. no. 69.218/1316, box 14, f. B64–10, v. 1*

internment. "[U]pon looking up the records of these men," he complained to the officer in charge of the British Columbia operations, "[I] find that the only reason given for their internment was being destitute, a cause in itself which is not sufficient for their arrest, and one can only assume that municipalities have been quietly getting rid of their unfortunate at our expense . . . Why such men were sent . . . to working camps I cannot imagine or understand."[124] Otter's outrage, however, apparently did not extend to the mentally unstable. An April 1917 list of prisoners considered ineligible for parole from Banff included Marcin Bysko; transferred to the park from the Brandon insane asylum, the thirty-four-year-old Austrian had originally been arrested by authorities because he was considered "unreliable."[125]

· · ·

The discharge of the Jasper prisoners began the second week of August. The majority were turned over to the Canadian Pacific Railway—some ninety men on 16 August alone—while smaller groups were paroled to the Grand Trunk Pacific Railway, local mining companies, or to individual farmers.[126] General Otter was evidently concerned about releasing prisoners who had identified themselves as reservists in the Austro-Hungarian army and had asked the Brandon and Lethbridge internment stations in mid-June for a list of those aliens who fell into this category and had been transferred to one of the park camps. Once the evacuation of Jasper commenced, however, most of these men were also paroled; of the 207 prisoners on the park roll in early August, only 22 were kept in confinement—including the 3 who had tried to escape—and transferred to Lethbridge at month's end.[127]

The breakup of the camp also affected military officials. Coming after weeks of tension, it touched off a petty spat, complete with recriminations, between the commandant and one of his officers over the refusal of the prisoners to work. The Jasper superintendent, on the other hand, was more sanguine about the camp's fate. In his report for that year, he conveniently forgot about any labour difficulties and attributed the wholesale release of the men to "their good behaviour."[128]

The entrance to Camp Otter, Yoho National Park. Although the camp buildings have since collapsed, one of the gates still stands today. *National Archives of Canada, C81357*

The Yoho camp at Boulder Creek was next to close. In mid-July 1916, Commandant Brock recommended that a request for prisoners from the Crow's Nest Pass Coal Company be turned down; the company's own workforce was on strike, and Brock questioned the wisdom of sending parolees into such a setting.[129] Little did he realize, however, that he would soon be facing serious labour problems of his own. Less than two weeks later, the Yoho prisoners, after being marched out to their worksite one morning, refused to pick up their tools and were promptly returned to camp. Upon being interrogated, the men complained about their unfair treatment—in the words of the park superintendent, they wondered "why they should be interned, while hundreds of other alien enemies are still allowed . . . to go free."[130] They also dreaded the prospect of spending another miserable winter at Camp Otter and apparently reasoned that the park would have to get rid of them sooner or later if they simply withheld their labour. Lieutenant Brock promised to place their grievances before General Otter if the men resumed work on the Ottertail–Natural Bridge road. They had no sooner returned to this task than they struck again on 10 August—this time in response to an unsympathetic reply from General Otter the day before. The commanding officer blamed this new strike on a handful of instigators who bullied the rest of the prisoners. The situation was further complicated by the fact that the men had recently been inoculated for typhoid, which had left many of them ill and thereby unable to do much work anyway. In the end it was decided not to discipline the prisoners—beyond the removal of canteen privileges—but to give them two weeks to recover before trying to get back to work. Construction of the road, in the meantime, was carried on by the project foreman and his supervisory crew.[131]

The situation at the Boulder Creek camp was little better by the end of August—if anything, it was worse. While recuperating, the prisoners had learned from inmates at Morrissey in southeastern British Columbia—ironically through censored letters—that they too were not working.[132] This knowledge only hardened the men's resolve not to co-operate, and as the deadline for the resumption of work approached, it became clear that they had no intention of finishing the road or doing anything else beyond regular duties around the camp. The continuation of the strike, in turn, greatly flustered the camp command. Whereas Lieutenant Brock had once believed that he could get the majority of the men back on the job, he now doubted whether they would ever work again "unless strenuous measures are resorted to; and it is very hard to determine just how far a commandant is allowed to go in that respect."[133] The only feasible solution, as far as Brock was concerned, was to reach a special arrangement with the prisoners. Knowing how much they did not want to put in another winter at Yoho, he suggested to General Otter that the men be told that if they completed the road and remaining bridge work over the next two months, they would not have to work over the winter.

The Parks Department was much more hard-nosed about the Yoho strike. Although the road clearing and bridge work was nearly complete, Commissioner Harkin was not prepared to maintain the men if they were not willing to work; it was an expense that his department's already limited budget could do without. When Superintendent Russell was approached in late August by the Columbia River Lumber Company of Golden, British Columbia, about the need for loggers, therefore, Harkin had no qualms in recommending the release of seventy-five Yoho prisoners.[134] He also wrote General Otter about the strike and advised him that "if the aliens are not going to work, or are not to be compelled to work,"[135] then the camp should be closed. Before acting on the commissioner's letter, however, Otter requested time to investigate the situation personally. He evidently believed that Yoho's troubles were largely the result of a weak command, and at the end of his one-day visit to the camp on 23 September—by now, the eighth week of the strike—he not only decided on a complete change of officers, but also ordered the return of the prisoners to their winter quarters.[136]

General Otter's intervention put the Parks Department in an awkward position. There was no guarantee that a new commandant would get the Yoho prisoners back to work; the superintendent frankly believed that no one could. And Camp Otter needed considerable attention before it could be occupied for another winter. If Commissioner Harkin insisted on the closure of the camp in the interests of economy, however, it could adversely affect relations with Otter, especially after the general had shown such personal concern over the situation. Harkin therefore adopted a wait-and-see attitude. The prisoners, meanwhile, were not so patient, and some of them decided to take matters into their own hands. Using a shovel and cutlery from the mess, some fifty-three men in a large tent near the compound fence started to dig their way to freedom, excavating a few feet each night and then trampling the dirt down on the earthen floor or hiding it under their bunks. They also began to arm themselves, in preparation for their escape, by fashioning crude dirks from table knives. By the time the guards discovered the prisoners' burrowing activities, on the morning of 28 September, the tunnel reached beyond the stockade wall and was only eight feet from the bush.[137]

The escape attempt convinced Harkin that there was little sense in keeping the Yoho camp open any longer, and he wired the superintendent about the impending closure on 7 October. The wisdom of the decision was confirmed the next day, when the new commandant, unaware of Harkin's telegram, reported that Camp Otter was poorly situated and should be abandoned in favour of building new winter quarters about a mile from the new Kicking Horse bridge.[138] The construction of a new camp was the last thing that the Parks Department was prepared to contemplate—especially when the prisoners still refused to work—and it was decided to transfer the men to another location before winter set in. Given the camp's continuing labour strife and the "unruly and surly"[139] attitude of the prisoners, the evacuation was personally supervised by a member of the Internment Operations Ottawa staff. On 23 October, almost a year to the day that the first prisoners arrived at Yoho, 114 men boarded a train for Spirit Lake in northern Quebec, while the remaining 14 were transferred to Banff. The garrison was marched out to Field the next day.[140] But all did not go smoothly. In a last act of defiance, 2 of the Quebec-bound prisoners escaped from the train as it travelled across the prairies and had to be retrieved by 2 Regina-based Mounted Policemen.[141]

Camp Otter in Yoho National Park. The camp was vacated in June 1916 and never occupied again. *National Archives of Canada C81373*

· · ·

The closure of the Jasper and Yoho camps left Banff as the only national park with internees. The size of the alien labour force, however, had steadily declined through the late spring of 1916, as small groups of men were paroled every few days to local companies and individuals. These releases continued through the summer, even after the prisoners had been moved back to their summer base at Castle Mountain; company representatives would visit the camp every week or so and interview prospective workers. There were also two large discharges. On 8 July, fifty men were handed over to the CPR; eleven days later, another fifty were taken away by the Crow's Nest Pass Coal Company. Life on the outside was not much better for the parolees—they tended to be abused by their new employers—and many simply ran away at the first opportunity. The Canadian Pacific Railway regularly complained to an unsympathetic General Otter about the number of desertions.[142] Strangely, one of the former Banff prisoners, Wasyl Perchaliuk, never lost faith in his adopted country and left his work contract with the Canmore Coal Company to enlist in the 211th Battalion at Calgary. When discovered, he was taken to the Calgary gaol on suspicion of having escaped; three days later, he was found dead in his cell hanging by his uniform puttee.[143]

The release of so-called nondangerous prisoners dropped the Castle Mountain population well below 200 men—the lowest number during the camp's brief existence. There was no intention, however, of phasing out the Banff operations, in large part because the men were still working. During the summer of 1915, the prisoners had managed to clear almost three miles of new highway to Lake Louise. In this second construction season, the Dominion Parks Branch wanted this work "pushed forward as rapidly as possible"[144] and assigned two engineers to the project, one at each end of the road. The more valuable addition, as far as the prisoners were concerned, was the arrival of a steam shovel in mid-July. This machine was to be used for ditching, removing rocks and stumps, and building bridges—the same work that the men had been expected to do the previous summer largely by hand. The road crews were also bolstered at the end of the month when the Brandon internment station was closed and half of the inmates—some 103 men—were shipped to their new home in the mountains. Banff's acquisition of these prisoners, at a time when other camps were closing and internees were being paroled, underscored the importance of the Banff–Lake Louise road and the influence it enjoyed with Internment Operations.

The prisoners toiled steadily on the new highway six days a week from early July until early November, when the weather finally forced a suspension of the work for the season. At the end of the four-month period, they had cleared, grubbed, and gravelled another four miles of new highway, complete with culverts, cribbing, and guard rails; they even scraped and painted the Bow River bridge at Castlé. A sergeant with the camp garrison spoke several decades later of "the marvels you can do if you just have the labour."[145] The aliens viewed things differently. Although strikes were not a problem at Banff as they had been at the other two national park camps, the prisoners attended to their various duties only grudgingly, and tried to work at their own pace. Some resorted to damaging shovels or feigning illness. Others continued to test the guards' vigilance and run away. At times, the escapes seemed to mock the camp authorities, such as when two men bolted while the new steam shovel was being unloaded. In most instances, though, the internees made a break for the bush along the new road right-of-way whenever they had the opportunity. It was during one of these escapes in August that one of three fleeing prisoners, Peter Konowalczuk, was shot below the hip and had to be hospitalized in Calgary; a subsequent search of the men revealed that they were carrying extra clothing and their personal belongings underneath their work overalls, and that they had stuffed their pockets with bread.[146] This was the first time that a guard had managed to hit his target, and it seemed to have a quieting effect on the prisoners, as the number of escapes declined dramatically and the men were generally more co-operative.[147] The same could not be said of the garrison's behaviour, and their antics—everything from refusing to obey orders to discharging a rifle during an argument—resulted in a steady number of disciplinary hearings and dismissals.

The Castle camp also became something of a curiosity that summer, as carloads of park visitors would drive out to see the tent compound, hoping to catch a glimpse of the prisoners at work. A number of government officials,

Indian Days at the Castle Mountain camp. *Glenbow Archives, Millican Collection, NA–1870–16*

including the minister of the Interior, also made the trip to Castle. The most distinguished among these was the governor general, the Duke of Connaught, who inspected the camp for the second time on 17 July (the first time was September 1915) and spoke approvingly of the operations. The prisoners probably did not care about this viceregal blessing, but undoubtedly appreciated the day off work that accompanied his visit. General Otter was not as impressed. After a mid-September inspection of the camp, he told the Calgary *Herald,* "The men do not as a rule hurry themselves."[148]

The prisoners and troops moved back to Banff on 14 November 1916 and took up residence again on the edge of the townsite near the Cave and Basin pool. Because of the number of men who had been paroled over the past half year, the bunkhouses were not as congested as they had been the previous winter, and part of one of the buildings was converted into a recreation room where the men could play cards and perhaps write letters or read. The garrison was also better quartered, for the simple reason that fewer prisoners necessitated fewer guards. The commander of the local military district emphasized these improved conditions in his December inspection report. If Brigadier General Cruikshank was to believed, life at the Banff camp was never better. "The physical condition of the prisoners of war appeared to be entirely satisfactory," he reported. "Only five men were sick at the time, and the remainder had every appearance of vigorous health and seem to be well fed and generally well satisfied with their food, clothing, and quarters."[149] Any complaints were "generally trivial and not well founded"—the consequence of a few "discontented men with abnormal appetites."

All was not well, though, either in the townsite or at the Cave and Basin camp. As the war entered its third year, local residents had come to resent the presence of the aliens, especially the cockiness of the work gangs as they made their way to and from the jobsites. Under the title "Compel Them To Be Decent," an article in the Banff *Crag and Canyon* warned that if the guards did not "suppress this growing evil . . . some muscular Canadian . . . will wade into the gang of foul-mouthed, leering Austrians, and armed with a club or some other persuasive weapon, teach the brutes a lesson."[150] The mood among the prisoners was equally stark, as many of them faced their second winter in confinement in the park. Poor Mike Pendziwiater, for example, was on the verge of a breakdown. While on sanitary detail one morning, he went missing, and then turned himself in a few hours later. The following week, he walked away again—this time under a hail of bullets—and returned to the compound in the early evening.[151]

There were also simmering ethnic tensions between the men. Internment Operations had tried to prevent any blow-ups by separating the Germans and Austrians as much as possible. As the *Crag and Canyon* observed, the Austrians blamed the Germans for starting the war and "developed a habit of knocking

Internee work party marching through Banff townsite. *Glenbow Archives, Harmony Collection, NA–841–172*

the spots off the Germans when opportunity arose."[152] And there were strong rivalries between the various nationalities of the Austro-Hungarian Empire, as evidenced by the sorry fate of George Luka Budak, a recent Romanian internee from Regina. Within two weeks of his arrival at Banff, Budak asked for special protection from the other prisoners and was given sanctuary in the guardroom. His imprisonment and anxiety about the other prisoners, however, soon proved too much for him, and on the afternoon of 24 December—Christmas Eve—he crawled under the bunk in his cell and carved open his stomach with a razor and then slit his throat.[153] At the insistence of the camp commandant, Budak was buried in a remote part of the Banff cemetery, well away from the plots of the two Internment guards—John Grindlay and J.H. Brearly—who had died earlier that year.[154]

Perhaps to help the camp get over the trauma of Budak's suicide, the prisoners were granted holidays in early January 1917, on their traditional Christmas and New Year's Days. Otherwise, it was work as usual. The internees built a new rock wall and widened the road between the Spray Bridge and Bow Falls, cleared along the Loop Drive, and eased a dangerous turn on the Tunnel Mountain road. They also did extensive underbrushing at the recreation grounds and in the animal paddocks, as well as cutting timber in Mount Edith Pass. And they served as the townsite's handymen, being called upon to attend to a myriad of duties. Their most unusual job that winter was the construction of an elaborate ice palace, complete with interior maze, for the Banff winter carnival. They also built a toboggan run in connection with this work, but it is not known whether the prisoners or their guards got to use it.

On 22 March 1917, Internment Operations asked for a listing of the Banff internees by name, number, and nationality. Just over a month later, the prisoners started to be released in small groups—109 men over nine days—to the Canadian Pacific Railway. Ottawa's request, followed by the loss of what amounted to half the camp population, was a warning that the Banff operations would soon be shut down. And the Parks Department made no effort to fight the camp closure, even if it wanted to; it was readily apparent by the spring of 1917 that the country's manpower crisis—both at home and overseas—was getting worse, and that all nondangerous internees had to be paroled.

In January 1917, the internees constructed an elaborate ice palace, complete with interior maze, for the Banff winter carnival. *Provincial Archives of Alberta, A4837*

Through the spring and early summer, then, the Banff superintendent tried to do what he could with a steadily declining labour force. A small gang of internees painted the new Spray River bridge, while another group did general maintenance work on the main highway between Banff and the east gate. It was also decided that spring to extend the park golf-course by another nine holes, and Commissioner Harkin was anxious that the bulk of this work be performed by the aliens, especially since the annual Parks budget had been reduced again. Although Superintendent Clarke assigned as many men as possible to the project, by mid-June he was grumbling to Harkin that "they work absurdly slow and are not making the headway I would like to see made."[155] By the time they finally ceased work on 10 July, they had done the initial clearing for three new holes. Five days later, the remaining forty-seven prisoners in camp—generally men who were considered troublemakers—were transferred by rail to the internment facility at Kapuskasing in northern Ontario. The Banff episode was over, exactly two years and two days after the first internees had arrived.[156]

. . .

The closure of the park camps and the loss of the alien workforce effectively brought the various road-building and other projects to a standstill. Banff, Jasper, Yoho, and Mount Revelstoke initially tried to complete what they could by day labour, but the continuing shortage of funds soon forced them, in the words of the Jasper superintendent, to do, "no work . . . beyond what was absolutely essential."[157] In the spring of 1918, however, it appeared that the national parks camps might be reactivated. As the war continued to sap Canada's energies, there was a renewed backlash against enemy aliens, accompanied by heated calls from patriotic organizations, newspapers, and politicians for mass internment. Conservative H.S. Clements told the House of Commons during a lengthy, emotional debate on alien labour policy on 22 April, "I see no reason why every alien enemy in the Dominion should not be conscripted and placed at work doing something for the State."[158] R.F. Green, who had been instrumental in securing internees for Mount Revelstoke three years earlier, endorsed Clements's call for "a strong iron hand" and argued that "the ordinary alien at large in this country" should be forced to "bear his fair share of the burden imposed by this awful war."[159] Newspaper editorials were no less strident. The *Golden Star* accused the Borden government of being "criminally weak" and warned that the enemy alien was "like a viper to [Canada's] bosom."[160] Ottawa, however, was still not prepared to assume the expense of a mass internment policy; at over a million dollars annually, the current operations had been costly enough.[161] Besides, as Justice Minister Doherty explained to the House, it made more sense to discharge the non-dangerous Austrians and apply their labour towards the war effort.

Commissioner Harkin had his own plan about how to resolve the national parks' manpower problems. When it became apparent in the spring of 1917 that he would lose the use of internees at Banff, he looked to another possible source of cheap labour–Canadian gaols. In his annual report for 1918, he described how prisoners in several American states were being successfully used to build roads and wondered why the same kind of work could not be carried on in Canada's national parks. As far as Harkin was concerned, it would be an ideal activity. The natural setting would do more to renew the men's mental and physical well-being than could any rehabilitation programme. And since the prisoners would be working in isolated areas, they would not only be kept from public view but would also be less likely to try to escape. These arguments flatly contradicted the parks' experience with internee labour. Harkin believed, however, that most of the camps' troubles had been caused by poor supervision, and in a thinly veiled swipe at Internment officials, argued in his report that the success of his new scheme would rest largely on the character of the camp officers.[162] Harkin's political masters, however, had no interest in the idea—the timing was all wrong—and nothing came of the proposal.

. . .

When the war ended in November 1918, there were approximately 2,200 prisoners still confined at four internment stations. The majority of the men were German; less than 500 were Austrian.[163] Although most of the internees had been held for several months, if not years, more than 130 so-called radical socialists had been recently rounded up and incarcerated by the federal government in the aftermath of the Bolshevik Revolution in Russia.[164] In January 1919, it was announced that those internees who were considered "dangerous, hostile or undesirable" would be repatriated—including the sick and insane.[165] This process commenced two months later and by the time it was completed in February 1920, over 1,900 men and some 60 women and children had been deported.[166]

In making the wonders of the national parks more accessible, the internees had known only exhaustion, suffering, fear, and desolation. *Glenbow Archives, NA-5263-1*

The question of what to do with the funds of the thousands of internees who had been paroled was also resolved at this time. Throughout 1919, while the peace treaty negotiations were underway, many of these men continued to report on a monthly basis to local police authorities. In March 1920, however, the government passed an order-in-council that allowed former internees to claim all outstanding camp earnings, as well as any confiscated money and valuables, by making a statutory declaration and handing in their release certificates.[167] When the Internment Operations Branch of the Department of Justice was transferred to the Secretary of State at the end of June 1920, there was an unexpended balance of $94,112.75 in the claims account. Six years later there was still over $35,000.00 in unclaimed earnings and cash being held by the Office of the Custodian of Enemy Property; approximately $5,500.00 was owed to men who had worked in the park camps. Very few claims were submitted thereafter—none after March 1939—and in 1951 it was recommended that the remaining funds be turned over to Consolidated Revenue and the Internment Operations records destroyed.[168]

As for the Dominion Parks Service, it looked back upon the internment camp experience as something of a mixed blessing. Parks officials had expected great things from the internees and were disappointed by what had been achieved in the end. They believed that the prisoners should have been forced to toil away—regardless of the circumstances and conditions—and resented not only the slow pace but also the prolonged work stoppages. At the same time, Commissioner Harkin had to admit in his 1918 departmental report that the nine hundred men, representing roughly 10 percent of the total numbered interned, had tackled jobs that would have been otherwise impossible during the war.[169] It was a case of some work or no work at all—the very reason Harkin had secured the internees in the first place. But many of the projects, especially the road building, would see little progress again until the Depression, when another batch of camps was established.

There was also a regrettably ironic aspect to the park Internment Operations. Throughout the war, Commissioner Harkin was forever extolling the virtues of the national park system and how these special places would provide much-needed sanctuary and salvation when the guns finally fell silent. Sadly, this vision did not apply to the aliens. In making the wonders of Banff, Jasper, Yoho, and Mount Revelstoke more accessible, the internees had known only exhaustion, suffering, fear, and desolation. They also learned about a darker side of Canadian life and their place on the margins of society. The cruellest blow was being confined in what were being widely promoted as Canada's national playgrounds. For several years thereafter, the words "These are your parks . . . Come and enjoy them"[170] would haunt many immigrants who, despite their wartime treatment, had decided to make Canada their home.

CHAPTER TWO

Relief Workers

P ARKS COMMISSIONER J.B. HARKIN WAS READY FOR THE DEPRESSION.
Not that he anticipated the economic collapse; no one could have
known the depths to which the country would slide during the early
1930s, when one out of every four working Canadians would lose
their jobs. But as the ranks of the unemployed continued to swell through the
summer of 1930, Harkin sensed that recovery was still several months away and
that his department's budget would be an easy target for the newly elected
Conservative government. He also realized from past experience that unless he
secured other sources of funding, ordinary park maintenance, let alone any
major development, would likely be curtailed. When a special session of
Parliament was convened in early September 1930 to revive the slumping
Canadian economy, Harkin was poised with a list of possible work projects in
ten national parks in western Canada. This was no collection of simple jobs.
The scheme called for a major construction programme, mostly new roads and
bridges, which would employ in excess of twenty-five hundred men over the
winter months. Nor was the price tag modest. It was estimated that the various
projects would cost almost two-thirds of a million dollars.[1]

This was not the first time that the Parks Department had tried to secure
the labour of the unemployed. In the closing months of the Great War, national
parks officials unsuccessfully floated the idea that demobilized soldiers could
be used to build sections of a national highway system through the mountain
parks until other work was found for them. "I see no reason," the Banff
superintendent told Harkin, "why a transcontinental highway that will provide
a play-route to these playgrounds cannot be developed hand in hand with our
Parks as a national project."[2] Two years later, in December 1920, with the
Canadian economy mired in a stubborn postwar recession, Harkin and his
officials drew up an ambitious winter works programme for consideration by
the Meighen government. Although the projects were ostensibly designed to

relieve the unemployment situation in western cities, particularly Calgary, the parks would be direct beneficiaries.[3] It was not until almost a year later, in the midst of the 1921 general election, however, that funds were finally approved. Even then, not all the proposed projects could be undertaken or completed; many of the same items would later appear on Harkin's 1930 list.

The national parks' need for additional funding only increased through the 1920s. In response to complaints about the concentration of parks in the mountains,[4] Commissioner Harkin decided to extend the national parks system east of Alberta and eventually have at least one national park in each province; the establishment of Prince Albert in Saskatchewan in 1927 and Riding Mountain in Manitoba shortly thereafter was part of an overall plan to develop a series of national playgrounds and thereby appease regional demands.[5] Harkin also recognized how the automobile was revolutionizing North American travel habits and that national parks, once the handmaidens of the railways, now had to accommodate visitors who holidayed by car or forfeit their share of this new traffic.[6] What was needed, then, were roads and lots of them—both to and through the parks—to bring "the national playgrounds within reach of thousands."[7] The costs of building these highways, especially in the mountains, however, would easily gobble up the parks' annual budget. The plan to create a truly national system of parks only compounded the problem; new parks such as Prince Albert and Riding Mountain would require not only roads but buildings and other facilities as well.

Harkin tried to improve his department's share of federal spending by arguing that park scenery could be marketed like any other natural resource—the only difference being that the natural setting could be sold year after year and never be exhausted. This was a strategy he had embraced from his first days as commissioner in 1911, and he continued to pursue it with a single-minded vigour after the war. Each annual report during the early 1920s trumpeted the growing importance of tourist revenue to the national economy, reiterating the fact that national parks could attract more visitors and their tourist dollars only if additional funding was available for roads and other developments.

This argument carried little weight with the federal government, however, largely because the link between parks and railways had been broken. Once automobile parks began to displace the more traditional railway parks of the late nineteenth century, the Parks Department lost a powerful ally and with it, whatever influence it had over the level of government funding.[8] At the very time, then, when the Parks Department wanted to expand the parks system, as well as make them more accessible by car, its budget remained static, if not smaller, relative to overall federal spending.[9] Harkin, meanwhile, was reduced to a kind of hapless cheerleader, whose message about the profitability of parks became more tiresome with each repeating.

· · ·

The coming of the Depression allowed for new tactics. As the number of unemployed leapt from the hundreds to the thousands in 1930, Commissioner Harkin was immediately reminded of what the enemy alien camps had accomplished in the mountain parks during the war years. Why not do the same thing with Canada's growing army of unemployed? The parallel between the two situations was, in fact, quite striking. Many of the aliens were out of work at the time of their internment and had been sent to the parks to do something useful. Relief camps could now be established in the parks for essentially the same purpose. Men would be removed from the cities and given work in a healthy setting until the faltering Canadian economy began to recover, while the parks would enjoy the kind of development that would otherwise have been impossible under the circumstances. It was an attractive idea in itself, but what encouraged Harkin even more was the fact that the new Conservative prime minister was R.B. Bennett, the Calgary West representative whose riding included Banff National Park. Bennett was no stranger to the wartime use of enemy aliens in the parks—he had been involved in the negotiations—and Harkin assumed that he would probably be sympathetic to a similar relief scheme. After all, Bennett had promised during the July 1930 election to end unemployment or perish in the attempt. Canadians took him at his word and swept the moribund Mackenzie King Liberals from office.

Less than six weeks after his election victory, Prime Minister Bennett summoned a special session of Parliament for early September to deal with the worsening unemployment crisis. Having promised action during the campaign, he was anxious to offer his prescription for Canada's economic woes. Harkin lost little time himself. Within days of Bennett's victory, he canvassed the park superintendents and then together with his chief engineer, J.M. Wardle, hurriedly pulled together a schedule of park relief projects, many of which had been contemplated for several years. The list included mundane tasks such as brushing campgrounds, cutting boundaries, hauling logs, laying sidewalks, digging water and sewer lines, and ploughing fireguards. The dominant item on Harkin's wish list, however, was road work—constructing new ones and upgrading or widening those already in existence. Once intimately tied to the railways, the national parks were now to be at the forefront of the automobile age. There was even provision for building the east leg of the so-called Big Bend Highway from Golden to Revelstoke, British Columbia, a surprising inclusion since not a mile of the road passed through a national park.

Submitting his relief list five days before Parliament convened, Harkin clearly expected the proposals to be favourably received by the new government and was more concerned about the timing of the projects; he warned the deputy minister of the Interior that if work did not get underway by the middle of September, winter weather, particularly in the mountains, could delay

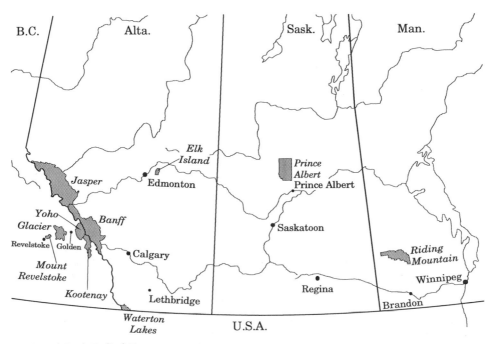

National Park Relief Camps, 1930s.

operations until the following year.[10] In the end, though, Harkin did not have to concern himself with the timing because none of the projects qualified for direct assistance. Under the terms of the Unemployment Relief Act approved during the special session, the Bennett government provided $20 million to the provinces to help them finance relief expenditures.[11] Affirming that unemployment was a local responsibility,[12] the act was also a temporary, emergency measure scheduled to expire the following spring. What particularly affected Harkin's plans, however, was the government's insistence that none of the funds could be used by any federal department.[13] The only way, then, that the Parks Department could get any of its projects financed was if a province agreed to use part of its share of the special relief appropriation to establish work camps in a national park.

The regulations governing the relief fund came as a severe blow to Harkin and his plans. And there was little he could do about it. His new boss, Thomas Murphy, was a small-town Manitoba druggist who would spend five inconspicuous years in the Interior portfolio. Although he had a strong local profile, particularly from his tenure as mayor of Neepawa, he was more likely chosen because he would do what he was told. Even sympathetic ministers, such as Harry Stevens of Trade and Commerce, carried little influence. In August 1930, the veteran parliamentarian toured his new British Columbia riding of Kootenay East and strongly endorsed the relief projects identified for Yoho and

Kootenay National Parks.[14] This backing did not sway the government from its course. As one commentator has observed, there was only one cook in the Bennett kitchen and that was the prime minister.[15]

But all was not lost. Both Manitoba and Saskatchewan opted to use a portion of their federal monies to provide temporary work in Riding Mountain and Prince Albert National Parks over the winter months. This decision made good sense for a number of reasons. Because the parks had just been set aside—Riding Mountain as recently as February 1930—there was a great deal of manual labour that could be done there at relatively little cost. And although the parks fell under federal jurisdiction, the provinces stood to benefit from their improvement and development through the generation of tourist dollars. Above all, the park camps would get the unemployed out of populated centres and thereby ease some of the strain on the already overburdened municipal relief agencies.

Work crews started to arrive at the park camps on a rotating basis in late October 1930. Most were married men from the surrounding towns and municipalities, while a few—single transients—had been sent from the larger cities. All were entitled to collect a maximum of $100 for two months' work, at which time they were to be replaced by another group of unemployed. This alternating arrangement did not please either the men or local park authorities. But work was work. Unlike the situation with the aliens who came before them, this new batch of park workers was generally happy to be given the chance to earn a decent wage and enjoy regular meals, whatever the location and job, and there were no complaints, except for the prospect of having to go home to no

One of the first jobs of the relief workers at Prince Albert was to build their own camps. *Prince Albert National Park Collection, 046-03*

Man attending to the laundry at Camp 5, Prince Albert National Park, January 1933.
Prince Albert National Park Collection, 046–48

job. One middle-aged businessman, when questioned by a Prince Albert reporter about his suitability for bush work, remarked, "Never you mind, just let me get behind one of those axes, and in a day or two I'll be as tough as the toughest. I'm looking forward to the experience."[16]

The parks also profited. In Prince Albert, the men enlarged the townsite campground by filling in muskeg, brushed along the main park highway, and cut seventy-seven miles of park boundary. At Riding Mountain, on the other hand, the men devoted most of their energies to running roads east and north from the townsite to Norgate and Dauphin respectively. When winter weather stalled this work, they cleared around Clear Lake for future cottage development. By the time the camps were shut down in late winter, roughly a thousand men had passed through the camps in the two prairie parks. One senior Saskatchewan civil servant lauded the experiment as "mighty fine."[17]

Although a beginning, the Riding Mountain and Prince Albert operations were a far cry from the kind of relief programme originally proposed by Commissioner Harkin. What made the situation even worse was that several parks faced an unemployment problem of their own. Because of severely limited funds, the Parks Department had to reduce its workforce in the fall of 1930. Park residents consequently faced a double whammy; not only were they unable to find local work over the winter months, but they were also deemed ineligible for provincial relief since they lived on federal land. Harkin estimated in mid-October that more than a thousand men could be out of work in the western parks, and pleaded with his superiors to fund some of his special projects.[18] Prime Minister Bennett eventually became involved in the matter—

most likely in response to complaints from his Banff constituents—and personally telephoned Harkin at his home on Saturday, 10 January 1931 to inquire about
the unemployment crisis in the parks.[19] Four days later, an order-in-council was
approved, authorizing the disbursement of $33,000 from the unemployment
grant for relief work for about 330 men for a month in Banff, Jasper, and
Waterton Lakes National Parks.[20] Although the sum fell more than $400,000 short
of what Harkin had targeted for the three parks, he scored a moral victory, as
the government retreated from its earlier position that the special relief funds
could not be allocated directly to the Parks Department. It also set a precedent,
for within a month, Riding Mountain also received a grant from the unemployment fund.

· · ·

The Bennett government's relief programme was to end in March 1931, when
it was expected that the ailing economy would be on the mend. Unemployment was not new to Canada in the 1930s—the country had experienced a series
of recessions in the past—and it was innocently assumed that the economic
storm could best be weathered by seeking temporary shelter under the umbrella of retrenchment and restraint.[21] The forecast remained bleak that spring,
however, as the international prices for Canadian commodities went into a free
fall, while the weekly tallies of the unemployed added up to unprecedented
amounts. Initially hit the hardest were the thousands of low-skilled workers,
many of them recent immigrants, who laboured on a seasonal basis in agriculture or resource industries. As the price of wheat, for example, nosedived to its
lowest recorded level in three hundred years, the demand for farm labour
simply disappeared and with it, the hopes of thousands of transient harvesters
for several weeks' steady work. Other Canadians began to suffer as well.
Because of Canada's heavy reliance on export markets, the depressed prices
sent shock waves through the rest of the economy; all industries—be they
construction, manufacturing, service, or transportation—felt the sting of lost
business. People who had enjoyed steady employment for much of their
working lives were sent home, while an entire generation of new workers
never got the chance to realize some of its hopes and dreams. Winnipegger
James Gray perhaps best captured the mood of those "winter years" when he
said, "Our world stopped and we got off."[22]

What made the Depression worse for most Canadians was the popular
attitude towards relief at the time. It was widely believed in early twentieth-
century Canada that there was always work to be had and that any able-bodied
person on relief was lazy. As a result, many of the jobless in the early 1930s
found it personally degrading to apply for assistance, even if they had a family
at home without food or clothing. Relief carried with it a stigma—it was a badge
of failure and disgrace. "The wounds of war leave scars," recounted one
survivor, "but the wounds of humiliation and lost pride leave their scars here,

up here in the mind. Oh, I could have wept for some of those people . . . with all that pride in them."[23] The problem was further compounded by the fact that the municipal relief structure was based on the English poor-law tradition. In other words, assistance was deliberately provided at the lowest possible level to encourage people to continue to work, even at the most menial, ill-paid job. The needy had to vouch, moreover, that they had no other resources to fall back on—such as a bank account, car, or relative—and that they were completely destitute. One of the jobless likened this declaration of poverty to signing away one's manhood.[24] The severity of the economic collapse, however, was such that even with these fiscal and psychological deterrents, the number of unemployed quickly overwhelmed the limited resources of municipal relief agencies.

Confronted with this dismal situation when Parliament reconvened in March 1931, the Conservatives naively asserted that although the recession was particularly persistent, traditional solutions would ultimately prevail. In the interim, in keeping with the government's ad hoc approach to the Depression, another dose of emergency relief assistance was prescribed. The nature and amount of this aid were the subject of considerable debate on the floor of the House of Commons, and even touched upon national parks. When the department's 1931-32 budget was being discussed in early July 1931, J.S. Woodsworth, the acknowledged saint of Canadian politics, suggested that the current crisis offered "a splendid opportunity" to undertake a major relief programme in the parks.[25] Liberal opposition leader William Lyon Mackenzie King, who was instrumental in setting aside Prince Albert National Park, echoed these sentiments, arguing that park relief work would serve "a double purpose": men would be doing something meaningful in return for unemployment assistance.[26] Other members agreed, the consensus being that the improvement of national parks was a good use of relief funds, especially if the parks were made more accessible to the general public. The only sour note was voiced by Henry Mullins, a Conservative backbencher whose Marquette riding included Riding Mountain National Park. Mullins had evidently been overwhelmed with requests following the 1930 creation of the park and would not have been upset to see it removed from his constituency. Thomas Murphy, for his part, was largely silent during the debate—even though the members were talking about one of his areas of responsibility—and simply expressed regret about the curtailment of the park relief camps.

The Bennett government's new relief legislation, the Unemployment and Farm Relief Act, was in place in early August 1931. Like its predecessor, the act not only affirmed that unemployment was fundamentally a local matter, but placed a time-limit on federal assistance. What was different about the legislation, however, was that the amount of money available for unemployment relief was left to the discretion of the government; it could spend whatever was

By January 1932, nearly thirteen hundred men were housed in one of ten camps at Riding Mountain National Park. *Riding Mountain National Park Collection*

deemed necessary. The act also specified that the funds could be used for public projects "and any other works and undertakings of any nature of any kind whatsoever."[27] This change effectively meant that the Parks Department could proceed with its own relief programme—separate from that of the provinces. And within a few weeks, the idea of running relief camps in western Canada's national parks over the winter received official blessing.

The approval of the park camps was a logical decision for the Conservative administration. Not only had the idea been favourably bandied about by all parties in the House of Commons, but civic boards and newspapers had also called for national park work camps.[28] The proposal would also provide some temporary relief until the anticipated recovery finally kicked in. Although the Bennett government was reluctant to assume direct responsibility for the unemployed and steadfastly believed that the crisis would soon be over, it had received a troubling assessment of the situation in western Canada from the minister of Labour, Gideon Robertson. During a special tour of the prairies in June 1931, Robertson was shocked by the almost total collapse of the grain economy and urged that the region's single unemployed be put to work in highway camps.[29] Since the Parks Department had already done its homework and many of its proposed projects involved road building, it made sense to give the park relief scheme the go-ahead, especially when the government lacked any other concerted plan of attack. The most important consideration, however, was probably politics. The Bennett-led Conservatives had wrested the prairies away from the Liberals in the 1930 general election and if they were going to consolidate this gain, they had to take care of the region. Park relief camps could serve this purpose, especially when the prime minister and other Conservative members represented ridings that included or bordered national

Chief Engineer J.M. Wardle (far left), Big Bend Highway, 1932. Wardle was responsible for coordinating the national park relief programme. *Whyte Museum of the Canadian Rockies, Byron Harmon Collection, NA71–1734*

parks.[30] The camps would get the unemployed off the streets, help beleaguered businesses, and provide local improvements for which thankful constituents could express their appreciation in the next election. And it was all possible because of the open-ended nature of the new relief act, which gave the Bennett government considerable discretionary power to use unemployment funds for patronage purposes.[31]

The man in charge of the national park relief work was James Wardle.[32] A graduate of the civil engineering programme at Queen's University, the twenty-six-year-old Wardle had joined the engineering service of the Parks Department in 1914, and within a year was named acting chief of the branch when his supervisor enlisted. This position was formalized in the early 1920s, at which time he was also briefly moonlighting as superintendent of Banff National Park. Wardle was a perfect candidate for overseeing the park camps and their work. His first love was building highways, and his technical expertise was often called upon to flesh out Commissioner Harkin's ambitious road-building schemes—it was Wardle who served as general supervisor for the enemy alien work projects during the war and who subsequently devised the preliminary list of park relief projects. As a native British Columbian, he also had an intimate understanding of the difficulties entailed by many of the park highway projects, and welcomed the challenge. In addition, Wardle had an uncanny knack for handling details, and his records betray a man obsessed with providing accounts down to every quarter cent spent and every yard of earth moved. He would need these organizing skills, for he was expected to coordinate relief projects in no fewer than ten national parks. The extent and nature of the activities, however, would be determined by the largesse of the Bennett government.

· · ·

The first funds for park relief projects were approved in early October 1931, once the fall harvest on the prairies was winding down; other monies were forthcoming at regular intervals over the next few months. One of the most favoured beneficiaries was Riding Mountain National Park, which was granted $200,000 for relief work—more than six times the amount Harkin had originally sought for the park a year earlier.[33] This sum reflected the size of the unemployment problem in Winnipeg, as well as the fact that Riding Mountain was the newest park in the system and required a lot of development, especially in advance of the official park opening. It also did not hurt that the Manitoba representative in the federal cabinet was the minister of the Interior, and although somewhat invisible on the national scene, he had enough political sense to take care of his home province. Murphy personally investigated the employment prospects in the park shortly after his appointment in August 1930[34] and was probably instrumental in getting the province to allocate some of its federal relief assistance to park work over the winter of 1930-31. The size of the grant from the 1931 unemployment fund was also undoubtedly a consequence of Murphy's influence.

The Riding Mountain relief operations were reactivated in early November 1931 and by Christmas, nearly a thousand men were housed in one of ten camps "humming with activity."[35] As during the previous winter, residents from the surrounding communities were sent to the park on a quota basis. Many were looking for work to help them get through the winter, while others were just out of school. Jimmy Brown of nearby Onanole, for example, was hired as a teamster and paid $1.25 a day for the use of his own team of horses.[36] Three young teenaged brothers from Brandon, on the other hand, had to go away to Riding Mountain so the rest of their family could get relief assistance.[37] A large number of transients and recent immigrants were also absorbed from the province's larger centres. Such was the case of Ed Turner, who had no sooner arrived in Winnipeg from England than he was shipped off to the park.[38] Priority was to be given to veterans, but this distinction was often ignored by overzealous relief authorities, who were more concerned with exporting the problem of the single homeless unemployed to the park. As a consequence, by early January 1932, Riding Mountain had a camp population approaching thirteen hundred, well in excess of the anticipated numbers. This development inflamed regional jealousies and caused one of the local newspapers to wonder whether the park was being used "for the sake of keeping Winnipeg's unemployed out of trouble."[39]

Not a word of criticism, however, was levelled against the work performed by the men, whether locals or transients. Construction was not only resumed on the Norgate road from park headquarters to the eastern boundary, but several hundred men were also kept busy over the winter, clearing and burning along the projected highway through the park to Dauphin. Work crews also performed a wide range of tasks in the Wasagaming townsite and around Clear Lake, such as laying water and sewage pipes, building kitchen shelters and food lockers in the campground, and brushing cottage subdivisions. Another batch of recruits, armed only with grub hoes, was kept busy over the winter improving and enlarging the park golf-course.[40] By the following spring, the Minnedosa *Tribune* reported that the park promised to be the "most remarkable zoo in the world";[41] it is not clear whether the paper was talking about the animals or the men.

Depositing rocks in the new Clear Lake breakwater, Riding Mountain National Park.
Riding Mountain National Park Collection

It was also relief gangs who erected some of the first government structures, both in the park townsite and along the north shore of Clear Lake. Under the watchful tutelage of local foremen skilled in stone and log work, the men immediately started work on a new administration building and superintendent's residence, and later a golf clubhouse and east entrance gate. All proved to be attractive, enduring facilities, but the centrepiece was a museum-community building situated on a slight rise of land between the new administrative centre and the entrance to the main campground. The one-and-a-half-storey log structure, with its stone and half-timbered detailing, dominated the townsite, even more so because of the extensive landscaping that completed the project. Men whose lives had come crashing down over the past few months found themselves creating an old English garden more in keeping with another time and place. They planted wildflowers and shrubs, erected a fountain and pergola, laid flagstone walkways, and constructed a summer cottage with a thatched roof. They even arranged in front of the museum a small flower bed in the shape of a crown and the initials of King George V.[42] Whatever the intention of its designers, the regal tribute was a testament to the men's pride, patriotism, and resilience. Many undoubtedly mused, though, as they passed the site each day, whether the system that had caused them to be there was worth saving.

These various activities required careful coordination, and it was readily apparent from the organization of the relief operations that the Parks Department had learned from its experience with the enemy alien camps some fifteen years earlier. All the services essential to the relief operations, such as administration, engineering, maintenance, and stores, were located at a central camp in Wasagaming and supervised by a member of Wardle's staff in consultation with the park superintendent. The other nine camps were established at or near the worksites—along the new road right-of-ways, the boundaries, and the northeast shore of Clear Lake—in locations that could be easily serviced during the winter. Camp buildings were either old, refurbished log buildings from prepark lumbering days, or new frame-and-tar-paper structures often constructed by the men themselves upon their arrival; the exceptions were the boundary operations, which had to make do with tents in order to be mobile. Each camp was more or less self-contained and featured two or more bunkhouses, a kitchen and dining hall, an outbuilding, wash house, root cellar, and stable. Camp supplies were secured from an approved list of local businesses and regularly trucked from Wasagaming to the outlying camps.

Camp survivors all declared the meals to have been wholesome and plentiful. They had to be. Not only did many individuals arrive at the park in poor physical shape,[43] but in the interests of providing work for as many as possible and as cheaply as possible, the men were expected to do as much as they could by hand; heavy machinery was used only rarely. A typical one-day menu featured good, basic food: porridge, bacon, toast, apricots, and cake for breakfast; roast beef, peas, potatoes, and pudding for dinner; and fried sausage, mashed potatoes, cheese, and various desserts for supper.[44] There was no shortage of fresh baking. One former cook at another park camp recalls making thirty-two loaves of bread daily (except Sunday), two to four cakes each day, and sixteen or more pies every other day.[45]

The men had fewer kind words for the clothing, in particular the footwear.

Park authorities ensured that the relief workers were well-fed—in large part because of the emphasis on manual labour. *Canadian Parks Service, Western Regional Office, Webster Collection*

Although new arrivals were issued a work outfit after two weeks, including wool pants, overalls, and a black sweater with orange or yellow trim, they were expected to get through the winter in gumboots.[46]

The most consistent complaint, however, was the housing. The bunkhouses were remembered as little more than tar-paper shacks—without insulation! Heat was provided by two large converted fuel drums that were constantly fed wood by a camp fireman, whose job was to tend the fire night and day. This arrangement made for uncomfortable sleeping conditions; the men in the bottom bunks were always freezing, while those on top were usually too hot.[47] The bunks were little better. One gentleman, who spent four consecutive winters in the park camps from the age of fifteen, suggested that only a horse could enjoy the bedding; the men stuffed their ticks with straw that had been brought in by local farmers and dumped outside the bunkhouses.[48] The real adventure, though, was the latrines. The men had to deftly balance themselves on a peeled pole that ran the length of the building above a deep trench. The outhouses at Waterton Lakes were even worse; there were normally no doors on the buildings, even in winter, and the seat next to the entrance was always cold, if not wet.[49]

For those injured on the job or otherwise taken ill, there was a small camp hospital in the townsite; serious cases were transported to one of the local hospitals. Transients had to contribute one dollar per month for what could best be described as medical insurance; local men, on the other hand, were

The men from the camps surrounding Clear Lake were paraded to the central bathhouse in the park townsite—even on cold wintry days—at least once a week. *Riding Mountain National Park Collection*

expected to go home if they were unable to work. At the end of their eight-hour day, the men could either read books and magazines, listen to gramophone records, or play cards and checkers, all of which had been donated by Winnipeg service clubs. Some gambled, but not on a regular basis, because it was difficult to find people with enough money to get a game going. A few continued their schooling; the youngest of the three Brandon teenagers completed his grade seven and eight while in camp.[50] The park administration also rented a local restaurant in Wasagaming—the Wigwam—and used it as a central recreation hall and commissary. It housed the only camp radio, and any interesting news items were typed and distributed to the outlying camps as the "Wigwam Daily."[51] Many men probably waited in vain for word that the Depression was over.

· · ·

Similar operations were carried out in neighbouring Saskatchewan at Prince Albert National Park, but with considerably less funds. The park received only a quarter of the relief monies that Riding Mountain did for 1931-32, even though the province was hit as hard as Manitoba, if not harder, by the Depression. Mackenzie King, the creator of the park, however, was no longer prime minister, and Prince Albert had to be thankful that its relief grant equalled roughly the amount that had been cut from its annual budget.[52] Things could have been much worse, but the Bennett government evidently decided that it was better to keep Mackenzie King quiet rather than give him an issue, especially one that directly affected his home riding.[53] Like Riding Mountain, the relief camp operations at Prince Albert were strategically located in the townsite or along the central highway, and directed by a resident engineer based at a headquarters camp at McKenzie Creek near the main park entrance. Much of the work was also the same—only on a smaller scale—and included road construction and maintenance, boundary demarkation, and campground development. Unlike workers in its sister park, however, the local men laboured in and around Waskesiu and were deliberately kept separate from the transients, who were given jobs along the park margins.

Elk Island used relief funds to undertake an extensive brushing and burning programme to improve the grazing capacity of the park. *Canadian Parks Service, Western Regional Office, Webster Collection*

The other prairie national park to benefit from relief work that winter was Elk Island in eastcentral Alberta. Although the park served as a regional playground for the surrounding farming communities, it had been established before the First World War as a game sanctuary, first for elk and then buffalo. Unlike other national parks, then, where relief projects were largely concerned with building roads and developing recreational facilities, Elk Island also wanted to use relief funds to undertake an extensive brushing and burning programme to improve the grazing capacity of the park.[54] This activity was more in keeping with the preservation principle underlying recent national parks legislation.[55] It was also the kind of labour-intensive work favoured by the federal government; it required limited skills, little equipment, and was best done over the winter, when unemployment was normally highest. Other national parks in Alberta, however, had greater prestige, and Elk Island—the poor cousin in comparison—had to make do with only 150 relief workers, the majority unemployed veterans from Edmonton. These men had no sooner got started in October 1931 clearing bush and building a new road to the south gate, than it appeared the operations would have to be discontinued at the end of the year. At this point, the mayor of Edmonton and the Alberta premier intervened and successfully lobbied the federal government for additional funding that would keep the Elk Island camps going until the spring.[56] Conservative back-bencher and former Edmonton mayor Ambrose Bury, whose federal riding included the park, likely played a role as well.

At Elk Island National Park, the men carefully banked hay bales around their sleeping tents in order to keep warm. *Canadian Parks Service, Western Regional Office, Webster Collection*

· · ·

The experience at Waterton Lakes, in the southwest corner of the province, was completely different. Established in 1910, the park had become a favourite recreational retreat for southern Alberta communities, despite the fact that it lacked a direct link, rail or road. This access problem was not uncommon for new national parks, particularly for recent creations such as Riding Mountain and Prince Albert. What made it a special concern in Waterton's case was the fact that the park was nestled up against Glacier National Park in neighbouring Montana. Park authorities from both sides of the border were anxious to develop a road link between the two parks, thereby creating an international playground for tourists from Canada and the United States. Added impetus arose in 1927, when the American-based Great Northern Railway, which already operated the Many Glaciers Hotel in Montana, built the Prince of Wales Hotel in the Waterton townsite; the only way that American guests could reach the new hotel, after detraining at Glacier Park station, was by a roundabout route via Cardston, Alberta. By the beginning of the Depression, however, a Waterton-Glacier link was still only an idea. Although a new road had been built southwest from the Waterton townsite to Cameron Lake in the late 1920s, British Columbia was refusing to give up land in the southeast corner of the province to allow the Akamina Pass highway to continue into Montana's Flathead valley. The other possible route, a highway southeast along the Belly River valley to the international boundary, had been crudely surveyed but was otherwise stalled until the necessary funds were found and more importantly, American co-operation was guaranteed; it made no sense to build a highway to the border unless there was an American road to meet it.[57]

National park relief work offered a chance to bring the Waterton road schemes a step closer to reality. And the Association of South Alberta Boards of Trade was determined to see that the park secured its rightful share of federal funds, especially since attendance was setting new records each year; between 1925-26 and 1929-30 the number of park visitors increased more than fivefold. At their December 1929 meeting in Pincher Creek, the trade boards had collectively passed a resolution calling on the Parks Department to undertake a number of ambitious improvements in Waterton—to the tune of $150,000. Although many of these projects were initially proposed with local tourism in mind, they were ideally suited for unemployment work and subsequently formed the basis of the Waterton relief programme.[58] Securing the necessary funds was another matter, and this was likely the handiwork of J.S. Stewart, the new Conservative representative for the region. A Lethbridge dentist, decorated Great War veteran, and experienced provincial politician, General Stewart supported the idea of park relief work and used his position to have men placed in the camps. He also had no qualms about promoting his own interests and regularly held political meetings at Waterton.[59] It really was no surprise, then, that the park received a healthy dose of relief funds from the Bennett government in the early fall of 1931.

The men sent to the Waterton camps were either local unemployed from the surrounding communities or homeless drifters in search of work. Some were living at the time in makeshift shelters in the coulees, digging into the banks and lining the hollows with whatever material was available; they would slip into town each day for a hand-out or a meal in a soup kitchen and then head back to their homes in the hills.[60] If, after applying for admission to the camps, they were confirmed by authorities to be without work or destitute *and* able to perform manual labour, they could be sent to the park. The trip to Waterton was usually made in the back of an open truck—even when it was snowing. "Upon arriving at the start of the Akamina Road in Waterton," one informant recalled, "we were told the snow was too deep for the trucks to go any farther, we would have to walk, this was just at dusk. We got to our destination, four and a half miles up the road, at 1:30 a.m., cold, wet, and very tired from slogging through the deep snow."[61] A few of the new workers arrived at camp looking and smelling like paupers, and if they did nothing to clean up their appearance, the other men would often wrestle off and burn their clothes and then give their new bunkmates a good scrubbing. Other problems were not so easily solved. The camp storeskeeper, an alcoholic, quietly consumed lemon extract and then peed into the empty containers; he was found out when one of his special bottles was accidentally shipped to camp four, where the cook there drank it.[62] More palatable treats were the whitefish and pike netted in the lower Waterton Lakes. When advised of the practice, Chief Engineer Wardle wondered whether this "somewhat novel departure" constituted an infringement of national park regulations; the fishing stopped in late February.[63]

The relief gangs performed a wide range of work in the Waterton townsite that winter. Small groups of local men cut and graded new streets, laid sidewalks and curbs, dug sump holes, brushed and levelled the campground, and installed sanitation facilities. They also partially rerouted and resurfaced the roads leading to the townsite. About a hundred single transients from Lethbridge, meanwhile, were put to work improving the Akamina Pass highway in anticipation of the day when the road would be extended into British Columbia. Here, they widened and cleared the right-of-way, installed faced rubble walling along the outside edge of the road to prevent erosion, and erected stone monuments for guard rails. It was heavy, treacherous labour, especially building the rock retaining wall—one slip and a worker could fall to his death. To the men's credit, though, it was accomplished with little equip-

Relief workers installed faced rubble walling along the outside edge of the Akamina Pass highway, Waterton Lakes, to prevent erosion, April 1932. *Canadian Parks Service, Western Regional Office, Webster Collection*

Some men did little more than clear snow or cut wood in the mountain camps. Eldon camp, Banff. *Canadian Parks Service, Western Regional Office, Webster Collection*

ment and few injuries. The greatest challenge came from a spell of "rough and wet" weather in late March 1932, which, if not for the hurried construction of a series of temporary ditches, might have washed away much of the winter's work. The timing could not have been worse, however, for the men were in the midst of dismantling the camps and shutting down operations for the season.[64]

. . .

Jasper also enjoyed its share of relief activity. In January 1931, along with Waterton Lakes and Banff, the park had received emergency funding for a number of small, short-term projects to help the local workforce get through the winter.[65] These operations resumed in September 1931 under the provisions of the new relief act, but, unlike the previous winter, many of the men who now made up the work gangs were railway workers who had been laid off by Canadian National. The numbers available to the park—some three hundred destitute souls—meant that several major road improvements could be tackled, in addition to work in the townsite. The Maligne Canyon, Edith Cavell, Pyramid, and Miette Hot Springs roads, as well as the Yellowhead highway, all received substantial upgrading, including work on the bridges and approaches.

This relief labour was paid at the standard rate of twenty-five to thirty cents per hour, depending on the nature of the work, for an eight-hour day, six-day week—less eighty-five cents per day for meals. It was not much, especially for the handful of former businessmen and professionals, who were not used to camp life and the daily demands on their strength and stamina entailed in the road work. But only a dozen men reportedly quit the park camps during the first two months.[66] The alternative, returning to Edmonton, evidently held little attraction. A journalist who spent twenty-four hours sleeping and eating with the unemployed in the city's old immigration hall found the occupants verminous and the food uneven. "One man," he reported, "was picking the lice from his underwear as he prepared for sleep."[67]

The Jasper operations proceeded without incident until the third week of November, when a blizzard swept through the region, leaving bone-chilling temperatures in its wake. Lacking adequate clothing, the men were unable to last more than an hour at the job before the cold forced them to retreat to their tents; even here they found little comfort and spent seemingly endless hours huddling together in home-made toques and with socks over their hands.[68] The harsh weather threatened to undermine relief activities in the park; not only were the men suffering, but they were paid only when they worked. Edmonton authorities warned the minister of the Interior about the problem by telegram— "no grumbling or unrest but real hardship"—and asked whether winter clothing and footwear could be advanced against the men's wages.[69] Before the matter could be quietly resolved, however, Reverend H.A. Edwards, the park chaplain, contacted the Edmonton newspapers about the desperate plight of the men— drawing special attention to the fact that many of them were veterans—and

Miette Hot Springs road camp, Jasper National Park, December 1931. *Canadian Parks Service, Western Regional Office, Webster Collection*

appealed for donations of warm clothing and boots; two hundred pairs of woollen socks and two dozen suits of underwear were shipped to Jasper by the newspaper's sunshine department over the next few days.[70] The adverse publicity caused the Parks Department acute embarrassment and in its defence, officials maintained that the park commissariat had always been well stocked with winter clothing at reasonable prices, but that the men chose to use their wages to pay off outstanding debts or for other purposes.[71] The damage had been done, however, and provincial authorities began to question the use of tents for winter quarters—even though relief operations in other parts of the province followed the same practice. Harkin and his chief engineer bristled at the criticism and privately called into question the experience and knowledge of the provincial inspector. In the end, though, they responded by seeing that all relief workers were properly outfitted and that frame and log buildings were erected wherever possible.[72] To prevent the men from spending their earnings on booze, the park superintendent also provided the Jasper liquor vendor with the names of those working on relief projects and asked him not to serve them in the interests of their wives and families and the community.

· · ·

Banff National Park, in the meantime, received special treatment. This was not surprising, since it was Canada's oldest, most famous, and most popular national park—it was in a class by itself. When it was learned that national parks would qualify for relief work under the new legislation, the Banff Advisory Council immediately sent the minister of the Interior a list of possible projects, mentioning the usual items such as road improvements and general maintenance activities. What was unique, however, was the request for funds to build a new bathhouse and pool at the Upper Hot Springs.[73] It was generally acknowledged that a new facility was required; the old Cave and Basin pool was not up to modern standards. Relief projects, however, were supposed to employ as many men as possible for as long as possible for as little money as possible. Major building ventures requiring special skills, equipment, and materials were generally to be avoided, unless the park had just been set aside, as in the case of Riding Mountain and to a lesser extent, Prince Albert. The proposed Upper Hot Springs pool was different, though; it involved the prime minister's home riding. And in early September 1931, the Parks Department found itself scrambling to complete plans and specifications for the new facility.[74] The estimated $75,000 cost represented almost half the proposed relief expenditure for Banff, and was well in excess of the amounts that would be eventually expended that winter in all other parks except Riding Mountain.

Work got underway at Banff in late September 1931, and over the next five months almost five hundred men were given employment. The majority of the workers were local unemployed, mostly veterans and/or married individuals with dependants, who laboured at various tasks in and around the townsite:

improving the Banff–Lake Louise highway, clearing a new scenic drive up Stoney Squaw Mountain, building a new road to the Upper Hot Springs, laying cement sidewalks in the townsite, and of course, constructing the new Upper Hot Springs bathhouse. Some fifty unemployed transients secured in Calgary were divided into two camps and put to work either widening the eastern park section of the Banff-Calgary highway or cutting the eastern boundary of the park. Although these gangs were gradually supplemented over the fall, the number of single homeless from Calgary remained small relative to the local workforce. Park authorities wanted not only to keep these unfortunate victims of the Depression separate from other workers—they were an underprivileged class—but balked at assigning them any jobs that would bring them even within sight of the townsite. A proposal to have them clear the underbrush on Sulphur Mountain, for example, was flatly rejected on such grounds.[75]

Pouring concrete for the foundation walls, Upper Hot Springs bathhouse, Banff, 1932. *National Archives of Canada, C141584*

The Banff camps—both local and transient—were models of activity that fall, and the superintendent spoke in glowing terms of the fine work being accomplished.[76] The new Upper Hot Springs bathhouse, however, soon presented problems. Because of the lack of plans and the search for a suitable site, work did not get started on the facility until mid-October, when local men began excavating the foundations and quarrying and hauling stone from Mount Rundle. By late November, when actual construction of the building and pool was ready to proceed, the park superintendent realized there was not enough relief money for both the bathhouse and the other park relief gangs. Materials for the new facility would cost an estimated $35,000, while the work itself would have to be done by skilled tradesmen at a wage in keeping with the standard construction rate. Knowing that the project had the blessing of the Banff Council and the prime minister's office, the superintendent recommended that sixty-five men be immediately released from other park relief work in favour of completing the bathhouse—even though the project would provide work for no more than fifty men over the winter.[77] This suggestion did not sit well with the Parks Department—Harkin and Wardle were still smarting from the recent Jasper fiasco—and it was initially decided to transfer $25,000 from the bathhouse appropriation in order to keep the Banff relief camps running.[78] Less than a week later, however, Parks officials reversed themselves and requested additional funding for the work camps. This money was forthcoming by cabinet order in two instalments, first in December and then January.[79] It was probably no coincidence that Chief Engineer Wardle had kept the prime minister's private secretary apprised of the situation over the winter.[80]

· · ·

The park relief funding also meant that one of Commissioner Harkin's favourite schemes would finally be realized—namely, a highway between Banff and Jasper. He had first proposed the idea after the war as a means of capturing tourist traffic for the region, but nothing had come of it. Now, with the number of unemployed steadily climbing in western Canada, it seemed a perfect relief project, especially since it could provide work for several hundred jobless men from both Calgary and Edmonton. It also posed, however, formidable engineering and construction challenges—all the more so since most of the work was labour-intensive—and one wonders whether the highway would have been tackled for several years if not for the availability of this large pool of idle labour. The Parks Engineering Service approached the proposed 147-mile highway with a healthy mixture of respect and trepidation, and it was not until after the project had received federal approval and construction actually started that the route was finalized in October 1931.[*81] Given the location of the highway and the obstacles involved, the announcement of the project attracted considerable newspaper attention. One enthusiastic reporter predicted that when the road was complete, in about two years' time, it would quickly become known as

---

* The road would traverse some of the most spectacular scenery along the eastern edge of the Rocky Mountains. From Lake Louise, the eighteen-foot-wide gravel highway would proceed north along the upper reaches of the Bow River to the Bow Pass (the highest point along the 150-mile route) and then down through the Mistaya River valley to the North Saskatchewan River. The road would then ascend again, skirting the Columbia Icefields, to the summit of Sunwapta Pass—what the engineers simply termed "The Big Hill." From here, it would drop down beside the Sunwapta River to the Athabasca River and then continue along the river, where it would eventually meet the Edith Cavell road, outside the Jasper townsite.

"The Highway in the Clouds." The relief workers were much less romantic about the job and sarcastically dubbed it "Bennett's Five-Year Plan."[82] Neither prediction proved even close. The so-called Big Hill caused big headaches and big delays, and the highway was not finished until the beginning of the Second World War.

The Parks Department planned to attack the highway from each end and have the two advancing forces meet at Sunwapta Pass, the boundary between the two parks. Beginning in late September 1931, gangs of labourers from Calgary and Edmonton began to take up positions at Lake Louise and Jasper respectively, while survey teams rushed ahead to locate and stake the route. It was initially assumed that a thousand men from the two major Alberta cities would begin work on the project and that the size of the force would eventually climb to twenty-five hundred.[83] This number, however, was never realized. At its peak in early December 1931, before the weather restricted activities, the labour force amounted to 750 men: 400 in eight camps at the Banff end and 350 in seven camps at Jasper. None of the workers assigned to the project were local unemployed. All were transients, mostly veterans, who had no choice but to accept their placement or lose what limited assistance they received; 8 men who refused to go to Lake Louise with the first work gang were immediately cut off relief and thrown out of the Calgary employment office.[84]

Because of the push to get the highway underway, camp conditions were less than ideal at the outset. Men had to sleep in tents and try to keep warm with two army blankets until log bunkhouses were erected. Many had also arrived in camp without suitable clothing for working in the mountains during late fall, and spent cold days on the job to go along with their cold nights. During the

The Banff-Jasper highway project provided work for hundreds of single unemployed men from Calgary and Edmonton. *Glenbow Archives NA-4775-31*

unusually frigid weather at Jasper that November, two highway workers evidently cut a deck of cards to see who would wear a set of donated underwear and pair of socks. Some shared whatever extra clothing they had, be it a shirt or sweater. Still others refused to swallow their pride and accept charity, "declaring they had come to work on the highway and wished to pay for what they received."[85] These shortcomings did not result in any serious labour trouble, in large part because it would not have been tolerated—a situation confirmed by men who worked in other parks. When a Great War veteran was released for the second time from one of the Jasper camps for complaining about the conditions, and twenty-one other men laid down their tools in a sympathy strike, all were discharged by the camp foreman. Not even the intervention of the Edmonton branch of the Ex-Servicemen's Association could get the strikers reinstated.[86] The message was plain and brutally simple: any worker who argued with project supervisors or bitched about camp life could expect immediate expulsion.[87]

Those who remained committed to their jobs faced two obstacles. On 24 December 1931, it was officially announced that the highway camps would have to close at the end of the year because of the exhaustion of project funds. The men were paid and plans made to evacuate them in the early new year. In a spirit more in keeping with the season, however, the Bennett administration pushed through an order a few days later giving the camps a reprieve until the end of February;[88] the government likely wanted to avoid the howls of protest that would have accompanied the return of the transients to Calgary and Edmonton. The other obstacle, which could not be so easily overcome, was the arrival of winter. By mid-December, there were twelve inches of snow at the Jasper end of the highway and over two feet around Lake Louise. The onset of winter brought grading to a standstill and hampered other operations as well. Thereafter, the men did their best to clear and stump the right-of-way, install culverts and ditches in anticipation of the spring run-off, and build tote roads for bringing in supplies and freight. Most of this work was done by hand. At one point at the south end, for example, where the road had been staked across a hillside, men perched atop ladders, hacking away mercilessly at the earth and loose shale, while a nimble gang below shovelled the debris into wheelbarrows; whenever solid rock was encountered, the men were called in, a dynamite charge set off, and the clearing resumed.[89] Someone stumbling upon the scene on a wintry day might have mistaken it for a kind of devil's workshop.

• • •

Weather also played havoc with the relief work at the national parks in southeastern British Columbia. At Yoho National Park, small groups of local unemployed—no more than twenty men to a crew—upgraded local park roads, widened sections of the new highway between Field and Golden, and built a new bridge over the Kicking Horse River at Leanchoil. All of this work, except

Snow—and lots of it—often forced the closure of mountain relief camps, such as this one at Yoho National Park. *Canadian Parks Service, Western Regional Office, Webster Collection*

for the bridge construction, lasted less than a few months before it had to be shut down because of deteriorating conditions. The same problem arose at Kootenay National Park. Here, in early October 1931, about fifty local unemployed men began making general improvements to the Banff-Windermere road. A month later, Chief Engineer Wardle wired Harkin about the urgent need to outfit the project truck with a snow plough; otherwise it would soon be impossible to service the camps, let alone perform the road work. In what surely ranks as a classic understatement of the men's plight, Wardle warned, "communication . . . must be maintained throughout winter . . . would be inhuman [to] allow these camps to be isolated in mountains."[90] Kootenay secured its plough, allowing relief operations to continue into the new year. The men must have wondered, however, whether their camps were going to be swallowed up by the snow, especially when their tents had to be overlain with boards to keep the walls from collapsing. Things eventually became so bad that it was decided in early February that closing the camps made more sense than trying to give the men a few weeks more employment. The wisdom of this decision was confirmed two weeks later when a snowslide swept across the Banff-Windermere highway near Vermilion Crossing and closed the road until spring.[91]

In February 1932, a snowslide swept across the Banff-Windermere highway and closed the road to Kootenay National Park until spring. The camp had been shut down only two weeks earlier. *National Archives of Canada, C141816*

The project that suffered the most from the mountain weather that winter was the Golden-Revelstoke road, popularly known as the Big Bend Highway. The project was also unique, in that it was the only national park relief operation that did not take place in a national park. In 1929, the federal and British Columbia governments had reached an agreement to build within three years a highway from Golden to Revelstoke around the wide, sweeping bend of the Columbia River—hence the name Big Bend Highway. The province would construct the western leg from Revelstoke to Canoe River, while the dominion government would contend with the section from Golden to Canoe Lake. This 190-mile stretch of road was the last major link in the western section of the Trans-Canada Highway[**][92] and was chosen over a more direct route through the Selkirk Mountains via Rogers Pass and Glacier National Park. Avalanches had played havoc with railway traffic through the pass and it was believed that a highway would suffer a similar fate.[93] The Big Bend route was also favoured because it was hoped that a connecting highway would someday be built from Canoe Lake to Jasper via Mount Robson, thereby opening a second route from the prairies to the Pacific. Responsibility for constructing the dominion leg of the highway fell to the Engineering Service of the National Parks Branch, which had performed this kind of work in western Canada for

---

[**] In the 1920s, the Banff–Lake Louise road had been pushed west through the Kicking Horse Pass to Yoho National Park. During the same period, the province of British Columbia had built a road from Golden to Yoho, and completed a highway up the Fraser valley to Revelstoke. By 1929, then, the roads on the east and west side of the Selkirks simply needed to be connected to provide a through route to the Pacific.

Hauling rocks from the roadbed of the Big Bend Highway beside the Columbia River.
Canadian Parks Service, Western Regional Office, Webster Collection

the federal Department of the Interior for the past two decades.

Construction of the federal portion of the Golden-Revelstoke highway began in October 1929, and within a year the dominion crews had pushed the road some thirty miles north of Donald. The Parks Engineering Service expected to complete the middle and acknowledged worst section of the highway by the fall of 1931. Funding cutbacks during the Bennett government's first few months in office, however, made a mockery of these plans, and Wardle found himself in the awkward position of having considerable heavy equipment for the project but not enough money to support any major construction activity; all he could do under the circumstances was to continue with the bridge work and try to prevent the deterioration of the existing grade.[94] The *Golden Star,* in the meantime, recommended that the road be finished as soon as possible "with the use of labour from those on the soup and bread lines."[95]

The situation looked as if it might rebound in the late fall of 1931, when the project received $20,000 in relief funding for the month of November.[96] About 130 local unemployed men, including miners from the Crow's Nest Pass area, were taken on and given the task of cutting a road through heavy timber towards Sullivan River. It was a formidable assignment, even for the well-equipped road gangs. The country was so wild that the highway locational team had to forge a new trail through much of the region before they could commence surveying. What made the job even more daunting, however, was the wet weather. Rain started falling in early September and continued every day until the snow arrived—by the foot—the second week of November. This mixture of mud and fresh, wet snow turned the right-of-way into "one frightful mess." The heavy equipment not only regularly broke down, but supply trucks could not make it through to the camps without the assistance of one or more tractors. Conditions were so bad that machinery was more often idle than running, while the horses had to be fed hay from the men's mattresses on several occasions. Numberless hours of overtime, meanwhile, were required just to keep the work going. It was enough to discourage even the most experienced, and by 15 November, the project superintendent was close to breaking. "This job has been nothing more or less than a nightmare," he privately confided to Wardle, "and I am absolutely fed up to the teeth."[97] The men themselves were much more sanguine about the state of affairs and were generally happy to have the work, given the desperate unemployment situation in the area.[98]

Wardle sympathized with his colleague, but reminded him that the Big Bend Highway was also a relief project and that he was to "keep this work going as long as humanly possible."[99] In the meantime, the chief engineer had

Heavy rains often turned the Big Bend grade into a frightful mess. Sections of the route quickly deteriorated and had to be regularly maintained. *Canadian Parks Service, Western Regional Office, Webster Collection*

problems of his own. The minister of the Interior could not understand why ploughs had been requested for the highway work when all the field reports indicated that the real problem was mud; a somewhat testy Wardle responded with a set of recent photographs of the incredible snow conditions in the region.[100] Continued financing also proved problematic. In late November 1931, the government approved another $20,000 in relief money for the highway. The funding came with a twist, though—it was to be taken from the budget of another park unemployment project. Neither Wardle nor Harkin believed there was any such "extra" money, and repeatedly sought direction from the minister as to what national park employment programme should be raided. In the end, the government decided to continue to finance the Golden-Revelstoke highway for the time being and wait and see whether any park projects would have to be closed down over the winter.[101] Ironically, this is exactly what happened to Big Bend road. With four to five feet of snow on the ground by mid-January, transportation problems simply became insurmountable and the men were sent home at the end of the month.

The closure of the Big Bend camps was followed over the next few weeks by the termination of relief operations in most other national parks. In fact, all projects financed through the 1931 Unemployment and Farm Relief Act were required to end by 1 March 1932. This deadline made little sense in the face of the growing unemployment crisis and in an effort to appease provincial leaders,[102] Prime Minister Bennett recalled Parliament in early February and extended the life of the act another two months. The Parks Department used the extra time to continue work on a few projects, such as the Upper Hot Springs bathhouse at Banff.[103] Most park relief activities, however, were scheduled to end in late February, when project funds would run out, and the extension was used in most instances to decommission the camps. Even large operations, like the one at Riding Mountain, were silent that spring.

· · ·

In retrospect, the 1931-32 national park relief programme was an overall success, especially when measured against those initiated by various municipalities and provinces. Many of the local employment projects were overly ambitious and were forced to shut down after only a few months because of funding shortfalls. Relief activities also suffered from a lack of coordination, consistency, and vision; solutions tended to be temporary in design and application and were better suited to serving political purposes than economic needs.[104] The national parks record, in contrast, was enviable. Harkin and his officials knew exactly what they wanted to do, and the ready availability of relief funds—a whopping $885,000 for the 1931-32 fiscal year—ensured that they were able to tackle a good portion of this work. Most of the park projects, moreover, were labour-intensive and thereby employed large numbers of men over the winter months.[105] These operations were not without their problems,

The Big Bend Highway project was "a life saver for people down and out on their luck." *Courtesy Robert Sime*

as evidenced by the complaints about inadequate clothing and accommodation, or the difficulties created by the weather. But once the projects were up and running and brought under Wardle's steady hand, the park relief programme ran smoothly and without major incident. And much was accomplished, albeit at a slower pace because of the emphasis on manual labour. As for the men, at a time when they could not fathom what was happening to the life they once knew, they came to value the food, shelter, and camaraderie offered by the park camps. They also welcomed the work, despite the hardships, and seemed to appreciate the fact that they were doing something useful. "The projects were a life saver for people down and out on their luck," one former Big Bend worker claimed more than sixty years later.[106] Similar sentiments were expressed by two of the three Brandon brothers who had been sent to Riding Mountain as mere teenagers.[107]

Sample Menu
Riding Mountain National Park
Relief Camp #6, March 1932

	Breakfast	Dinner	Supper
Monday	Porridge	Roast beef with	Cold beef
	Fried sausage	brown gravy	Hot roast pork
	Fried potatoes	Baked beans	Macaroni & cheese
	Stewed figs	Pickled beets	Stewed figs
	Corn bread	Boiled potatoes	Jelly
	Cake & cookies	Sago pudding	Assorted cakes
Tuesday	Cornflakes	Roast pork with	Cold roast pork
	Fried bacon	dressing	Cold ham
	Fried potatoes	Parsnips	Spaghetti & tomatoes
	Stewed figs	Mashed potatoes	Boiled potatoes
	Drop cakes	Cheese & sodas	Prunes
	& cookies	Apple pie	Layer cake & fruit cake

Included with all meals: Bread, butter, milk, sugar, tea, coffee (breakfast only)
Catsup, mustard, pickles, pepper, and salt

Source: *National Archives of Canada*, RG22, v. 588, f. RM2.

What kept the men going was the belief that things would soon get better and that national park relief work would help carry them through to that day. Whether this kind of activity would continue, however, was not clear in the spring of 1932. Not that the economy was starting to turn around; if anything, the jobless rate was getting worse and the downturn would not bottom out for another year. Relief work also remained a popular idea. During the budget debate in the House of Commons that March, for example, J.S. Woodsworth called for the emergency recruitment of a so-called "peace army" of the unemployed, which would perform meaningful work across the country at a decent wage. "More than anything else such an arrangement might help to save the morale of these men," Woodsworth admonished the government.[108] Prime Minister Bennett had other concerns. He found the cost of providing work for the unemployed to be an expensive drain on the federal treasury and was worried that budget deficits would undermine the country's financial standing. Instead of continuing to fund provincial public works projects, then, the Conservative leader forgot past concerns about the sanctity of the work ethic and opted for direct relief—in other words, the dreaded dole.[109]

Bennett did not, however, as is often suggested, entirely turn his back on public works projects.[110] During a federal-provincial conference on relief in early April 1932, Premier Brownlee of Alberta spoke privately with the prime minister about the critical need to reopen the Banff-Jasper highway camps before trouble erupted in Edmonton and Calgary. Bennett could easily have ignored Brownlee's request, given his blinkered determination to reduce federal expenditures. But the national park relief programme had been one of the few successes in an otherwise dismal attempt at public works, and there was no reason to believe that the resumption of the project could go wrong. The road work would also benefit his home province and, it was hoped, defuse some of the growing unrest among the unemployed. While his government was urging the provinces to bring their spending under control, then, Bennett convened a special meeting with Thomas Murphy, James Wardle, and George Headley, an Alberta cabinet minister, to consider the possibility of continuing relief work on the Banff-Jasper highway over the coming summer. In characteristic form, the prime minister dominated the discussion and made all the decisions. Opening the conference by affirming that the project was of national benefit and therefore a worthy recipient of relief funds, he then brushed aside a number of Wardle's concerns about the opening and operation of the camps and told him that "the country was in a grave emergency" and that he was "to do everything possible to get the work under way and some men taken on." After a brief review of construction-related matters, the meeting concluded with Bennett's personal assurance that the necessary funding would be available as soon as it was required.[111]

· · ·

This behind-the-scenes decision to proceed with the Banff-Jasper highway was transformed a few days later into a formal renewal of the national park public works programme. According to the new relief act introduced in late April, the government was to be given the discretionary power to "Provide for special relief, works, and undertakings, in the National Parks of Canada."[112] Bennett spoke forcefully in support of the provision; using the Banff-Jasper highway as an example, he argued that park relief projects would provide work for the hundreds of single homeless men congregating in cities and towns and at the same time promote Canadian tourism and thereby help the balance of trade.

Liberal leader Mackenzie King also approved the idea but in a swipe at his Conservative opponent, wondered if park work was so much better than the dole, then why could the concept not be extended to other areas.[113] This jousting made no difference to the bill's fate, and on 12 May 1932, one day before the legislation became effective, the minister of the Interior instructed the Parks Branch to begin work immediately on the highway.

The Engineering Service lost little time in getting the Jasper and Lake Louise camps ready for occupation again, and within a week the call went out for physically fit, single unemployed men from Edmonton and Calgary. Few men, however, were willing to trade their labour for the new lower wage of $7.50 per month, and it was only when threatened with being struck off the relief list that they accepted a posting to one of the road camps. Some still refused, and lost their benefits; according to an internal RCMP report on the matter, 85 men from Edmonton accepted work on the project, while a whopping 199 refused.[114] This kind of trouble came as no surprise to the Parks Branch. During the April meeting about the highway, the prime minister had indicated that the men would essentially be working for their board and a small allowance, and that he expected them to "cooperate with the efforts of the Government to keep them from starving."[115] Wardle, in turn, foresaw nothing but grief for the project—the recruitment problem was just the beginning—and tried to warn his political masters that the highway foremen would get more work out of the road gangs for an hourly or even a daily wage rather than magnanimous gestures. The men also made their feelings known when a delegation representing the Lake Louise camps told Parks officials on 26 May that they planned to work only four hours starting the next day. This mutiny resulted in a mass meeting that evening at which the camp spokesmen presented their case against the piddling remuneration. Wardle, who had driven out to Lake Louise to head off the trouble, then coolly informed the congregation that any man refusing to work the prescribed hours would be evicted and permanently cut off relief. The ultimatum had the desired effect; all men reported to work the next morning.[116]

Wardle provided Harkin with a sober assessment of the situation a few days later, informing the commissioner in a lengthy telegram that half the eligible men had refused to go to the highway camps, that the project would probably not be fully manned for several more weeks, and that it might be necessary to release a large number of disgruntled individuals. His most telling observation, however, was that unemployed, single veterans were not interested in any special preference.[117] What he forgot to add was that the men had become little more than prisoners; they not only had to accept work on the highway, but had to stay at the job or lose their relief assistance. The very nature of the park relief programme seemed to be changing. Whereas many of the unemployed had once gone to the park camps voluntarily and wanted to stay there as long as they could, they were now being forced to work at the projects at a wage that many

Midday meal on the Banff-Jasper highway project. *Jasper National Park, Martin Rossander Collection, H2591*

considered an insult. It was as if their jobless state had become a crime and their removal to the park camps a kind of open-ended sentence, more in keeping with the treatment that enemy aliens had endured some fifteen years earlier.

This new reality was reflected on the Banff-Jasper highway that summer. When Wardle tried to solve the manpower shortfall by securing permission to recruit men from other parts of Alberta, Premier Brownlee was quite adamant that the project was intended solely to reduce the number of single unemployed on the relief rolls in Calgary and Edmonton. It was a callous though simple way of helping the two cities evade their relief responsibilities, and local officials took full advantage of the situation to the point where they even sent individuals who were medically unfit for heavy road work.[118] The project, in the meantime, experienced further labour strife when the men at the Jasper camps began agitating for a clothing and tobacco allowance and talking of a possible work stoppage. Once again the men were sternly warned about the consequences of any strike action, while the RCMP were instructed to investigate whether any of the foreign workers might be deported.[119] The clothing issue would not go away, though, and workers at the Lake Louise camps took up the cause a few weeks later and began complaining about being poorly outfitted for work in the mountains. This time the grievance was taken seriously—largely in the interests of averting a public scandal—and the local Red Cross was called upon to organize a clothing drive.[120]

Surprisingly, these various disputes did not affect highway construction. The camps not only surpassed their eight-hundred-man target, but by early August 1932, Wardle reported that the amount of work being accomplished exceeded the Engineering Service's expectations.[121] This headway was even more remarkable given that, in the interests of keeping expenditures to a minimum, the road gangs were forced to do as much of the cutting and clearing as possible with pick, shovel, and wheelbarrow. For local newspapers the project was nothing less than an epic tale—down-and-outers pitted against the environment. The Calgary *Herald,* for example, spoke of "the toils, difficulties, resistances of the wilderness" of the "great feat of construction."[122]

For the men involved it was a different story. Although they laboured long and hard, they were consumed by an increasing sense of bitterness about their fate, a bitterness made only worse by the niggardly allowance. And as Wardle correctly predicted, once the fall harvest began, they abandoned the highway camps en masse in the belief that they could earn a better wage in the fields. These desertions—the Lake Louise operations dropped from 415 to 167 men in two weeks[123]—brought about a consolidation of the road work until early October, when there was once again a ready supply of single unemployed in Calgary and Edmonton. By this time, however, snow was already on the ground in the mountains, and Wardle was reluctant to bring the camps back up to full strength for only a few weeks' work. Only a small portion of the available men were consequently taken on for the balance of the construction season.

. . .

Looking back over the past two years, Commissioner Harkin had good reason to be pleased. While the country was gripped by a seemingly unshakable economic malaise and the government searched vainly for a cure, the Parks Department enjoyed the luxury of several hundred labourers, who toiled at a variety of development, recreation, and maintenance projects. These were not "lost years" for the national parks in western Canada; the national playgrounds would be ready for the return of prosperity. And so too would the relief crews who worked there. Out of work and in many instances out of hope, many of these men, in spite of the conditions of their employment, found in the park camps a temporary refuge from the worst ravages of the Depression. The Edmonton *Journal* said as much in describing the jobless stationed at Jasper. "Bracing air, regular living conditions and wholesome food have benefitted them greatly," it reported. "When jobs are offered to them again they will be fit and ready to take them."[124] When that time would come, however, was anything but certain in the fall of 1932, for the Depression seemed to tighten its grip on the country. And it was far from clear whether the Parks Department would continue to provide relief work, let alone sanctuary, for Canada's unemployed.

CHAPTER THREE

Transients

T *HEY SEEMED TO BE EVERYWHERE. THEY LINED UP FOR HOURS,* in soup lines or outside relief offices, waiting to be fed or perhaps offered a few hours' work. They were at back doors, cap in hand, asking if there was anything they could do to earn a meal or some unwanted clothing. Or they were in the rail yards, coming or going, hoping that things would be better down the line at the next stop. No one seemed to know what to do with Canada's jobless. And the problem was getting worse. By October 1932, the unemployment rate had reached an unprecedented 28 percent of the working population and would not peak until the following spring, when it hit a staggering 30 percent in March. Many of the people behind these statistics were homeless single men who up until the Depression had managed to eke out a living in Canada's resource sector, moving from job to job and from region to region, depending on the season and the demand for their services. There were also several thousand young people–fresh-faced teenagers who had quit school to help support their families and then left home so they would not be a burden.[1] Together, they dominated the ranks of Canada's unofficial corps of unemployed, who wandered the country atop freight cars, on the backs of trucks, or on foot, trying to survive as best they could. It was a harsh, at times demeaning, existence, made worse by the numbing sense of waste and utter desolation. "Wherever they go they feel they are not wanted," wrote a Vancouver minister in 1932. "There is no work, no hope, no place for them. They are Canada's Untouchables."[2]

Most single transients eventually made their way to larger cities in search of work, and more importantly, relief. Here, they were initially granted emergency assistance, but the demands of the needy soon became so overwhelming that many western cities faced the prospect of bankruptcy if they continued to help the homeless, in addition to their own citizens. In May 1932, for example, the federal minister of Labour was secretly advised by the Royal

Canadian Mounted Police that the monthly relief bill for the city of Edmonton alone had averaged a whopping $100,000 for the past six months and was expected to rise if work programmes were discontinued.[3] This kind of expenditure could not be sustained, even with special supplementary funding from Ottawa, and prairie centres had no choice but to enforce residence requirements and cull their relief lists if they were to continue to fulfil their social welfare obligations.

Some of the first victims of these cost-cutting measures were recent immigrants, many of whom had been brought to Canada in the late 1920s by the country's two major railway companies. Under the federal Immigration Act, any non-Canadian who was convicted of vagrancy or otherwise became a public charge could be deported. Local authorities now took advantage of this provision to get rid of foreign relief recipients in record numbers—a mean-spirited process that one author has aptly described as "shovelling out the unemployed."[4] Just as workers from Austria-Hungary had been discriminated against and mistreated during the Great War, many of the deportees in the early 1930s were also from central and eastern Europe. Those unnaturalized immigrants who remained in Canada, meanwhile, were little better off. Painfully aware that a simple application for food, clothing, or fuel could mean a deportation ticket, they were effectively forced to get through those dark years with little more than their wits and prayers.[5]

Canadian-born transients were treated almost as heartlessly. The introduction of residence requirements—in most cases, six months—may have helped municipalities reduce their welfare costs, but in human terms it effectively sentenced the single homeless unemployed to a life of constant motion and uncertainty. Disqualified from regular relief and with no other resources, they moved about the country in a determined though somewhat naive search for work—a fluid mass of humanity trying to make sense of what was happening when not trying to figure out what to do next. There was little time to put down any roots, even in the makeshift hobo jungles that sprang up, like stinkweed, on the outskirts of communities. Private charities, such as church-run hostels, would normally provide only a few meals of watery soup and bread, and the men were then expected to move on to the next town. City and railway officials, meanwhile, constantly harassed the transients—often at cross purposes—as if they carried some dreaded plague. Local police would shoo the men away rather than arrest them as vagrants, while special patrolmen chased them from the freight yards back towards town. It was as if the men were pinballs in the game of life, constantly being hit by the flippers. "Them railroad bulls is mean bastards," vouched one young man who had crossed the country twice. "They always carry a big club and they like to use it. We always try to git off the freight before we git to town, otherwise you're liable t' git a beatin."[6]

. . .

By the summer of 1932, the question of what to do with Canada's single homeless had become the subject of considerable concern but little action. It was proposed, for example, that all male transients should carry identification cards and be assigned to a particular municipality as part of a countrywide registration programme. It was also suggested that mass feeding stations, such as one at the former Edmonton penitentiary, be established in western cities for the coming winter. Using a line of reasoning more appropriate to animals than men, it was argued that the displaced workers were essential to the agricultural and industrial well-being of the country and at least deserved to be fed.[7] The most popular idea, especially among civic and provincial authorities, however, was that the federal government should assume sole responsibility for single men. Their plight had become a national scandal, and as such, Ottawa should have to deal with the problem. This sense of emergency, though, did not extend to single unemployed women, even though they were part of the transient population. Not only was their contribution to the national economy undervalued, but it was generally assumed that the care of the female jobless was a family duty.

The suggestion that the Bennett government attend to the growing transient population—estimated to number around seventy thousand—clearly went against the thinking that had defined the Conservative administration since it came to power some two years earlier. Relief had always been regarded as a purely local matter, and any federal assistance during this time of crisis was simply a temporary contribution—nothing more. The prime minister would likely have continued to disclaim any responsibility for single homeless men, if not for the activities of the Communist Party of Canada. The Depression had saved the moribund party from probable extinction, giving it a relevance and vigour unparalleled in its short, decade-long history. The massive layoffs and accompanying hardships seemed to fit what the Communists had been saying about the perils of capitalism, and they now went on the offensive in what they saw as the final battle for the hearts and minds of the Canadian working class. Through its umbrella organization, the Workers' Unity League, the party tried to sign up labourers in traditionally nonunionized sectors of the economy. It was also the first and only group to attempt to organize the unemployed in a common fight against the bastions of wealth and power.[8] Prime Minister Bennett was deeply troubled by these developments—the Reds were nothing less than a threat to country, church, and family—and vowed to crush the party and its nefarious disciples with "an iron heel of ruthlessness." In stamping out this scourge, however, Canadian authorities, including the prime minister, tended to see any form of public dissent or protest by the unemployed as the work of Communist agitators.[9] They were also afraid that disillusioned veterans and impressionable youth, many of whom made up the ranks of the single

Placing a culvert along the Banff-Jasper highway at the Lake Louise end, August 1932. As much of the road work as possible was done by hand with shovels, picks, and wheelbarrows. *Canadian Parks Service, Western Regional Office, Webster Collection*

jobless, might fall into the clutches of the Communists—a fear confirmed in the weekly Mounted Police security bulletins of the period.[10] For many, indeed, revolution probably seemed more likely than recovery. In one of the saddest developments of the Depression, then, Canadian officials, blinded by their Communist phobia, came to see the single male transient as a potential menace and not as a casualty.[11] And it was only because of the apparent threat these men posed to Canadian law and order, and not because of their wretched condition, that the Conservative government gave serious thought to the question of what to do with them.

Searching for a solution, Prime Minister Bennett met with Chief Engineer J.M. Wardle of the National Parks Branch in Calgary in mid-September 1932 to discuss the possibility of further relief work in various western parks over the coming winter.[12] He also conferred with General Andrew McNaughton, chief of the general staff, who had recently completed an inspection tour through the West. Alarmed by the growing numbers of single unemployed men and their seemingly wasted lives, McNaughton recommended that the Conservative administration establish a system of national work camps for the physically fit, run by the Department of National Defence; these camps would remove transients from the cities, where they were easy prey for the Communists, while at the same time providing the homeless men with the basic necessities of life, including a princely twenty-cent daily allowance, until the economy recovered. McNaughton's proposal appealed to the Bennett cabinet and on 8 October 1932, just two days into the fourth parliamentary session, the scheme became official government policy.

What is overlooked, however, in the accounts of the Department of National Defence camps, and McNaughton's role in particular, is that the idea was not a new one. Not only had municipalities and provinces been calling for the creation of relief camps during the past year, but such camps already existed in Canada's national parks—surely McNaughton must have been aware of the park work camps, as well as those that had been operated by Internment Operations during the Great War. The DND camps, moreover, were initially to accommodate no more than two thousand men over the winter of 1932-33. That still left several thousand transients. And on 22 October, less than two weeks after approval of the McNaughton plan, the Parks Department also received $200,000 to establish camps for homeless single men. As the country entered the bleakest winter of the Depression, then, there were two kinds of relief camps for the transient unemployed—a situation that naturally led to comparisons and, less fortunately, petty rivalry. Ultimately, however, the national park operations did benefit. The dissatisfaction and unrest that had characterized the Banff-Jasper highway camps during the summer of 1932 would come to be concentrated in the DND camps. Parks officials were also extremely protective of their share of the transient labour, and were forever trying to demonstrate that they could do a better job of looking after the men.

With relief funds readily available, Commissioner Harkin and his officials lost little time in getting the camps up and running again. Harkin briefly toyed with opening camps at Glacier and Mount Revelstoke National Parks to take in some of the thousands of men who had flocked to the west coast because of the warmer weather. It was decided in the end, however, that the expense of trying to keep mountain camps open through the winter would greatly out-weigh the value of any work that might be done.[13] Transient camps were therefore restricted to the same parks that had benefitted from relief activities the past winter—with one exception. Homeless single men were also sent to Point Pelee National Park in southwestern Ontario, the only park outside western Canada where relief work was undertaken during the Depression.[14] Under the terms of the government order, the camps were limited to homeless single men and could not include anyone who might have met residence qualifications in a neighbouring town or city and thereby be eligible for local assistance. The Bennett government was prepared to assume direct responsi-bility only for transient relief, and Wardle was regularly reminded by the

The sleeping tents had wooden floors and walls. Spray Camp "D," Banff National Park, January 1933. *Canadian Parks Service, Western Regional Office, Webster Collection*

Interior Department to ensure that this was the case.[15]

The men were required to work an eight-hour day, six days per week in return for food, shelter, a free issue of "standard" clothing, and a monthly allowance of $5.50 less 50¢ for medical care. As in past practice, the projects were to employ as many men as possible for as little as possible. Little equipment could be purchased beyond small hand tools, kitchen and dining utensils, and tents. To keep expenses down, the men were also to be fed at a maximum cost of 50¢ per day per man (including the kitchen staff's wages). This figure is all the more incredible when it is realized that two people today can rarely dine at a restaurant for $25.00—the daily cost of feeding a fifty-man camp in 1932, including the cooking crew's wages![16]

Parks personnel rarely complained about these constraints; they were generally pleased to have the transients at their disposal, while the cities were more than happy to be rid of them. As for the men, their new home represented quite a change from the nightmare they had been living for several months, if not longer. They discarded their worn-out clothes for a new winter outfit, slept in a bed—and the same one at that—every night, and could eat all they wanted three times a day. They were also well out of reach of city and railroad bulls, and could enjoy something of a settled life in a place where they—or at least their labour—were wanted.[17]

There was also a down side to the park camps. Many believed that they had been misled by Prime Minister Bennett and his promise to end unemployment, and felt a collective sense of isolation in the out-of-the-way locations—as if they had committed some crime. The men, moreover, still had their pride, and although they were never pushed hard on the job, they expected a decent wage and not some miserly allowance that seemed to suggest their labour no longer had any value.[18] Most probably wondered about the future and what it held for them. The park camps were being touted as a stopgap measure, something to get the men through these troubled times. And in retrospect, they did.[19] But in the fall of 1932, things looked quite different, as the Depression that was supposed to be only a temporary phenomenon dragged the Canadian economy down to even lower depths. Coming to terms with this disheartening situation would test the men and their work supervisors.

· · ·

The Banff and Jasper camps were the first to open that fall. As construction of the Banff-Jasper highway wound down through November, several of the men were simply transferred to park work, where they were joined by fresh recruits from Calgary and Edmonton. At Banff, brush camps were located at Healy Creek, Castle Mountain, and the Spray River valley, while a road camp was stationed in the Eldon Hills to carry out a revision of the Lake Louise highway. Similar clearing and road work were done in Jasper at Pyramid Lake, Lake Annette, and Maligne Canyon. In both parks the men were housed and fed in large tents with stoves for the first part of the winter, until log or frame kitchens and bunkhouses could be erected.

Transients were also sent to Waterton Lakes, where they made further improvements to the Akamina Pass highway, and assisted with the survey and preliminary clearing of the Belly River highway to the international boundary. In the fall of 1932, the Canadian and American governments had created by concurrent legislation the Waterton-Glacier International Peace Park; part of the agreement included a connecting highway (the Chief Mountain International Highway) between the two parks via the Belly and Kennedy River valleys. This project would keep the single unemployed busy for the next few years. In the early new year, however, a small group of men, who identified themselves as mostly veterans, also turned their hands to letter-writing and sent a formal protest to General J.S. Stewart, the Conservative MP for the region. Although they expressed their willingness "to carry on until such time as there is a change for the better," they did not want to create the false impression that "the men are in any way satisfied with conditions here."[20] They complained about favouritism and incompetence, denounced the clothing issue as cheap and inadequate, and wondered why men who occupied key positions in the camp were paid at the standard market rate while the single homeless, who did the real work, had to be satisfied with a five-dollar allowance; the "only bright spot," according to the signatories, was the food. Wardle responded to the letter a month later by taking the high ground. Dismissing the complaints as misguided, he argued that relief camp policy for the single homeless had been set by the federal government, that all national park relief operations had to abide by these guidelines, and that the men were not forced to go to the camps—if they had some other means of support.[21]

Grumbling was also heard at Elk Island, where the men were expected to continue with the general underbrushing and clearing that had begun the previous winter. In early November, the first contingent of forty transients arrived by truck from Edmonton and were assigned to one of two tent camps in the bush. The prospect of spending a cold, dreary winter with several hundred elk and buffalo, however, was apparently too much for six of the new arrivals, and they tried to start a general protest against the conditions by "stirring up unnecessary strife." When the park superintendent ordered them to leave, they were joined by about half the men, who, despite their desperate condition, evidently decided that there were limits to what they would do.[22] The defections effectively ended the trouble, and replacements were easily secured in Edmonton. The only other commotion during the following months was caused by the resident buffalo, which liked to graze on the hay bales the men had carefully banked around their tents to keep warm.[23]

· · ·

The two largest national park transient operations that winter were based at Prince Albert and Riding Mountain. As parts of the southern prairies were reduced to a desert and wheat prices dropped to unimaginable lows, more and more communities sent their homeless unemployed to the parks. They arrived in regular instalments in groups of ten to fifty, so that by late December 1932 there were more than a thousand men at each location—more than the total transient population in all of the Alberta national parks. At Prince Albert the men spent their first few weeks on the job constructing their own permanent quarters at one of ten sites along the main highway and the southwest shore of Lake Waskesiu. The bulk of the workforce was then put on general brushing or road work, while smaller crews tackled a number of planned improvements in the townsite and main campground, including recreational facilities.[24]

Despite the size of the operations at Prince Albert, there was little unrest and few desertions—mainly because there was nowhere else to go. Six homesick young men, all from Moose Jaw, learned as much when they left the park in mid-January 1933 and were subsequently arrested in Prince Albert and charged with vagrancy. During their hearing, two of the defectors, W. Bevan and John Johnson, claimed that they had suffered frostbite wearing the rubber footwear they had been issued. Another, H. Sims, told the magistrate that he was incapable of doing any kind of physical work and that he had originally been advised by a doctor not to go to the park. The most pathetic case was that of C. Innes, who said that he had left camp because of the food; when questioned, though, it was learned that he could not eat properly because he had no upper teeth. All six men pleaded guilty, and despite an offer from Park

Superintendent James Wood to take them back, all chose to return home when given the alternative of going to gaol.[25] The men's hearing hinted at an appalling health record, a situation confirmed in the spring when official camp statistics were made available. In a May 1933 address to the Prince Albert Rotary Club, the superintendent reported that 1,778 cases of sickness—mostly flu—and 336 cases of injury had been treated by the camp first-aid men and doctor during the winter.[26] In other words, every camp member was ill at least once, while 1 in 3 sustained an injury of some nature.

The Norgate road gravel pit, Riding Mountain National Park, August 1933. The park orchestra was drawn from the ranks of these men. *Canadian Parks Service, Western Regional Office, Webster Collection*

• • •

The other large winter relief operation was at Riding Mountain. The park got an early start when it received a special federal grant in late September 1932—probably Thomas Murphy's doing—to provide relief work for two hundred local unemployed. These men worked on the new park golf-course and in the townsite before being joined by the first batch of transients in early November. The park relief population thereafter grew rapidly and by the new year, Riding Mountain was providing refuge for almost twelve hundred men. According to a mid-January survey of the camps, the only surviving record of its kind, 90 percent of the men were of British extraction and of these, one quarter had served overseas during the Great War; only a small number were immigrants from central and eastern Europe and even fewer were from Scandinavia. Six out of every ten men had been sent from Winnipeg; the rest were from the larger neighbouring towns or outlying rural municipalities. One in two identified themselves as labourers; the other men were listed in more than a hundred different occupations, from gardener and prospector to civil engineer and shoemaker. Neither their ages nor period without work was recorded. Nor were their names given.[27] Hidden in the survey were also a number of deaf-mutes; one former relief worker, in fact, learned how to "sign" in the camps.[28]

Unlike Prince Albert, which had placed its relief workers in one of ten camps throughout the southern half of the park, the men at Riding Mountain were heavily concentrated around Clear Lake: more than three hundred in the Wasagaming townsite along the southeast shore, and another six hundred in one of three camps along the north shore. About one hundred were also stationed along the Norgate road. This distribution made sense, since the men would be working on various projects in the region, such as brushing the cottage subdivisions, clearing and grubbing the golf-course, or gravelling the Clear Lake road. The camps were also relatively easy to service—no small point given the size of the relief population and the logistics involved. The speed with which the camps were occupied and the numbers involved, however, led to problems. And on 22 November 1932, J.S. Woodsworth, the member for Winnipeg North Centre, stood up in the House of Commons and proceeded to read into the official record a damning indictment of the Riding Mountain operations. The letter, provided by a Winnipeg man on behalf of a group at the park, described how eighty-eight men occupied "a tar paper shack 79 feet by 24 with no windows" and slept in twos in narrow, straw-filled, double bunks that had to be crawled into, like animals entering dens, from the foot end. The passageway between the row of bunks, meanwhile, was so small that it was difficult to move about when the men were sitting at the bottom of their beds. It also reported that the washing and toilet facilities were "thoroughly filthy," and that the night air in the crowded bunkhouse was "simply fetid." Most troublesome, according to the author, was the fate of the young men. "The terrible thing about it," Woodsworth quoted, "is that many of the men who are congregated in this camp are teenaged Canadian boys forced into close association with mature men, who have tramped the streets and bummed their way through the country, with the result that the outlook of these boys stands a good chance of being completely warped and their characters so degraded and demoralized that their future is unquestionably seriously menaced."[29] The letter closed by noting that men would have fled the camps if the nearest rail line was closer, and that complaints would have been voiced if not for the presence of paid informers among the men, who reported any attempt at organization.[30] By the time Woodsworth finally sat down, members were

At Riding Mountain, the men slept in twos in narrow, straw-filled, double bunks that had to be crawled into from the foot end. *Canadian Parks Service, Western Regional Office, Webster Collection*

probably wondering whether Riding Mountain had been mistakenly confused with Manitoba's Stony Mountain Penitentiary.

H.A. Mullins, whose riding included the park, was immediately on his feet, overflowing with indignation, and yelled at Woodsworth: "When I tell him it [the letter] is wrong, it is wrong."[31] The next day, Thomas Murphy, the minister of the Interior, provided a more reasoned response to the charges. Armed with a file of clippings from various Manitoba newspapers, he read article after article that lauded the Riding Mountain operations and what was being done for the men. "I could secure hundreds, yes, thousands, of men in Manitoba to live under those conditions," Murphy assured the House at one point. "The trouble is . . . we are unable to provide work for all those who want to go." He also reported that he had personally telephoned the park superintendent that morning and that no complaints had been voiced. Finally, in keeping with the Bennett government's strategy of dealing with dissent, the minister of the Interior called into question Woodsworth's motives, and denounced the information as scurrilous and absolutely false. "We have merely a letter," Murphy sarcastically concluded, "by some unnamed and unknown committee."[32]

The matter ended there because of the adjournment of Parliament for the Christmas break. Parks Commissioner J.B. Harkin was privately worried, however, that the national parks could lose their relief workers to the DND camps if a similar scandal ever erupted again, and asked for a full report on the Riding Mountain situation before the session reconvened. He also spent considerable energy trying to identify the author of the letter—even though its contents had been dismissed by the government as unreliable. It was later discovered that the writer was a British-born landscaper and suspected Communist, R.E. Thompson (alias Grey), who had been released from the Riding Mountain camps for trying to foment unrest, especially among the younger men.[33] This finding certainly comforted Parks officials, but what they did not expect was the 10 December report in which a somewhat sheepish Superintendent James Smart confessed that there was some truth to the letter's contents. Men were indeed sleeping in double-barrelled, double-decker, straw-filled bunks (measuring four feet, five inches wide and six feet, six inches in length), which were butted together, with the heads to the outside walls, along both sides of the bunkhouse. The men entered their bunks in the same fashion that shot was fed into a muzzle-loaded gun—hence the term double-barrelled. Smart defended this arrangement by arguing that it was the best way to accommodate a hundred bodies in the standard bunkhouse (twenty feet by sixty feet), and that the men actually preferred to double up to keep warm, whatever might have been thought about the practice. At the same time, he advised Harkin that he had started to rebuild several of the bunkhouses, making them ten feet wider and placing the double bunks head-to-head down the middle of the building; these modifications not only created space for tables and benches down each side of the bunkhouse, but also allowed for the insertion of windows. For those bunkhouses that could not be enlarged, the row of bunks along one side of the building was simply removed. Smart assured Harkin that the reconstructed bunkhouses were much more comfortable and that the men would have absolutely no grounds to "kick"—especially since there had been no objection to the sleeping arrangements in the past.[34]

As for the letter's other charges, Smart insisted that they were unfounded. He carefully outlined the camps' sanitation practices: the bunkhouses were regularly swept and scrubbed, the bunks sprayed for vermin and the straw replaced every two weeks, and the men paraded to the central bathhouse in the townsite—even on cold wintry days—at least once a week.[35] He also claimed that the relative isolation of the camps shielded the men from any "outside interference, exploitation or contamination," and that the veterans were "more inclined to correct the characters of the younger men rather than degrade or demoralize them."[36] And he vehemently denied that the men were spied upon—even though informers had been secretly recruited in each of the camps for just this purpose the previous winter.[37]

Smart's trump card, however, was the ambitious recreation programme sponsored by the park; he was not exaggerating when he boasted to Harkin that "we are doing everything in our power to make camp life congenial to the men."[38] He explained how hockey sticks and footballs had been distributed to the camps around Clear Lake and that once the ice had formed, the work gangs put together teams and began to play a regular schedule of games against each other. Intercamp champions could look forward to a personal team photograph and tobacco.[39] The park also equipped through private donations an all-star hockey team and hosted an exhibition match against one of the neighbouring communities every Sunday afternoon before a crowd of a thousand spectators; future Toronto Maple Leaf goalie Turk Broda got his start guarding the pipes at Riding Mountain. And Walter Crossman of Brandon actually wanted to be admitted to the park camps so he could play hockey with some of the best talent in the area.[40] There were also boxing tournaments, with the champions in the various weight classes being decided at a special evening card at the Wasagaming dancehall. For those who preferred a more sedentary form of relaxation, radios, reading material, playing cards, and checkers and cribbage boards were supplied to each of the camps. The performing arts were not neglected either. Every camp organized its own concert company, and these performers would take turns entertaining the men with their singing, acting, and other hidden talents. There was even a park orchestra, made up mostly by men who worked in the gravel pit, which gave regular Saturday night concerts in the main camp recreation hall or nearby Danceland, and travelled with the motion picture outfit to the camps to provide music during the changing of reels.[41] As Superintendent Smart neatly summed up the situation, "To be in one of the camps . . . is a God Send . . . in every way you want to look at it."[42]

Riding Mountain equipped through private donations an all-star hockey team and hosted an exhibition match against one of the neighbouring communities every Sunday afternoon before a crowd of a thousand spectators. The football and hockey leagues at Riding Mountain were made possible because of the proximity of the camps—some nine hundred men were housed in a three-mile radius. *Canadian Parks Service, Western Regional Office, Webster Collection*

Future Toronto Maple Leaf goalie Turk Broda (front centre) got his start guarding the pipes at Riding Mountain. *Canadian Parks Service, Western Regional Office, Webster Collection*

Whether the men would have agreed with such an enthusiastic endorsement is debatable. Many welcomed the food, shelter, and camaraderie; others simply reconciled themselves to their fate. Repeatedly mentioned in personal reminiscences, however, is that the recreation programme filled a void in the men's otherwise empty lives. In August 1991, for example, Charles Sim of Brandon attended an evening talk on the relief camps, carrying a cherished photograph of his athletic team taken almost sixty years earlier. Ed Turner, who had been sent to Riding Mountain from Winnipeg, confessed that he had wanted to stay there as long as he could.[43] And Lorne Burkett, who lived on the edge of the park in the 1930s but was never in the camps himself, fondly recalled the Saturday evening concerts in the townsite, when he and several hundred others were treated to a minstrel and vaudeville show by the "Clear Lake Darkies."[44]

What is particularly ironic about these contemporary testimonials is that at the time, Chief Engineer Wardle wondered whether the park was doing too much to try to keep the men contented in their spare hours. "There is always the possibility of over doing matters of this kind," he advised Commissioner Harkin, "and that anything further . . . might be subject to criticism."[45] This is exactly what happened in the early spring of 1933 when Captain Alfred Hall, a resident of Kelwood, Manitoba, wrote to former Conservative Prime Minister Arthur Meighen to complain about residents of relief camps playing sports on the sabbath.[46] Smart vigorously defended the programme, arguing that Sunday recreational activities did not interfere with camp religious services, and that the friendly competition helped the men forget—if only for a few hours—the pain of where they were and what they were doing. Harkin could also see no wrong, and in an effort to demonstrate that transients were better off—both physically and mentally—for being in the park, it was decided to open the camps to the local media in the belief that the operations would benefit from some favourable publicity. This promotional work was facilitated by the fact that Smart was already involving the outlying communities in park recreational activities as much as possible, while men from the camps often competed in local contests. In March 1933, for example, Spooky Ballantine won the Minnedosa boxing tournament.

Sleeping arrangements, meanwhile, continued to be a contentious issue. In late December 1932, another letter of complaint was received—this time by the prime minister and the minister of Labour. The author, simply identifying himself as a member of camp six, argued that "the plight of the men here is quite bad enough without subjecting them to housing conditions that . . . no self-respecting farmer would tolerate . . . for his cattle," and that as veterans, they deserved "living and working conditions more worthy of the Dominion of Canada."[47] This note resulted in a ministerial order to speed up reconstruction of the bunkhouses, and by late January most of this rebuilding was complete. It still did not settle the issue, though, as there was continued debate over whether men should be sleeping together in the same bunk, especially when there were no women in the camps. Smart could not understand what all the fuss was about, reporting that most of the men preferred the double bunks and that any concerns were being raised by prudish outsiders who had no under-

Religious services were held weekly in the main camp recreation hall (the Wigwam restaurant) at Riding Mountain. *Riding Mountain National Park Collection*

standing of the situation. This assessment was confirmed by Frank Goble, who, starting in August 1932, two month's shy of his seventeenth birthday, worked out of every camp on the Chief Mountain highway project at Waterton Lakes throughout the entire life of the programme and heard not a single complaint about the use of double bunks. Nor was he ever approached by any other man or aware of any homosexual activity.[48]

The Riding Mountain controversy caused Harkin to take a look at park relief operations in general, and he instructed Wardle not only to prepare a detailed report on the camp conditions at the five other national parks, but to make regular inspections as well. Steps were also taken to ensure that there were no legitimate grounds for any future criticism. The parks were told, for example, to carry larger stocks of clothing and to replace worn-out items, especially footwear. Potential problem areas, in the meantime, were singled out for action. The superintendent at Waterton Lakes was reproached for taking too long to erect bunkhouses for the men, while his counterpart at Prince Albert had to be reminded to secure more reading material for the camps and to make a greater effort to get along with the resident engineer for the relief projects. There was no desire, however, to try to duplicate the Riding Mountain recreation programme at any of the other relief operations; the aim was simply to keep the men contented, but not necessarily happy. Nor could it easily have been done. Riding Mountain's programme was only possible because of the proximity of the camps—some nine hundred men were housed in a three-mile radius. A similar situation did not exist at any other national park. The men at Prince Albert had to make do with Ensign W. Hraniuc of the Salvation Army, who toured the ten camps with his concertina, banjo, cornet, gramophone, and unbridled faith, and led the work crews in singing and prayer.[49] But this was certainly better than the situation of those men in the mountain camps who watched national park films at night of some of the same scenes in which they laboured by day.

· · ·

By the time the 1932 Relief Act expired on 31 March 1933, the Parks Branch had secured almost $700,000 for park relief work, of which $400,000 was specifically earmarked for the single homeless. This latter amount compared favourably with the Department of National Defence operations; although the DND camps received nearly half a million dollars for transient relief, there were half as many more men housed in the park camps over the winter, and a correspondingly higher number of man-days of work.[50] The Parks Branch was naturally pleased with the level of relief activity, especially since few, if any, of the projects could have been financed from its own drastically reduced budget. In effect, what the Bennett government took away with one hand, it was giving back with the other. The work also enjoyed widespread public approval—a complete contrast to the enemy alien experience during the First World War. In a lengthy editorial

The interior of the Riding Mountain commissary (the Wigwam restaurant) at Christmas. *Riding Mountain National Park Collection*

on the value of the Riding Mountain camps, the Dauphin *Herald and Press* spoke glowingly of "the purposeful movement of groups of men . . . who apparently had something to do and were intent upon doing it."[51] The assessment of the Prince Albert newspaper was more to the point. "The jobless single men," it bluntly observed, "are fortunate to have these havens of refuge."[52] The Edmonton *Journal,* on the other hand, attributed a rejuvenating influence to the park camps. "The men for the most part realize how much better they are in Jasper," it reported, "and the malcontent is conspicuous by his absence."[53]

This self-congratulatory publicity was hard to dispute; the park camps were providing much-needed refuge for the transient unemployed. What also needs to be recognized, however, is that the national park relief programme was just as important—perhaps more so—to the surrounding communities. Many of the projects tackled by the single homeless were initiated or endorsed by park associations often made up of prominent citizens. Local businesses and farmers also benefitted from the mass purchasing for camp operations. And summer visitors enjoyed new tourist facilities that would probably never have been built until the Depression was over. These multiple advantages more than likely explain why the Bennett government continued to provide for national park relief operations in the new 1933 Relief Act—a virtual copy of the 1932 version. At the same time, the government also looked favourably upon General McNaughton's work-camp experiment over the past winter and decided to consolidate responsibility for the bulk of the single homeless unemployed under the Department of National Defence. And it did so in a big way. At the end of March 1933, on the same day that the new relief act became effective, the Defence Department received the first instalment of what would eventually amount to nearly $9 million over the 1933-34 fiscal year.

The Parks Branch saw no problem with the existence of two separate relief camp programmes under the control of two different government departments, as long as it was allowed to run its projects without interference. Parks authorities privately prided themselves on the fact that their operations employed "as many men as we could properly handle and obtain reasonable results,"[54] while the Defence Department, in comparison, seemed primarily concerned with caring for the maximum number of transients whatever the outcome. General McNaughton believed, however, that all the camps for single homeless men should be subject to the same rules—his rules—and at his insistence, he and two other officers met with Harkin and Wardle at his office in late May 1933 to try to arrive at a common policy for the administration of the camps. During the wide-ranging discussion, McNaughton raised a number of minor details where the two programmes differed. In the end, though, Harkin and Wardle were only willing to adopt the Defence Department's twenty-cents-per-working-day allowance for the single homeless camps. On all other points the two parties grudgingly agreed to continue to follow their existing practices, on the understanding that the differences would not affect the welfare of the men.[55] As Harkin candidly advised the deputy minister of the Interior about the outcome of the meeting a few days later, it made no sense to modify arrangements that had worked so well to date just to suit McNaughton. He also noted that Defence officials had had little practical experience operating highway construction camps—the DND relief work over the past winter had been largely confined to building landing strips—and that McNaughton's policies in these circumstances were largely untried.[56] Harkin's smugness aside, he knew that the park camps would be closely monitored by the Defence Department, and that more than ever, everything had to run smoothly.

Because of complaints about the use of tents during the winter months, log bunkhouses were erected wherever possible. Spray camp, Banff, 7 February 1934.
Whyte Museum of the Canadian Rockies, V488/138(1)

While the Interior and Defence Departments were wrangling over relief camp policy, several western national parks were formally authorized to resume work projects for homeless single men.[57] This government order represented quite a change from the previous summer, when relief activity was confined to the Banff-Jasper highway. Indeed, park relief had always been largely a winter activity. The unemployment situation, however, remained bleak—it would continue to hover around 25 percent during 1933—and the Bennett government apparently reasoned that it was best to try to keep several hundred transients at work in the national parks, in addition to those being absorbed by the DND operations. The Parks Branch was also given special relief funding to hire needy, permanent park residents on a quota basis at the rate of thirty cents per hour; those unable to join these crews, such as residents' sons, were assigned to the park transient camps and placed on the new twenty-cent daily allowance. This sum did not even come close to what could be earned in the regular labour market—the going rate for a carpenter, for example, was forty dollars per month—and the men, particularly those in the DND camps, mockingly referred to themselves as the "Royal Twenty Centers." Chief Engineer Wardle did not like it either—he still preferred to pay the men a nominal hourly wage—but he knew that the Parks Branch would lose its access to transient labour if it did not match the DND allowance. The most outspoken critics, however, were the newspapers located near the park camps. The *Golden Star* suggested that park labourers' only options under the Bennett government's new "slavery" policy were "submit or starve."[58] And the Banff *Crag and Canyon* angrily observed, in an unprecedented attack on the park relief programme, that the new daily allowance would have a demoralizing impact on the men's pride. "No one can believe," the paper charged, "that Canada is in such desperate straits that it is necessary to cut working men down to such a low standard of living."[59]

· · ·

Not since the Great War Internment Operations had the Parks Branch had such a large workforce available to it as during the summer of 1933, and it decided to take advantage of the weather conditions and concentrate on a number of outstanding park highway projects. For the past few years, Wardle had been monitoring road-building activity in the United States, such as the new trans-Montana highway, and was concerned that these new American routes might capture the lion's share of future tourist traffic unless the Canadian roads were quickly completed.[60] Construction was consequently resumed at the north and south ends of the Banff-Jasper highway, as well as on the Stoney Squaw Mountain and Miette Hot Springs roads in Banff and Jasper respectively. At Elk Island, the South Gate road was completed, while the long-awaited highway link from Waterton Lakes to Glacier National Park, the Big Belly road, was pursued in earnest. Highway work also figured largely in the relief operations at Prince Albert and Riding Mountain, in particular the roads from Waskesiu to the Narrows and from Clear Lake to Dauphin. Even the eastern leg of the Golden-Revelstoke highway reverted to being a national park relief project that summer, after a somewhat disappointing construction season the previous year on regular government appropriation.

The progress on these projects initially failed to meet expectations. Part of the problem was the lack of workers. The Burkett family of Clear Lake, Manitoba, was a good example; although his two brothers worked at the Riding Mountain camps as a teamster and a cook, Lorne Burkett believed that he could do better on his own—and did.[61] Those who had worked on the Big Bend Highway at regular wages during the summer of 1932 also balked at the new daily relief allowance. Who could blame them? At mile sixty on the eastern leg, the road had to pass through a dense cedar swamp. The huge trees, up to ten feet in diameter and two hundred feet in height, had to be sawn in manageable lengths and then quartered. Removal of a single stump sometimes required an entire case of dynamite and left a huge water-filled hole resembling a shell crater. It also cost at least one life—that of a powderman who blew himself up.[62] The other major problem was equipment. Because of funding limits and the continuing emphasis on the virtue of manual labour, the projects had to make do with as little heavy machinery as possible, including bulldozers. This

At mile sixty in the eastern leg of the Big Bend project, the road had to pass through an enormous cedar swamp. The huge trees had to be sawn in manageable lengths and then quartered. *Canadian Parks Service, Western Regional Office, Webster Collection*

restriction seriously handicapped the road projects—it was akin to working with one arm—and actually prevented Wardle from bringing the crews up to full strength in a few parks for several weeks.[63] By early September 1933, however, he had resolved the worst of the equipment difficulties and reported to his own apparent surprise, "We are actually getting work done . . . in spite of the fact that they are relief projects at sustenance wages."[64] He probably privately wondered what might have been achieved had the men been paid regular wages.

These results were even more remarkable given the obsession that summer with trying to keep camp expenses to an absolute minimum. Although the Parks Branch had been providing some form of relief employment since the fall of 1930 and had always kept a watchful eye on its budget, it now seemed to be locked in an unofficial contest with the Defence Department to see who could run its camps most cheaply. A number of money-saving measures were therefore implemented. Buffalo meat from Wainwright Park became a regular feature on camp menus; dental work was restricted to extractions; and men with chronic health problems or serious ailments were shipped back to the urban centre they had come from. The December 1933 report of the Waterton Lakes medical officer, for example, suggested that Lethbridge relief authorities were not adequately screening workers and were more concerned with simply getting the single homeless out of the city: one recent arrival at the park had influenza and had to be hospitalized; another was suffering from appendicitis; one was a severe epileptic; and another was "a cadaverous looking individual" who had been injured in a fall.[65] Perhaps the meanest act was the confiscation of the summer clothing ration from men who were evicted from the camps. As far as park authorities were concerned, though, it all added up. And that's exactly what Wardle did each month. For July 1933, for example, he calculated that each man-day of park relief work cost exactly $1,794; he regretted that the figure could not have been lower, but the Big Bend project had required close to $5,000 in explosives that month.[66]

The other main concern that summer was possible strike action or some other form of trouble. Commissioner Harkin had always feared the infiltration of the camps by trained agitators—however good conditions might be—and urged Wardle from the outset to provide some form of entertainment or recreation to keep the men busy when they were not working or sleeping. "Roughly one-third of their time . . . would be on their hands and probably few of them would know how to employ it," he had cautioned his chief engineer.[67] Wardle, who was always looking for ways to improve the operation of the camps, believed that the best way to keep the men contented was through their stomachs, especially since they were receiving only a small cash allowance. "A well fed man is not so receptive to red propaganda," he reasoned, "as a man poorly or insufficiently fed."[68] Parks officials' biggest worry, however, was that the unrest that was taking hold in the DND camps would spill over into the national park operations. Unlike the park camps, the DND programme placed greater emphasis on where the men were and not what they were doing. As a consequence, instead of protecting Canada's single unemployed from possible subversive contamination—as General McNaughton had argued the previous

Czar Creek camp, Big Bend Highway, 15 July 1933. *Canadian Parks Service, Western Regional Office, Webster Collection*

fall—the DND relief camps became natural breeding grounds for discontent and therein easy targets for Communist organizers. The men not only felt isolated but began to question the value attached to their labour—how else could one explain the make-work projects at slave wages? Many came to believe they were being deliberately punished for their misfortune. "It was jail, you know. What else would you call it?" recalled one former DND camp inmate. "All the fresh air and sunshine you could stand, but no women, no music, no streets and people, no place to buy anything . . . and no sounds of streetcars and kids playing. Just the wind through the fir trees, it blew all the time, and guys lying around bullshitting. After a while you forgot what you looked like."[69]

Harkin and Wardle tried to prevent contamination of the park camps by carefully monitoring all operations and taking immediate corrective action whenever necessary. When a circular was discovered in July 1933 in one of the Lake Louise camps calling on the men to organize in preparation for a general strike, local officials visited the workers and asked whether there were any grievances.[70] There was also a newspaper report that Russian-paid agitators were thwarting the efforts of the Salvation Army representative in the Prince Albert camps; it turned out, however, that Ensign Hraniuc likely sang one too many hymns for the men.[71] The Parks Branch tried to ensure that the men were occupied during their idle hours; in particular, it proved receptive to a request from Frontier College to offer evening education classes where possible.[72] Above all, the camps were run with a firm hand and the men subjected to a heavy dose of paternalism. Although fed wholesome meals, for example, they had to sit in the same seat in the dining hall and were forbidden to talk during the meal.[73] They were not allowed to leave the camps and had to get special permission to go into town.[74] This practice prompted one veteran to ask whether they were there as "Government workmen or Government prisoners."[75] These travel restrictions also applied to certain areas of the parks. One Riding Mountain worker and his buddy were stopped on the beach at Clear Lake in the late spring and told by a warden to get back to camp and not to mix with the tourists; the two men left the park the next day.[76] Potential troublemakers, including those who complained, were closely watched. The superintendent at Prince Albert National Park had a rather innovative way of dealing with suspected agitators; he sent them to small outlying tent camps in the bush, where they could "talk to their heart's content without doing very much harm."[77] The more common practice, and one that was regularly threatened, was simply to ask a worker to leave. This action intimidated the other men, for if they were dismissed from camp they would lose whatever meagre support they had.

· · ·

In October 1933, Wardle and his staff began preparing for another season of winter relief work. Although the process had become fairly standard, the chief engineer went out of his way that fall to remind the superintendents to keep two things in mind: the work was to employ only those numbers of men who could be used to advantage and who could be accommodated with the available camp equipment. The planning was also overshadowed by General McNaughton, who continued to think and act as if he knew what was best. First demanding to know how many transients would be involved in park work over the winter, he then started to complain again about the discrepancies in camp policy and how these differences could lead to trouble in the future.[78] Interior officials, however, were not about to be bullied, and after a private meeting with their minister in late November, advised General McNaughton that there would be no change in park camp policy, that the men were "well satisfied," and that the Parks camps would compare favourably with the Defence Department camps under any method of evaluation.[79] This rebuff simply bounced off McNaughton, who demanded once more a meeting with Parks officials. Some two weeks later he finally got his way, when Wardle and his assistant were dispatched to Defence headquarters during a visit to Ottawa. The meeting had the same outcome, though, as the one in the spring. Even though both parties claimed to have the welfare of the men at heart, they were unable to get beyond petty bureaucratic wrangling and could only agree to disagree on camp policy.[80]

Most of the relief work that fall was a continuation of the summer road-building programme, carried on in the parks—including Kootenay beginning in December—and on the Golden-Revelstoke highway for as long as weather permitted and measurable progress was being made. The men also constructed a wide range of recreational facilities, enlarged and improved campgrounds, and attended to a number of special tasks in the various park townsites. In several parks, work gangs were also sent into the bush to haul out logs for future building projects. The activity that led all others through the winter, however, was brush clearing—whether it be along roadways, in cottage subdivisions, or on new golf-courses. It was the one job that could be done under most conditions and at the same time provide employment for as many men as were available. It was also the kind of work that pleased local park associations. Once unemployment relief became a regular feature in the national parks, these associations would submit to Ottawa a list of possible work projects, which invariably included brushing and clearing of one sort or another. The strangest case was probably that of the Elk Island Park Golf Club, which came into being during the summer of 1933, even though there was no golf-course in the park. The president of the new club wrote Ottawa in September about "the very immediate need" to build a park course.[81] Commissioner Harkin approved the idea as a winter relief project—no doubt in part because he himself was an avid golfer.

Despite the size of the park relief operations that winter—some three

Riding Mountain construction projects drew on the skills of local log builders and stone masons. *Western Canada Pictorial Index, 442–14220*

thousand men—and the growing unrest at the DND camps, little trouble was experienced in the national park camps. In mid-September 1933, the Calgary *Albertan* carried a somewhat lurid story about the squalid living conditions in Camp 4A at the Lake Louise end of the Banff-Jasper highway. In particular, it wondered why some of the bunks had dirty old pieces of canvas drawn around them—in the words of the paper, "presumably to keep out draughts, but suggestive of other motives."[82] An internal investigation revealed that the author of the report had not visited the camp, that the tent was regularly cleaned and aired, and that some of the men shrouded their bunks for warmth and privacy. It did admit that the men were urinating outside the tent at night, but contended that it was difficult to stop this practice, especially when a night-time trip to the latrine necessitated a cold trudge through the snow.[83] What probably prevented the incident from becoming a serious issue, however, was the fact that it paled in comparison to the number and nature of complaints emanating from the DND camps. Whereas the Defence camps had been bedevilled by a series of strikes—fifty-seven between June 1933 and March 1934—there were only two short-lived protests in the park camps that winter, and both were easily resolved: one over working in deep snow and the other over a mistaken menu change.[84] The closest thing to a serious work stoppage occurred in mid-April 1934, when the men at Healy Creek camp in Banff informed their supervisor that they would no longer work Saturday afternoons since the DND camps, located just east of the park, were not required to do so. After joining the men for their midday meal, the superintendent told them that working hours would not be changed and that the camp would be closed and the men returned to Calgary if they refused to turn out for work that Saturday afternoon. This warning had the desired effect and a hurriedly convened secret vote on the matter returned only two ballots in favour of strike action. The superintendent then heard from a delegation, which asked for a football and a baseball and bat; according to the men's representatives, the days were getting longer and they had little to do at night but sit around and listen to agitators.[85]

The more serious problem that winter was the weather, especially in the mountain parks. It started to snow around the middle of December and continued to do so almost every single day until it peaked on the twenty-second. The weather cleared for the Christmas holiday, but the temperature plummeted—it was -43°F at Banff on Christmas morning. Luckily, the men were no longer living in tents. Towards the end of the month, another wicked storm swept through the region and deposited several more inches of fresh snow. At the Lake Louise headquarters of the Banff-Jasper highway, for example, there were four feet of snow on 29 December; all communication to Waterton Lakes, meanwhile, was disrupted for several days. Relief work came to a standstill, and the men spent their time loading wheelbarrow after wheelbarrow with snow, just trying to keep the camps operating. Things were so grim that at one point

Bunkhouse interior, Healy Creek camp, Banff, January 1933. *Canadian Parks Service, Western Regional Office, Webster Collection*

in early January, Commissioner Harkin sought ministerial assurance that it was the government's desire to keep the men in the camps.[86]

The other problem—more of an irritant—was General McNaughton's constant grumbling. He continued to gripe throughout the winter about the discrepancies in the administration of the two relief camp systems and the need for a uniform policy. Chief Engineer Wardle, who had a passion for statistics, happily joined the fray and produced an endless stream of figures to show that the park camps were more economically operated, despite the fact that the men were offered a more varied meal standard.[87] Harkin, on the other hand, grew increasingly exasperated with McNaughton's constant sniping, and in a heated memo to the deputy minister of the Interior, claimed that the general's harassment was "entirely out of place" and constituted nothing less than "an attempt to cause the lowering of our operations standards."[88] He also drew attention to the seemingly chronic labour troubles in the DND camps—even though the men received a number of special conveniences and privileges, including Saturday afternoons off, cots with mattresses, and free tobacco—and argued that the Parks Branch was better qualified and more experienced in operating work camps. These arguments were incorporated into a lengthy March 1934 report on park relief operations, which was later used by the minister of the Interior in the House of Commons to praise the national park camps and the work being done there.[89] And to General McNaughton's chagrin, when the new 1934 Relief Act was finally approved on 20 April, it continued to support relief work for single homeless men under the direction and control of the Parks Branch.

· · ·

The key ingredient in the national park relief programme for the summer of 1934 was once again roads. This was nothing new; roads had been at the heart of park relief plans since the beginning of the Depression. Wardle's selection and ranking of the projects, however, was influenced by two other factors that spring. Although the chief engineer enjoyed sparring with Defence Department officials over relief camp policy, he shared Harkin's concern that the Parks Branch might eventually lose access to the labour of the single unemployed, and proposed that major park road projects be given priority that summer. In the case of Banff and Jasper, for example, he argued that the Banff-Jasper highway be given first call on men, and that other projects, such as the Stoney Squaw Mountain or Miette Hot Springs roads, make do, if necessary, with a smaller workforce.[90] The other factor affecting the summer programme was the possibility of a new federal public works initiative. Although the exact details of this rumoured programme were not clear in the spring of 1934, it did not make sense to proceed with park buildings that might later qualify for funding and manpower under the terms of new public works legislation. Wardle therefore steered clear of new building projects in favour of roads and to a lesser extent, recreational facilities, hoping even then that many of these undertakings would be included in the new public works programme. In the meantime, he decided to push ahead with his priorities and do what was possible as long as the single homeless men were available.[91] And by the end of May 1934, the summer programme was in full swing in no less than eight national parks and on the Big Bend Highway, employing almost 2,800 transients and 150 local residents.

These arrangements all had to be reworked two months later, following the passage of the Public Works Construction Act (PWCA) in early July 1934. The long-awaited legislation was the result of several different but interrelated forces. Throughout the latter half of 1933, the Canadian construction industry had hammered away at the Conservative government with calls for a public works programme that would restore lost jobs and stimulate growth.[92] The idea also had the support of many leading Conservatives. Fellow cabinet ministers R.J. Manion and H.H. Stevens visualized public works spending as an essential component of any recovery scheme.[93] So too did Thomas Murphy, the minister of the Interior. In late January 1934, he confidently told the prime minister that a public works programme in the national parks would serve to generate millions of tourist dollars.[94] The most important influence on the Bennett government, however, was the New Deal programme of American president Franklin Roosevelt, in particular his $3-billion commitment to new public works initiatives. The broad appeal of this bold scheme was not lost on the prime minister or his advisors, and in November 1933, during a national radio broadcast, Bennett promised a similar public works programme–a pledge he repeated during the April 1934 parliamentary debate on the new relief act.[95]

The recently completed museum building, Riding Mountain National Park, 1933.
Canadian Parks Service, Western Regional Office, Webster Collection

Before the new programme could be implemented, the cabinet had to decide on the size of the commitment, and this proved to be a source of delay and then disappointment.[96] When the Public Works Construction Act was eventually tabled in the House of Commons, it made available only $40 million in supplementary spending for public works projects. Although this was almost four times the Department of Public Works budget for 1934, it was a far cry from what was actually needed for effective priming of the battered Canadian economy.[97] As a result, the programme did little, in the words of the act's preamble, "to accelerate recovery to more normal economic conditions."[98] It also smacked of patronage. Not only were most of the projects in Conservative ridings—88 percent of Alberta's PWCA projects, for example, were located in Bennett's Calgary West constituency—but the selection of architects and contractors had less to do with competence and more with political connections.[99] At best, the programme was a baldfaced attempt—and a poor one at that—to emulate the success of the Roosevelt plan.

For the Parks Branch, however, the Public Works Construction Act was a boon. Among the myriad of projects and estimates listed in the act's appendix was a $2-million budget entry for the Department of the Interior. Harkin and his staff were not caught flat-footed by the introduction of the programme. More than four months earlier, when the cabinet was agonizing over the size of the public works allocation, Murphy had asked for an inventory of "useful" building projects that might be undertaken in the national parks.[100] Harkin gladly obliged with a detailed list containing both new and old projects—it must have seemed like Christmas—and the Parks Branch had a clear idea of what it wanted to do by the time the programme was finally in place. The more pressing concern in the first few weeks of July, however, was deciding what to do with the transients now working in the park camps. Once the various projects went on a PWCA footing, married men with dependants were to be given preference at all jobsites. The obvious answer was to give the Department of National Defence sole responsibility for the care of single homeless men. And in a formal exchange of letters between Thomas Murphy and General McNaughton on 1 August 1934, this policy change was officially recognized. At a strained though amicable meeting between department representatives that same day, it was agreed that any single men who could not be retained on national park projects on a wage basis would be transferred to the Defence camps—provided they were willing to go.[101]

Ironically, the consolidation of the single homeless camps under DND control did not end the feud with the Parks Branch. Defence officials insisted that all transferred men had to undergo a medical inspection to ensure that they were physically fit and free of communicable diseases. They also requested the return of any materials, such as blankets and tents, that had been loaned to the park relief camps; when it was learned that much of this equipment was worn out, they demanded financial compensation.[102] As many as four hundred men, meanwhile, had decided that they wanted nothing to do with the DND camps and their reputation, and headed off in July.[103] Most of the remaining men in the park camps were also reluctant to join the Defence operations, especially when there was the possibility of wage employment on Parks projects—starting at forty-five cents per hour for labourers. Wardle, in fact, was terribly uneasy about the mood in the park camps in early August and warned Harkin by wire that any attempt to transfer the men en masse could result in "sabotage forest

The English Garden, constructed beside the new museum building at Wasagaming in 1934. *Riding Mountain National Park Collection*

fires property damage and strikes."[104] Treading carefully, then, the Department of the Interior instructed camp officials to employ single homeless men on the PWCA projects until they were displaced by workers with domestic responsibilities. This decision not only prevented any serious disruption in camp operations, but also allowed for an early start on many of the new building projects. And in many instances, the Defence Department had to wait until early 1935 before some of the single homeless men were identified for possible transfer.

The introduction of this programme had symbolic significance, in that it sent the relief operations of the Defence Department and Parks Branch off on separate paths. When the Department of Defence secured sole responsibility for the single unemployed, McNaughton finally won a battle he had been waging tirelessly with the Parks Branch ever since the DND relief programme had first been established. The DND camps, however, increasingly became the focus of all that was wrong with the Bennett government's handling of the unemployment crisis, as the internees began to challenge the seemingly meaningless nature of their lives and demand changes. This discontent eventually led to a mass walkout by the British Columbia DND camps in the spring of 1935, and culminated in the On-to-Ottawa Trek and the Regina Riot—events that gave the DND relief scheme a black eye from which it has never recovered. The national park camps, on the other hand, entered a new phase in their history. The public works grant meant that the national parks administration could now proceed with a number of pet building projects that would have been otherwise impossible during the straitened times. It also meant that park relief workers could do more than perform mundane tasks such as clearing brush, and could put into practice their various skills and get paid at a reasonable rate for doing so. Most important, it meant that a number of outstanding projects that had moved along at a slow, albeit steady, pace over the past few years might see completion in the foreseeable future after all.

· · ·

One of the greatest beneficiaries of the Public Works Construction Act was Banff National Park—not a surprising development given that the park was part of the prime minister's home constituency. Some of the current relief projects, such as the enlargement of the golf-course, fell under PWCA funding and were continued in this new capacity; others were modified. Construction of the Stoney Squaw Mountain road, for example, was temporarily suspended while engineers decided on the best location for a new spur road to the Mount Norquay Ski Club. There was also a wide range of new construction and improvement work, including a bridge over the Cascade River, a landing field, a central garage, and a sewer system from the Tunnel Mountain campground to the townsite; all this activity qualified under the provisions of the public works act. The most celebrated work at Banff, however, was a trio of projects—a gateway registration building, administration building, and land-scaped garden—designed and supervised by renowned Canadian architect Harold Beckett.

The need for a new entrance gateway building at Banff dated from 1929,

Construction of a new East Gate registration complex at Banff was made possible thanks to the Public Works Construction Act. *Whyte Museum of the Canadian Rockies, V488/313(12)*

when the eastern boundary of the park was moved westward some twenty-two miles. Although local Parks officials originally hoped to undertake the building as a relief project, construction was set aside until the park budget was restored to pre-Depression levels. The special public works funding, however, introduced a new set of ground rules, and the Parks Branch responded as if it had been finally cut loose from some great restraint. Harold Beckett, a highly successful private architect, was immediately engaged to design the East Gate, and conceived a three-building cottage complex featuring both rustic and Tudor Revival styles. Construction of the split fieldstone and timbered buildings commenced in April 1935, but because of delays in securing materials, the project was not completed until the following year. In the end, though, Banff boasted what was probably the finest entrance gate in the national park system—built by relief labour.[105]

Beckett also designed the handsome, three-storey stone administration building that today commands the south end of Banff Avenue in the park townsite. This project was also made possible by PWCA funding, but because it was to include a post office and customs house in addition to park administrative offices, it was financed as a separate project with its own $150,000 budget. And whereas the East Gate complex was constructed on a day-labour basis, the administration building was undertaken by contract. Parks officials, however, were extremely conscious of the public image to be projected by the structure and oversaw all aspects of the construction, including making minor revisions

Public works funding in 1934 enabled major building projects, such as the Banff administration building, to be undertaken in the parks. *Canadian Parks Service, Western Regional Office, Webster Collection*

One of the most intriguing park relief projects was "The Cascades of Time" display behind the new Banff administration building, July 1935. *National Archives of Canada, C141813*

to Beckett's original Tudor Revival design.[106] In keeping with one of the project's purposes, moreover, the local unemployed were taken on wherever possible, especially in quarrying limestone from nearby Mount Rundle for the outside walls. The park kept a careful record of these men—their place of residence, nationality, and marital status—in the event that there were any questions about their eligibility for relief work.[107]

Beckett did more than design buildings at Banff. He also doubled as a landscape architect and took a personal hand in developing the spacious grounds around the new administration building. This was no ordinary arrangement of flower beds interspersed with the odd shrub or tree. An amateur geologist, Beckett had always dreamed of using his landscaping skills to depict the evolution of time, and when he saw the terraced grounds behind the proposed site of the administration building during his first visit to Banff in July 1934, he knew he had found his spot. Beckett immediately put together a proposal, which seemed to have no bounds except for the limits of his imagination. Dubbed "The Cascades of Time," the rock-garden was to portray the different geological periods, from the Precambrian to Upper Cretaceous, by means of a series of interconnecting pools, rustic pavilions and archways, stone bridges and flagged walkways; there was even provision for trout spawning beds, imported perennials, and models of prehistoric animals. Parks officials got caught up in the vision—it was seen as a one-of-a-kind tourist attraction—and excavation of the first of the pools, the floodlit Reflection Pool in front of the future administration building, got started to considerable local fanfare in early October 1934.[108]

By the following summer, though, the Cascades project had become something of a nightmare for the Parks Branch. Although it provided several thousand hours of local relief work, it also gobbled up large sums of money, especially since Beckett had a penchant for devising new features as the project took shape. By the end of the 1935 construction season, almost $25,000 had been expended—two years earlier this amount would have covered the monthly allowance of five thousand transients working in the park system. Some of the relief workers probably wondered whether Beckett realized they were in the midst of a Depression; others likely thought that they too might go the way of the dinosaurs on display if things did not turn around soon. Harkin tried to rein in the architect, but it was to no avail. Beckett felt slighted by any suggestion that he scale down his creation and told the commissioner, "Not to complete my original plan would be like leaving the roof off the new home."[109] The constant need for cash infusions for the project, however, proved its undoing, and following the completion of the administration building in 1936 and Beckett's departure from Banff that fall, work on the Cascades quietly came to an end.

·   ·   ·

A number of buildings were also erected in several other western national parks under public works funding. Unlike Banff, though, all of these structures were designed by the architectural division of the Parks Branch. At Jasper National Park, approval was secured for a new superintendent's residence and gateway registration building. Steps were also taken to expedite the Miette Hot Springs project. Work gangs finally completed the road to the site, cleared a campground and parking lot, and then turned their hands to constructing a concrete pool and chaletlike bathhouse.[110] At Waterton Lakes, meanwhile, it was decided to build onto the existing administration building and then renovate the exterior of the enlarged structure in a half-timbered motif, the architectural trademark of most Parks buildings during this period.[111] The same Tudor Revival style was featured in a graceful registration building erected at the junction of the Pincher Creek and Cardston highways in 1935.[112]

The story at Prince Albert and Riding Mountain was much the same. Because these were two relatively new national parks, however, a certain amount of building activity had already been undertaken by relief workers in the early 1930s, particularly at Riding Mountain. The PWCA funding accelerated this construction work so that both parks emerged from the period with a full complement of administrative and recreational structures. At Prince Albert, work gangs erected a large garage, golf clubhouse, staff quarters, and museum to go along with a registration building and community hall. At Riding Mountain, on the other hand, the key buildings were already in place by 1934, and the

The museum building at Waskesiu nearing completion, 16 October 1935. *Canadian Parks Service, Western Regional Office, Webster Collection*

public works programme allowed for some finishing touches—a tennis pavilion, bandstand and pergola, and recreation shelter. In both instances, the Tudor-Rustic style, with its horizontal, peeled spruce logs and fieldstone, continued to be employed throughout, giving the buildings a common yet distinctive appearance, and also enhancing the parks' image as prairie playgrounds. In addition, it made good use of local materials and local skills—still key considerations for relief work.

The public works act funded more than just new buildings. The wording of the $2-million grant was open-ended, and the Parks Branch used the funds to complete or expand the visitor facilities at a number of parks. Whereas the nine-hole golf-course at Elk Island, for example, was completed with PWCA monies, those at Prince Albert, Riding Mountain, Waterton Lakes, and Banff were enlarged and upgraded. Local men were also put to work laying out tennis-courts, recreation fields, and children's playgrounds in the park townsites, as well as erecting kitchen shelters, washrooms, and refrigerator houses in the nearby campgrounds. There were also special projects, such as a new breakwater at Lake Waskesiu to improve boating facilities, an extension to the Cave and Basin pool at Banff, and the clearing and grooming of a bridle-path at Riding Mountain. There was very little the relief crews did not do. The public works initiative offered an unprecedented opportunity to enhance the tourist potential of the western parks—once the Depression was over. And there was good reason to believe that the people would come. By 1935, Riding Mountain was already drawing more than one hundred thousand people annually, and other parks were enjoying a similar popularity as Canadians sought an affordable family holiday by car.

Riding Mountain golf-course clubhouse. *Riding Mountain National Park Collection*

• • •

The public works funding also gave a much-needed boost to park road construction. At Prince Albert, the road to the First Narrows on Lake Waskesiu was finally punched through; although the route had been surveyed in 1927, less than half the distance had been cleared by 1933. Construction was also pushed ahead on the Clear Lake–Dauphin highway in Riding Mountain; this road would not only provide a scenic drive through the heart of the park, but would also allow direct access to the townsite from the north. And the dream of an international highway link between Waterton Lakes and Glacier National Parks was finally realized when the Belly River (Chief Mountain) highway was completed to the boundary in 1936 under PWCA auspices. The road crews also doubled as fire-fighters, being pressed into service whenever a blaze broke out. The men on the Belly River project, for example, battled two international fires: the August 1935 Boundary Creek fire that threatened the village of Waterton, and the September 1936 Kennedy Creek fire in Montana.[113]

The two major park road projects of the period—the Banff-Jasper and Big Bend highways—were also beneficiaries of the public works programme. Even though both roads would not be finished until the end of the decade, the special funding effectively rescued the projects from the doldrums and provided the momentum that had been lacking. In the case of the Banff-Jasper highway, only fifty-seven miles of road had been graded by the end of July 1934 when it was switched over to a public works basis; there were still another ninety miles of mountain wilderness between the south and north ends.[114] The additional funds—and more importantly, additional equipment—breathed new life into the project, and by the time the camps were shut down for winter that November, considerable headway had been made on another twenty miles of highway.

This work was not without its problems. Many of the married unemployed lacked road-building experience; some could not work in the high altitudes and had to be released. There was also a minor uproar when two relief workers, who went home to Calgary for Thanksgiving, returned to camp by taxi.[115] The most common concern among several Alberta communities, however, was that the road was not being built fast enough. In an October 1934 editorial on the value of the Banff-Jasper highway, the Edson newspaper spoke for many when it suggested that the early completion of the road should be a federal priority: "We cannot sell our wheat; we cannot sell our beef, but we can sell our Mountain Scenery to tourists for millions of dollars if we provide good highways to this scenery."[116] The road remained, however, a formidable challenge under any arrangement, and it was not until June 1939 that a truck managed to rumble over the incomplete grade from Banff to Jasper.[117]

The Big Bend Highway was also in trouble by the time it became a public works project. By the fall of 1934, the national park construction crews were still some fifteen miles from the apex of the Columbia River, and had yet to start construction of the steel bridge that was supposed to join east and west legs of the highway. Even worse, Chief Engineer Wardle could not say with any certainty how much completed road there was because of the extremely muddy condition of the grade; some sections of the road were wet all summer;

Ferrying a shovel across the Columbia River, Big Bend project, August 1936. *Canadian Parks Service, Western Regional Office, Webster Collection*

others had to be corduroyed.[118] The provincial or western section of the project was even further behind schedule. The British Columbia government abandoned work on its share of the highway in November 1932 because of funding problems, and nothing more was done until the following summer, when it became a DND relief project for single homeless men. These workers spent the remainder of the 1933 season refurbishing the old provincial camps, repairing bridges, and clearing debris from completed sections of the highway in preparation for the resumption of construction; at one point, a rock slide had wiped out almost seven hundred feet of road. Despite their best efforts, however, little was accomplished the next year. In March 1935, General McNaughton reported that only two-thirds of the western leg—from Revelstoke to Goldstream—was fit for one-way traffic, and that those sections of the road that met the standard twenty-four-foot-wide grade totalled just six miles.[119]

The Big Bend Highway was specifically named in the 1934 public works legislation as one of the projects that would be financed from the $2-million Department of the Interior grant. And it appeared that the dominion leg of the road would eventually be completed, thanks to the assistance. That still left the western, or provincial, section, and in early November 1934, British Columbia's minister of Public Works made an unsolicited offer to Thomas Murphy: if the federal government assumed responsibility for the completion and maintenance of the entire highway, then the province would turn over a quarter-mile strip of land along both sides for a national park. The proposition did not interest the Bennett administration—the Parks Branch was more interested in a new park along the Pacific coast—and the government began to worry that the completion of the Trans-Canada Highway in western Canada might be held up for several years, especially since British Columbia was tacitly admitting that it could not fulfil its side of the Big Bend agreement.[120] The federal government also realized that it could not count on much being done as long as the provincial section remained a DND relief project. It was therefore decided, effective 6 July 1935, to turn over construction of the western leg to the Department of the Interior and have the entire highway from Golden to Revelstoke built by national park relief crews on a regular wage basis. The formal details of the transfer were worked out at yet another testy meeting between Defence and Interior officials in Ottawa in the early spring. McNaughton seemed uncomfortable, if not embarrassed, by the episode.[121] After all, it seemed to confirm what Parks officials had been arguing for some time: that the Defence Department lacked the experience and expertise to manage construction projects of this nature on a relief basis. Wardle and his engineering staff, however, had little to gloat about. It would take another five years before the road was open to traffic.

Court Neville, one of the youngest men in the Big Bend camps in the late 1930s, worked on both legs of the highway as a truck driver and remembered being on the move every day, no matter what the weather or road conditions. He also recalled how at night the men had to find their own recreation, such as washing dishes or taking a Charles Atlas body-building course.[122] Someone even composed a six-verse ballad about the road, which ended:

> Some day this Highway will be opened wide,
> And from Golden down to Revelstoke we'll ride,
> We'll always remember, in our good old Ford,
> How we travelled 'mid the wonders of the Big Bend Road.[123]

There were also exciting moments, such as when a group of men had gathered to hear a prizefight on the radio in a recently winterized tent—the walls had been wrapped with tar-paper and then braced with a load of gravel—only to discover that two skunks had been accidentally trapped beneath the platform floor.[124]

Through it all, the men tackled the job with a determined grit, as if they owed it to the gangs of single homeless who had laboured there before them to complete the project. The Big Bend seemed a personal symbol for the road crews—that something good could come out of the Depression. And there were probably few prouder men than those who ringed the opening ceremonies at Boat Encampment, the northernmost point on the bend of the Columbia, on 29 June 1940. Sadly, the road fell into disuse in the early 1960s, when the Trans-Canada Highway was opened through Rogers Pass. It now lies several feet under water, the valley having been flooded by the Mica (1973) and Revelstoke (1983) Dams.[125]

· · ·

The assumption of the Big Bend Highway project by the Parks Branch was made possible by the passage of the Supplementary Public Works Construction Act in mid-June 1935. Approved during the final few weeks of the Bennett administration, the legislation provided an additional $18 million for new or continuing public works projects. And once again the Interior Department was given a share of the largesse—this time, $1.5 million. The Parks Branch used this sum, along with any unexpended monies from the 1934 grant, to fund a number of ongoing concerns. The Big Bend Highway, for example, received an injection of $285,000, while its Alberta rival, the Banff-Jasper highway, secured an additional $215,000. Work also continued on a number of park structures, such as the Banff administration building, which had been started during the past year. Several smaller, new projects were also embarked upon, particularly improvements and extensions to the water and sewage systems in some of the park townsites. These various activities brought total park relief employment to thirty-six hundred men that October. It was an unprecedented level, and one that would never be reached again. This kind of work, however, did not fall off

Relief crew replacing storm sewers in the Waskesiu townsite, Prince Albert National Park, 16 October 1935. *Canadian Parks Service, Western Regional Office, Webster Collection*

completely in the following months. Although Mackenzie King's Liberals swept the hapless Conservatives from office in the October 1935 general election, the new government did not cancel projects financed by the two public works acts, but allowed them to be completed over the next few years. Between 1935 and 1939, moreover, the Liberals continued their predecessors' practice–albeit in a slightly modified form–and approved a separate Department of Public Works budget for relief purposes. The Parks Branch was awarded a portion of these "special supplementary estimates" to provide "emergency" employment for needy park residents.[126] In many instances, this work involved the continuation or completion of projects that had been started by the relief gangs.

The Mackenzie King government did not look as kindly on the DND relief operations, but regarded them as a political liability, especially after Bennett's bungled attempt to arrest the leaders of the On-to-Ottawa Trek in Regina had sparked a riot. Before the Liberals could shut down the camps, however, the men at Dundurn, Saskatchewan, went on strike in early December 1935. Anxious to defuse the situation peacefully, Saskatchewan attorney-general T.C. Davis secured federal approval to transfer the men to Prince Albert National Park. He then laid the plan before the strikers, asking for volunteers. By coincidence, many of the Dundurn men had worked at Prince Albert before being displaced in the fall of 1934 under the PWCA provisions, and were now anxious to return to the park.[127] As a result, Prince Albert became the only national park to operate camps for the single unemployed during the winter and spring of 1936.[128] This turn of events was significant in itself, for it enabled local park officials to initiate two new, major road-building projects. It was also representative, however, of the great gulf between the relief activities of the Defence Department and Parks Branch. The transfer of the Dundurn men to Prince Albert undoubtedly galled General McNaughton, who was instructed in the spring of 1936 to dismantle the DND relief camp system.

•   •   •

The national park camps were also silent by 1937, and little time was lost removing the structures and clearing the sites. It was as if the buildings were a blight on the landscape, and any reminder of them had to be wiped out.[129] The final tallies for the programme were also done, and for the six-year period ending in March 1936, it was reported that more than $6 million—in relief funds and public works grants—had been expended on relief activities.[130] This was eight times greater than what Commissioner Harkin had originally sought in the fall of 1930, and he probably would never have believed at the time that the

Parks Branch would eventually have this level of funds at its disposal. They were certainly needed. Obsessed with balancing the budget and maintaining Canada's credit rating, the Bennett government had slashed department budgets and imposed a rigid economy. The relief funds not only made up for these lost resources, but enabled the Parks Branch to proceed with a number of projects and activities that would have otherwise been delayed or postponed for at least a decade, if not longer. The situation at Riding Mountain

Special public works funding made possible an extension to the Cave and Basin pool at Banff. *Whyte Museum of the Canadian Rockies, V488/303(22)*

National Park was a case in point. While the park budget for 1933-34 dropped by almost half from the previous year to just over $50,000, it received more than a third of a million dollars for unemployment work for the same period. Other western national parks benefitted in much the same way.

But the story of the park relief operations was more than about budgets and figures—or yards of earth moved or miles of road cleared, for that matter. It had a human side. It was about thousands of men, who, through no fault of their own, found themselves out of work and in many cases, out of hope. These men were not in the strict sense of the word prisoners; they were dispatched to the park camps, however, on the understanding that if they refused to go or quit the camps, they would be cut off relief assistance. Clearly, they had to accept their posting or face possible starvation. Park relief work, for these men, was not without its problems or shortcomings. The camps were administered with a firm hand, and any protest was usually greeted with intimidation or expulsion. In general, though, most men tolerated the conditions because they had no other alternative, and they were at least being sheltered, fed, and clothed.

That these camps even existed during the Depression is scarcely known today. Most students of Canadian history, on the other hand, have probably heard of General McNaughton's relief scheme. And for good reason—more than one hundred and sixty-seven thousand single homeless men passed through the DND camps. The national park camps, in comparison, were a relatively small operation. While the DND camps had an average *monthly* population of fourteen thousand during the programme's three-and-a-half-year existence, the park camps never housed more than six thousand men in any given year. In fact, more men were probably expelled from the DND camps for disciplinary reasons (17,391) than occupied the park camps for the same period.[131] These statistical comparisons are deceiving, however, as they fail to give a full appreciation of what the relief workers meant to Canada's national parks during those bleak years. In 1931-32, the jobless performed a quarter of a million man-days of work in western parks; two years later, this number had tripled.[132] The cumulative result of this labour was a level of development that has rarely been matched in national park history.[133] The men were also tackling projects that had meaning and purpose. Whereas Defence officials had to find work for the single homeless and were more concerned with keeping the men busy whatever the results,[134] the Parks Branch had a specific list of activities, particularly road building. And although the work was undeniably hard, even harsh, especially during the early years of the camp operations, the men had a sense that they were doing something worthwhile. This became even more evident after the various park projects were switched over to a public works footing, and the unemployed applied their skills to various building projects— many of which have been recognized today as heritage structures. "Any man I talked to over the years, and I talked with hundreds in the Waterton Relief

Camps," asserted Frank Goble, who has written an account of his experiences in the park camps, "was very happy to have the opportunity to be working there."[135] Court Neville shared these sentiments. When asked about the Big Bend project and how he regarded the experience today, he talked about how the work was a saviour for men like him, and how the road could not have been built any better, given the available equipment. What greatly saddened him, however, was that the highway and the men who toiled on it have been forgotten. For Neville, it was "a dirty shame."[136]

CHAPTER FOUR

Conchies

*I*T WAS ALL HAPPENING TOO FAST. AND ROY GIBSON, DIRECTOR OF THE Lands, Parks, and Forests Branch,[1] was not pleased. On 6 June 1941, the Mackenzie King government passed an order authorizing the establishment of work camps for conscientious objectors. Three days later, in one of his last acts as National War Services minister, Jimmy Gardiner requested that such camps be organized in western Canada's national parks. This much had been known for weeks; officials from the two departments had been busy working out the details of the programme since early March 1941. What bothered Gibson was that formal approval had been delayed so long, especially since the camps were supposed to be operational by early June. It would have been "more convenient," he told the associate deputy minister of National War Services in a pointed letter on 11 June, to have established the camps in the early spring, before the beginning of the park tourist season. He was equally perturbed that funding for the camps had not yet been authorized, and that any national park expenditures under the proposed programme would have to be reviewed by a National War Services official. Had not the national parks an enviable record in this regard, he wondered, particularly during the Depression? The most frustrating aspect of the arrangement, however, was that the men were already being ordered to report to the camps while there were still so many unresolved questions. "We know nothing whatever about these men," an exasperated Gibson complained, "and . . . we are finding great difficulty in knowing how many will arrive."[2]

That western Canada's national parks would become the surrogate home for several hundred conscientious objectors almost two years into the war represented quite a change in government policy. From the beginning of hostilities in September 1939, Prime Minister Mackenzie King and his Liberal administration had steadfastly pursued a "limited liability" policy in the interests of maintaining national unity. There would be no conscription for overseas service—no commitments that involved large manpower requirements—and therefore less chance of precipitating the kind of national crisis that had irreparably scarred the country in 1917. The German offensive in the spring of 1940, however, changed the entire complexion of the Second World War, and with the fall of France and the Nazi occupation of western Europe, Canada emerged as Great Britain's foremost military ally. King's limited liability approach to the war no longer made sense under the new circumstances. And in an effort to answer the growing number of critics who began to call for a greater mobilization of Canada's human and material resources, while also trying to avoid alienating French Canada, the Liberal government introduced the concept of conscription for home defence. Under the terms of the National Resources Mobilization Act [NRMA], approved on 21 June 1940, all men and women over the age of sixteen could now be called upon for home guard duty or some other essential service; only volunteer members of the armed forces, however, could be sent overseas.[3]

King's handling of the first conscription crisis of the war met with general approval. It created problems, though, for conscientious objectors. Although the prime minister vowed during the debate on the NRMA legislation that existing exemptions from bearing arms would be respected, members of religious groups such as Mennonites and Doukhobors were still required to participate in the national registration programme that August, or face a fine or possible imprisonment. The regulations governing how registrants were to be called up or exempted from service seemed to make matters worse. According to the National War Services Regulations, approved by government order on 27 August 1940, a man could claim conscientious objector status only if he belonged to a recognized peace church; even then, his military training was simply postponed until he was required for home duty.[4]

These narrow conditions prompted representatives of religious and pacifist groups to seek a broader definition of conscientious objector status, as well as some form of alternative service work in lieu of military training. Given the bleak mood of the country, they realized they could not avoid some type of service, but their preference was for alternative work similar to that performed by some of their relatives in Russia, which would affirm their status and beliefs but make no direct contribution to the war effort.[5] At a series of meetings with National War Services representatives that fall, therefore, they called for the creation of a special work programme on government land under civilian supervision. Government officials were initially cool to the proposal, and there was at least one heated exchange. When General LaFleche tried to unnerve the delegates by suggesting that they could be shot, Jacob H. Janzen, who had survived revolutionary Russia, snapped back, "I've looked down too many rifle barrels in my time to be scared that way. This thing is in our blood for four hundred years and you can't take it away from us like you'd crack a piece of

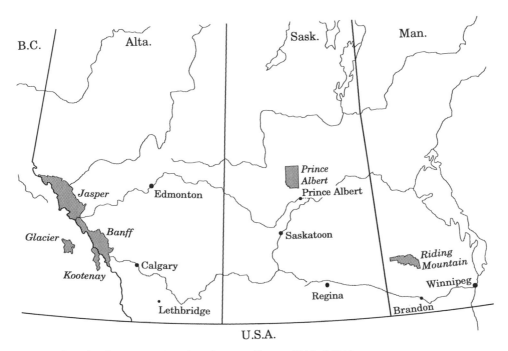

National Park Alternative Service Camps, Second World War.

kindling over your knee . . . We believe in this."[6] Once it became apparent that the Defence Department was not interested in providing noncombatant military training for "conchies," those sections of National War Services Regulations dealing with recruits were amended. As of 24 December 1940, conscientious objectors—now defined as members of any religious organization—could be called upon to provide some form of civilian labour for the same period as military training. The government's Christmas present lacked any substance, however, because there was no alternative service programme in place. Many conscientious objectors summoned before divisional registrars in the early months of 1941 were therefore ordered to undertake military training.[7] It was not until late May 1941—a little more than two weeks before the camps were supposed to open—that the King government finally announced the first call up of conscientious objectors for alternative service work.

· · ·

The man responsible for finding work for the conscientious objectors was T.C. Davis, associate deputy minister of National War Services. A former mayor of Prince Albert and Saskatchewan cabinet minister, Davis had been brought to Ottawa by Mackenzie King because of his political ability, and would later serve as Canadian ambassador to China, West Germany, and then Japan. He would need these diplomatic skills in trying to devise an alternative service programme that would accommodate, if not satisfy, all concerned parties. He would also draw upon his long, intimate association with Prince Albert National Park.[8] Not only had Davis been instrumental in getting the park established, but he had also used his influence to see that the park received its share of relief funds and workers in the early 1930s. And it was Davis, in his capacity as Saskatchewan's attorney general, who early in 1936 had convinced the striking Dundurn relief camp inmates to relocate to Prince Albert and work on projects there.

The associate deputy minister now proposed a similar solution for the problem of the conscientious objectors. Since places such as Prince Albert and Riding Mountain had provided refuge for victims of the Depression, why not use them to provide sanctuary for Canada's so-called peace soldiers? National parks, Davis reasoned, would be ideal places for these men to fulfil their training obligations, since they would be working in relative obscurity in a healthy environment. It was also the kind of labour that would make no direct contribution to Canada's military effort—an important consideration in convincing the men to report. Above all, the national parks had considerable experience running this type of camp and already had most of the equipment and facilities. As recently as the summer of 1939, the Parks Bureau had sponsored a National Forestry Programme to provide training in forestry management for young men aged eighteen to twenty-five.[9] The war, however, effectively killed the scheme, and several parks were left with a list of unfinished projects but no men to take up the tools—conscientious objectors could now fulfil this role.

The Department of War Services first approached the Parks Bureau about the possible use of conscientious objector labour on 3 March 1941. Major-General L.R. LaFleche, the other associate deputy minister, indicated that the government would soon be calling up twenty-one-year-old men for a four-month period of military training, and that his department was prepared to place about seven hundred conscientious objectors, mainly from western Canada, at the disposal of the national parks for the same period of time.[10] There the matter rested until early May, when LaFleche once again communicated with Gibson—this time with more details. Conscientious objectors, or alternative service workers as they were officially called, would be required to work the equivalent of four months basic military training—forty-eight hours per week at 50¢ per day, a rate well below regular army pay of $1.30. The parks, in turn, would be responsible for devising the work projects, as well as housing and feeding the men; clothing, though, was not to be provided. LaFleche also suggested that the men be kept together where practicable, that supervisory personnel be drawn from their own ranks in order to keep costs down, and that the men be given evening instruction in citizenship and first aid[11] in addition to forestry management practices. This much was certainly achievable, including the request that the camps be operational by June, but what shocked Gibson was the fact that LaFleche now expected the parks to absorb twice as many men as he had first indicated.[12]

These increased numbers left Gibson scrambling, and he recommended that the conscientious objectors be called up at staggered times. Even then, not all the men could be accommodated within the parks; according to Gibson's revised figures, 744 would be assigned to one of five summer camps, while another 263 would serve their terms in two winter camps.[13] The remainder were expected to do highway work either in the Montreal River area of northwestern Ontario or between Prince Albert and La Ronge in northcentral Saskatchewan. Gibson also reported that the operations would now cost close to half a million dollars, especially since additional equipment would have to be purchased "to make the work effective"; the days of trying to do as much as possible by hand were apparently over. The Parks Bureau was hopeful that the value of the work performed by the men would be at least equal to the cost of establishing and running the camps.[14]

General LaFleche responded favourably to Gibson's new proposal on 19 May 1941, reporting that the national park alternative service programme was finally going before the cabinet war committee, and that the camps should be readied for immediate occupation. "If anything is to be done this year," LaFleche counselled, "not a moment is to be lost."[15] Nothing more was heard

The first batch of conscientious objectors arrived at Riding Mountain on 12 June 1941.
Courtesy J.M. Unrau

about the matter until 29 May, when National War Services minister Jimmy Gardiner announced in the House of Commons that the King government would immediately be calling up men for alternative service work in several national parks.[16] This public statement was the first confirmation that the Parks Bureau had received regarding the employment of conscientious objectors. But there was still no formal agreement between the Departments of National War Services and Mines and Resources—not even a government order approving the arrangement. There were also a number of unanswered questions. The same day that Gardiner had committed the government to an alternative service programme, Parks Controller James Smart had drawn up a lengthy list of outstanding issues related to the camps. It was not clear, for example, whether the men could be transferred from one park to another, whether they were to be paid only for work days, or whether the parks were responsible for men who fell sick or were injured.[17] These questions led to another round of discussions and eventually figured in the wording of the 6 June order-in-council, which set out the terms and conditions under which conscientious objectors could perform alternative service work in lieu of military training. Three days later— and three months after the Parks Bureau had first been contacted about the matter—Gardiner formally asked Thomas Crerar, the minister of Mines and Resources, to establish alternative service work camps in the national parks.[18] As far as Gibson was concerned, this request was several weeks too late. General LaFleche had already instructed divisional registrars to begin dispatching men to the parks. The special funding for the camps, moreover, had still not been approved—and would not be for some time. Most frustrating for the Parks Bureau, which had only become involved in the programme at the behest of the Department of National War Services,[19] was that the scheme was not under Parks control. It was an inauspicious beginning.

· · ·

The first batch of conscientious objectors arrived at Riding Mountain National Park on 12 June 1941, a mere two days after the minister of Mines and Resources had officially agreed to operate summer work camps. Special buses left Altona in southern Manitoba at eleven that morning and slowly worked their way westward to Boissevain—stopping to pick up more passengers at places such as Plum Coulee, Manitou, and Pilot Mound—before turning north to Brandon and then on to the park. It was almost sundown by the time the men reached their new home in the woods, and they were immediately assigned to a tent, shown a pile of straw to fill their mattresses, and then instructed to bed down for the night.[20] As they tried to sleep, many were quietly overcome by the reality of what had happened to them and what they were doing there; a few were likely gripped with fear. Although they had known for several months that they would be called upon to perform some kind of alternative service and had been encouraged by their families and community leaders to report, their faith had probably never been more tested than that first night in their tents—alone with their thoughts.

Although the park had had little time to get the camps ready, and the men themselves little advance notice of their assignment, registration proceeded without incident the next morning, the superintendent's only complaint being that some had been late reporting.[21] According to the official record, the workers were between the ages of twenty-one and twenty-five, single (as of 1 July 1940[22]), and mostly from Mennonite villages and farming districts that had first been settled in the 1870s. It is only by talking to the men, however, that the human side of the story can be fully understood. For many, the spring of 1941 was one of the most stressful periods in their lives. In order to secure conscientious objector status, they had to appear before Judge J.E. Adamson of the provincial War Services Board. This process was described by several informants as altogether unfair and inconsistent. John Klassen, for example, was asked a few simple questions at his hearing in Altona, while others that same day were treated harshly by the judge.[23] Some of the men came under verbal attack for their beliefs and were subjected to rigorous questioning, if not challenged outright, for the stand they took. Henry Sawatzky, for example, became extremely worried when he overheard the man ahead of him being given a rough time for his position against military service.[24] It was equally difficult for the men to leave family and friends for the camps. A good many, such as Sawatzky and Anton Dyck, had never been away from home before. Others, like Klassen and Jake Unrau, had worked off the family farm but had had little interaction with the larger community. What made things worse was

Many of the young men had never been away from home before. *Courtesy H. Sawatzky*

that many of these young men were oldest sons in their families, and their departure was a cruel blow—emotionally and economically—to parents and siblings. Anton Dyck's two older sisters, for example, had to learn to operate the binder and do other chores in his place.[25] The men also did not know what lay ahead of them. Although told they were being sent to Riding Mountain to fulfil their terms of service, they had no idea what they would be doing—it was all left to their imaginations.

The first group of conscientious objectors, numbering more than 100, occupied one of two tent camps: Camp One, eight miles east of the park townsite on the Norgate road; or Camp Two, seventeen miles north on the Wasagaming-Dauphin road (present-day Highway 10). A third camp was established at mile 13 of the Norgate road in early July, when another group of call-ups was ordered to report to the park. This second instalment brought the total camp population to 202 men—it would eventually reach a high of 206 later that summer. The men slept in groups of 10, in 20-by-24-foot tents with wooden floors; belongings, such as suitcases, were usually placed under their cots. They rose at 6:15 a.m. and washed up at a basin stand in the centre of the camp; pit toilets were located nearby. Breakfasting in the mess tent starting at 7:00, they then walked or were trucked to the jobsite; sometimes the first part of the workday was spent sharpening tools. The men toiled from 8:00 to 5:00, with an hour midday break, six days a week, including Saturdays. Unless they were working too far away to return for lunch, the men were fed their meals at camp, and by all accounts, the food was good.[26] The men who were interviewed about general camp conditions at Riding Mountain that summer voiced no complaints and seemed resigned to their fate—even fifty years later—a far cry from the situation that had existed in the enemy alien camps during the last war.

After spending their first few days fixing up the camps, the men were assigned to general improvement or maintenance chores, work the park superintendent feared might otherwise never get done because of wartime shortages and cutbacks. He also believed the farm boys could be counted on for a good day's work, given their backgrounds, and wanted to take advantage of the manpower.[27] The men consequently applied their muscle to a wide variety of tasks. They hauled several hundred cubic yards of sand for the Clear Lake beach, weeded the townsite and cottage subdivisions, fenced the golf-course and resurfaced the tennis-courts, cleaned fish ponds, cut and put up hay for the buffalo paddock, and improved the Moon Lake campground. They also toiled on existing park highways—whether it be brushing rights-of-way, rebuilding shoulders, or replacing culverts—and cleared and gravelled a new seven-mile access road to the Whirlpool warden station. Sometimes this work had its unexpected perils. One day, John Eidse was working alone at the edge of the Dauphin road when a carload of women, returning from the nearby air

The conscientious objector crews applied their muscle to a wide variety of tasks, including brushing along park highways. *Courtesy H. Sawatzky*

training school, stopped to verbally harass him; he was rescued when the foreman came along and chased the hecklers away.[28]

Despite initial plans, none of these projects had anything to do with forestry conservation; the only work remotely related to forestry management during this period was the refurbishing of an old forestry experimental station and the collecting of insects for the dominion entomologist.[29] Ironically, this had also been the case with the short-lived 1939 National Forestry Programme. Although the trainees were supposed to learn conservation practices, the Parks Bureau missed the days of the relief worker and tended to look upon the young men as a cheap labour force during the brief life of the programme. The conscientious objectors were now employed in much the same capacity and had been placed at the discretion of the park superintendents to do whatever was considered most beneficial; in most cases this involved picking up where the work gangs of the 1930s had left off.

The Department of National War Services did not seem disturbed by the fact that the conscientious objectors were being used as national park handymen. Its chief concern was that the men were working; what they were doing was secondary. What surprised officials, however, was the volume of work they accomplished, especially considering that they were there under compulsion. George Tunstell, a department forester who doubled as alternative service camp inspector, marvelled at the determination of the internees as they went about their tasks. "There is no shirking or holding back," he reported in early August after a week at the different park camps. "They only require direction and driving seems to be unnecessary."[30] The Winnipeg divisional registrar, who had been responsible for sending the men to Riding Mountain, was equally impressed following an inspection tour of camp operations later that same month. Although he readily admitted "a prejudice against conscientious objectors" and that he "would like to see these young men in uniform," he told General LaFleche that the improvements being made at the park vindicated the programme and should silence any criticism.[31]

Besides being hard workers, the men were also commended for their exceptionally good behaviour; inspection reports were full of praise for the men and how they had settled into camp routine without incident. Part of the explanation for their conduct was that many of the Mennonites were away from their tightly knit communities for the first time and were somewhat uneasy—if not frightened—about their situation.[32] They had also been counselled by church leaders and family members that if they did their terms of service and stayed out of trouble they would soon be home; otherwise the government might be forced to cancel the programme and make them—and everyone who followed—take military training.[33] These fears made the men willing workers, all the more so since they were deliberately played upon by supervisory personnel. Ed Brooks, the foreman at Camp One, portrayed himself as a heartless bastard who never spoke a kind word when a job was well done and always used rough language or threats. He also gave disparaging nicknames to anyone who crossed him, such as referring to the bearded Holdeman Mennonites as Santa Clauses.[34] Privately, many of the men knew that Brooks appreciated their efforts, but they never challenged him. "In my day there," recounted John Klassen, "it never got beyond his bark, and we danced to his tune."[35] One day, for example, one of the men shovelling sand at Clear Lake beach reported to Brooks that he had strained his shoulder and wanted to know what happened to those men who were unable to work. The foreman's response was simple: "We shoot them."[36] On another occasion, Brooks ordered all the men to take a bath—and they did, including one shy young man who finally relented and went into the water wearing his bib overalls.[37]

Camp officials also tried to keep the men in line by attending to their recreational needs. Remembering how important it had been to keep the relief gangs occupied after working hours, especially during the long days of summer, the superintendent supplied the camps with bats, balls, boxing gloves, and horseshoes. Playing baseball in the bush, however, presented problems, and most of the men restricted their athletic endeavours to pitching horseshoes. They also exercised their lungs singing hymns, often to the accompaniment of musical instruments they had brought themselves. Many others spent their spare time walking, visiting, and writing home. Henry Sawatzky, for example, penned no less than sixty-nine letters during his four-month stay at the park.[38] Jake Unrau, meanwhile, welcomed the chance to spend some time with other men his own age; the eldest of twelve children,

Pitching horseshoes at Camp One, Prince Albert, 1941. *Courtesy J.M. Penner*

he had known only the company of girls on the small family farm.[39]

The National War Services Department also made arrangements to allow ministers from the different Mennonite churches to take turns staying with the men. These spiritual leaders often led short evening readings and prayers, in addition to regular Sunday services. Their presence in the camps, however, was soon regarded by some officials as harmful. Colonel J.G. Rattray, a National War Services inspector, complained in mid-July 1941 that the Mennonites at Riding Mountain were being intimidated by their ministers into maintaining the pacifist values of their community. As evidence, he reported that the men held spirited boxing matches as soon as the minister left the camp in the evening, and that many secretly expressed a desire to do something to help win the war and would have enlisted if they had been allowed to follow their conscience. He also argued that the men preferred their new life and predicted that their transition from alternative service work to a regular military camp would be easy—if only they could be encouraged to take up arms.[40] What Rattray did not seem to appreciate, though, was that friendly sparring between spirited camp mates was not the same as going to war and possibly killing others. If anything, the Riding Mountain experience was a test of the young men's faith and served to confirm and strengthen their beliefs. Besides, most were too homesick to consider breaking away from traditional teachings and practices. What kept them going, according to Henry Sawatzky, what made separation from their families bearable, was the knowledge that "We could go home in four months . . . and we just put up with it."[41] The enemy aliens and transients who were held in the parks before them never enjoyed this prospect.

• • •

The tension between putting conscientious objectors to work and persuading them to join the active army was nowhere more pronounced than at Prince Albert National Park. The call-ups—once again, mostly Mennonites—began arriving at the park in mid-June and were dispatched to one of four fifty-man canvas camps in the southern half of the park. It would have been much easier from an administrative and operational point of view if former relief camps along the main highway had been utilized and the men transported from there to their jobsites. But the new superintendent, Herbert Knight, a hard-headed Great War veteran, was more concerned about keeping the camps as isolated as possible from the townsite and visitors, as well as from each other. Camps Three (Rabbit) and Four (Boundary), for example, were sixty and ninety miles away from Waskesiu by road. Knight also did not want to make the men too comfortable—in the belief that they might be induced to take military training—and refused to provide wooden floors for their tents. One might even have

Walking home for dinner, Prince Albert, summer 1941. The four Prince Albert camps were kept as isolated as possible from the park townsite and visitors. *Courtesy P.K. Fehr*

suspected that the electrified wire fence around the cooking and dining tents at Camp One was not so much for the bears as for the internees.

The Prince Albert camps were in operation for only a few weeks when a minor furore erupted over the use of the German language during religious exercises. Superintendent Knight and the Saskatchewan divisional registrar had made a brief inspection tour of the operations in early July 1941 and were appalled to find the internees worshipping in their native tongue. The two men immediately put an end to the practice, sending a copy of their decision to General LaFleche, who in turn sought the advice of the Royal Canadian Mounted Police, the agency responsible for handling any trouble in the camps.[42] Commissioner S.T. Wood replied by secret letter that the internees did not need to speak German; "undoubtedly if they are liable to military service," he reasoned, using some perverse logic, "then they are fully conversant with the English language."[43] He also warned that the use of the enemy language during religious services might provoke a public backlash not only against the park camps but their administrators as well. Taking the assessment seriously, the Parks Bureau on 31 July 1941 issued a directive officially banning the German language in the park camps—except during visits from family members. It made for some interesting sermons. At Riding Mountain, Jake Unrau recalled a visiting minister telling the men in his best broken English that God would wipe away the "trains" from their eyes.[44]

Superintendent Knight also resented the idea of a Mennonite minister serving in the camps and tried to limit his movement and activities, maintaining that any church official sent to the park should live in the townsite, several miles from the camps. He also insisted that the clergyman refrain from interfering with any young man who changed his mind and decided to take military training.[45] This latter point was particularly important to Knight since he believed that it was part of his unwritten duty as senior camp official to see that the internees were given every encouragement to volunteer for active service. And he did this job well. Prince Albert had the distinction of having fourteen internees volunteer to join the army during the first weeks of the camps' existence, a remarkable figure given that only one other man—at Banff—came forward during the summer. What is not mentioned in the annual Parks report, however, is that in early July a recruitment officer personally spoke to the men on at least two occasions about army life, and left enlistment forms with the camp foremen.[46] Although this constituted a violation of camp policy, Knight saw nothing wrong with it, and the men were afraid to complain.[47] His only regret was that leaders of the Mennonite church had prevented the enlistment figure from being higher. "If the elders are permitted to visit the camps throughout the week and stay overnight to hold religious services," he advised the district recruiting officer in total disregard for the reason behind the establishment of the camps, "there is very little hope of the young men

One of the Prince Albert camps after a summer hailstorm. *Courtesy P.K. Fehr*

responding to our way of thinking, namely, to bear arms for the country."[48]

Once Knight overcame his initial suspicions, however, he quickly discovered that the internees were a gentle group of young men quietly committed to completing their terms of service. Like their counterparts at Riding Mountain, most of the Prince Albert call-ups were from small farms in the vicinity of the parks, in this case between the two branches of the Saskatchewan River north of Saskatoon, and had not travelled much—if at all—outside their home communities. They no doubt left for the park with mixed feelings, although it was not that they did not want to fulfil their obligations. All of them had appeared that spring before the War Services Board in the Saskatoon courthouse and endured the pointed questioning of Judge J.F.L. Embury. Art Dueck of Rosthern, for example, recalls standing his ground when the judge "wondered why I would do alternative service work for fifty cents a day when there were better options."[49] What made the men apprehensive, however, was that the park seemed so far away, and many felt they were going into forced exile. Leaving home that June was therefore one of the hardest things these men had done in their young lives. It certainly was for John Driedger of Osler, since "I had just married and my wife was pregnant."[50]

Once settled into camp, the men faithfully observed the rules and gave no cause for complaint, let alone a reprimand. Far from happy to be there, however, the simple truth of the matter was that the men were far too homesick to cause any trouble. Peter Fehr of Hague, who served as a straw boss at Camp Three, remembers that the first few weeks of camp proved extremely rough on men who had never been away from home before.[51] Their four months would probably have seemed like a life sentence if they had not been able to go home for weekend visits. Unlike the men at Riding Mountain, who were too far away to visit their families, the Prince Albert call-ups went home at least once or twice during their term of service—or in the case of Jacob Penner of Hague, every second weekend.[52] For fifty cents—one day's pay—a hired truck from the men's home communities would pick up anyone with a pass when work ended on Friday and bring them back Sunday night. This privilege was never abused, and those on leave always returned—on time.[53]

The men's recreational demands, meanwhile, were modest. Some of those stationed in the Sandy Lake area (Camp Two) learned to swim, while others spent their free time pitching horseshoes or playing baseball. The men at Camp

The Prince Albert workers were too homesick to cause any trouble. *Courtesy P.K. Fehr*

Three organized three ball teams and used a nearby meadow for the diamond.[54] In general, though, they seemed content to pass their idle evening hours visiting with one another. Art Dueck, for example, reported that he was able to cope with the separation from his family in part because of the sixty new friends he made in camp.[55] Walking was also a popular pastime. For many of the men raised on the prairies, the boreal forest was a new and strange place; they never wandered too far from camp, though, and on instructions from the superintendent, never visited the park townsite.[56]

The men also proved to be hardened labourers. In the interests of improving fire and game protection in the southern portion of the park, a large part of the work programme during the summer of 1941 was devoted to clearing, upgrading, or widening some sixty miles of trail. Camps One and Four worked their way east and west respectively along 57 Trail, while Camps Two and Three did the same along Elk Trail. More could have been accomplished if the men had had access to machinery. Only Camp One had this luxury; the others had to make do with hand tools, mainly grub-hoes. Instead of clearing the trail with axes or saws, the men had to root out trees with a hoe, limb and cut the trunk into cordwood lengths, and then carefully stack it beside the trail, where it was picked up by truck and taken to the public campgrounds as firewood.[57] Although the men hated this grubbing process, nobody ever refused to work because they were afraid of the consequences—military training. Most of the supervisory personnel, moreover, were Great War veterans, and the workers, already upset about being away from their families, were easily intimidated by their gruff language and manner—and occasional threat of a longer term of service. Peter Fehr recalls one man who was so frightened of the foreman that he kept working with his hoe even while trying to light a cigarette.[58]

This trail improvement work was more in keeping with the kind of activity that had been originally visualized for conscientious objectors. But as in the case of Riding Mountain, Superintendent Knight could not resist the temptation to use the men for routine maintenance, especially when physically fit men were prohibited from working in the government service as of June 1941. As the summer progressed, then, the internees were called on to provide help in a number of areas. They brushed along the main highway, cut firewood, removed rocks from the Narrows road, erected new patrol cabins, and rebuilt or relocated several miles of telephone line. They also helped salvage the metal from a number of dinky engines abandoned since the logging days in the park area.[59] Knight even allowed the men to work in the townsite, where they serviced the main campground, levelled and rolled the tennis-courts, and groomed the golf-course. Their value to the park was perhaps best demonstrated, however, when a group was flown to the northern boundary to fight a fire that threatened Lavallee Lake, the site of the second largest white pelican colony in Canada.[60]

• • •

The other two western national parks to serve as temporary homes for conscientious objectors were Banff and Jasper. Since both had run extensive relief camp operations in the past decade and had a number of outstanding projects to be completed or inaugurated, they welcomed the opportunity to secure their share of alternative service work. The Banff camps were occupied by mid-July and eventually numbered around 125 internees by the time all the call-ups arrived; approximately one-half were Saskatchewan Mennonites. The men were divided among three tent camps—at Healy Creek, Lake Louise (on Pipestone Creek), and Stoney Creek (in the Cascade River valley)—and were to spend most of the summer making improvements or additions to existing trails to provide easier access for fire-fighting equipment. They were frequently taken from this work, however, to do special jobs around the park or in the townsite. The men built a new two-storey chimney for the central equipment building, demolished old relief structures, enlarged the Lake Louise campground, erected a radio transmission tower outside the administration building, cut and peeled more than a hundred logs for a new teahouse addition atop Sulphur Mountain, landscaped several warden stations, dug a large garbage pit at the Johnson Canyon campground, and brushed several miles of saddle trail. They also assisted with wildlife management—their most noteworthy tasks being the digging of a four-thousand-foot canal-like ditch and the construction of a thousand-foot wooden flume to carry water from Fortymile Creek to sheep in an enclosure. Sadly, the completion of these projects did not endear the

Unloading hay for the Banff buffalo paddock. *Courtesy A. Dick*

internees to the local population. Although the men provided invaluable service to the park and townsite, their refusal to take military training seemed a blot on their character. When a group was taken by truck to the Cave and Basin pool for a Sunday afternoon swim, for example, an editorial in the *Crag and Canyon* titled "Is This Justice?" questioned not only why the men did not walk the ten-mile distance, but also why they were even granted the privilege. "There should be a different way of handling these people," the writer observed, "a far different way."[61]

Some of the Jasper internees experienced the same prejudice even before they were sent to the park. Paul Poetker had been teaching in the Grande Prairie district for two years when he received his call-up. At his Lethbridge hearing, the board members not only tried to confuse him by speaking at the same time, but one of them threatened to revoke his teaching certificate as he left the room.[62] Peter Unger, from Coaldale, fared little better. Not only was he called a coward at his hearing, but when boarding the bus to go to Jasper, several of his former school chums taunted him about his manhood.[63] This kind of treatment represented the prevailing attitude of the Canadian public towards conscientious objection. As the war approached its second anniversary, loyalty, sacrifice, and commitment were expected—even demanded—and there was little room in the national consciousness for those who refused to do their duty for the country. This attitude dominated the mobilization boards, and several members, such as Horace Harvey of Alberta, steadfastly believed that young Mennonite men would have chosen active service if not for the influence of their parents and church leaders.[64] There was some truth to this position. Many of the men interviewed about their experience, such as Nick Thiessen of Edmonton, would gladly have gone into the noncombatant service as a stretcher bearer or ambulance driver *if* they had been completely exempted from any form of military training, such as rifle drill.[65] Unfortunately, this option did not exist at the time, and many men who would otherwise have served their country were sent to the national parks.

At Jasper, Poetker, Unger, and Thiessen were among 160 men who were put to work on three road projects—upgrading the ten-mile Maligne road (between Medicine and Maligne Lakes) for automobile traffic; widening the Medicine Lake road (between the Maligne Canyon teahouse and Medicine Lake); and pushing a new road west from Geikie across the Miette River to the interprovincial border with British Columbia. This road work represented quite a change from work done in the other parks, where internees served more or less as caretaker crews moving from job to job. But despite initial plans, the projects turned out to be too ambitious because of the lack of machinery. The tools they had were fine for forestry duties, but totally inadequate for the kind of clearing and levelling they were being asked to do; the internees' best friend, in fact, was dynamite. In a scene reminiscent of Depression days, then, the men toiled

The Union Jack flutters over the camp at Geikie, Jasper National Park, September 1941. *National Archives of Canada, C141834*

away as best they could with picks, shovels, crowbars, grub-hoes, and jack hammers, while the superintendent tried to scrounge whatever machinery he could for the projects. After only a few weeks, however, a number of temporary camps were established where smaller gangs of men relieved from the heavy road projects did trail work or upgraded campgrounds, especially along the Jasper section of the recently completed Banff-Jasper highway.[66] According to Nick Thiessen, the men worked at a consistently "steady pace" and were "never pushed" by their foremen.[67]

The camp arrangements at Jasper were similar to those at the other parks. The men were housed in tents on wooden platforms and were kept comfortable at night by wood-burning stoves; laundry left hanging in the tents to dry during the day, though, sometimes froze in the cold mountain air.[68] The food was reportedly good and plentiful—although the men stationed at Geikie took it upon themselves one night to get rid of an unsanitary cook with a perennially dripping nose by pretending to be a bear outside his tent.[69] Unlike Riding Mountain and Prince Albert, there was no recreation equipment at the Jasper camps, and the men put in time after work playing music, reading, or simply resting in their beds after a hard day on the grade. Because of the distance from their home communities and the relative isolation of the camps, the men never went home during their four months of service; nor were they ever visited by their families—it was simply too far to travel. On at least one occasion, however, three men, dressed in suits, visited another nearby camp on bicycles one Sunday afternoon.[70] Traditional habits persisted, even in the bush. Hiking was also popular, and the men were regularly given permission to tackle the surrounding mountains on weekends. One of these outings nearly ended in disaster. Five men, including the visiting minister, left Geikie after Sunday service and set off for a distant peak. By the time they had clambered to the top, the sun was setting, and the men tried to find their way back through the darkness along a different trail. The foreman, meanwhile, was in a panic, and kept bellowing over the telephone to park headquarters, "FIVE MEN MISSING!" The group eventually made its way down to the rail line, well east of the townsite, and straggled into camp early Monday morning. The four men went to work that day, while the minister was summoned to Jasper to explain the incident.[71]

Hiking near Banff townsite. *Courtesy A. Dick*

• • •

By early October 1941, small groups of men began to be released from the park camps as they completed their four-month term of service. This process quickly gained momentum, and within six weeks the alternative service workforce had dropped by almost two-thirds.[72] Everything did not go smoothly, though, such as when John Eidse's father showed up a day early to take five men home from Riding Mountain. The camp had already been paid for the next working day, and only after Eidse and his friends had each handed over fifty cents were they allowed to leave.[73] Overall, the Parks Bureau was extremely pleased with the experience—and for good reason. The men were a bargain. According to the park superintendents, the workers provided the same amount of work normally performed by regular workers, but at a considerably lower cost. This favourable assessment was confirmed by George Tunstell, the department officer in charge of camp inspections, in his report on summer camp operations. For the period ending 15 November 1941, the conscientious objectors provided 80,029 man-days of park work at an average cost (including *all* expenses) of $1.30 per day.[74] Riding Mountain and Prince Albert were the greatest beneficiaries of the programme, each averaging around 25,000 man-days of work. But all parks received a good return from the men, especially since they willingly went about their tasks and there were no major injuries or bouts of sickness. Tunstell recommended that further economies could be realized if more alternative service workers were used as camp clerks, truck drivers, or cookies; some already served in this capacity. He also argued that no matter how hard they laboured, the men could not compete against heavy machinery, and strongly urged that suitable equipment be obtained for the various road projects.[75]

The bigger question for the Parks Bureau that fall, however, was whether it was worthwhile to operate camps over the winter. With many of the men completing their terms of service, senior officials began to wonder whether it would be best simply to shut the camps down unless there were enough future call-ups to replace the departing men. Canvassing the superintendents in late September 1941, the Parks Bureau found that all the parks except Prince Albert favoured winter camps. Arguing that winter operations would be difficult, if not expensive, and that it would be more practical to resume work in the early spring, Superinten-

The men had to clear the Prince Albert fire trails by hand. *National Archives of Canada, C131651*

A winter's cutting activity, Riding Mountain, March 1942. *National Archives of Canada,*
C141823

dent Knight sought permission to close the tent camps on 15 November, before
the arrival of cold weather made it necessary to relocate the internees to more
permanent housing along the main park highway.[76] The other superintendents
did not share Knight's concerns. They were not only anxious to make use of
the men—as long as they had a claim to their labour—but proposed a number of
projects that could best be done by small crews during the winter months. They
also recalled how the relief camps had been principally winter operations, and
that many of the men had lived temporarily under canvas until wooden
bunkhouses had been erected. Why should conscientious objectors deserve
better? If anything, many Parks officials believed, the men should be happy to
do whatever was asked of them, especially if they were not prepared to serve
in the armed forces.

The decision to operate park camps through the winter was made at a
meeting between National Parks Bureau officials and their National War Services counterparts at General LaFleche's Ottawa office on 1 November 1941.

Reviewing the summer programme, the two parties agreed that every conscientious objector should be required to work for a four-month period and that
he had to go wherever he was assigned—even if it meant working in another
province. As General LaFleche bluntly told the gathering, "It is hardly for those
concerned to pick and choose where they will work."[77] The officials also
decided that any man who subsequently chose to enlist voluntarily but was
found to be medically unfit would still be required to complete his term of
service in an alternative service camp; the same ruling applied to any man who
was convicted and imprisoned for being a defaulter. Finally, they considered
the possibility of keeping conscientious objectors at work for the duration of
the war, and tentatively approved the idea of creating a mobile, civilian work
corps—if and when the men were called up for a longer period of time. Policy
matters having been discussed, Parks Director Gibson tabled a request for 450
men for a winter works programme in four national parks (Riding Mountain,
Banff, Jasper, and Kootenay) and at the forestry experimental station at
Kananaskis, Alberta. This exercise seemed a mere formality, for unanimous
approval of the scheme was forthcoming after only a few minutes—once it was
ascertained that the men would continue to be responsible for clothing
themselves and be paid at the same fifty-cent daily rate, even if they were now
married and had dependants.[78] It did not seem to cross the bureaucrats' minds
that such conditions might create incredible hardships.

· · ·

Riding Mountain National Park was initially assigned 100 men for cutting and
sawing lumber and fuelwood. Because of the large number of conscientious
objectors still awaiting their call-up in Manitoba, however, the park quota was
increased in early November by another 50 at the expense of the Kananaskis
operations. Superintendent Heaslip decided to use the extra men to establish a
second park camp, in addition to the one originally slated for the old relief
facilities in the townsite. And one of the first jobs of the new batch of recruits
at Wasagaming—once they had refurbished their own quarters and made them
liveable again—was to erect a set of wooden buildings at the site of the summer
tent camp on the Norgate road.[79] The remainder of the winter conscripts were
then issued call-up notices and by early January 1942, the two camps were up to
strength. At Wasagaming, about 75 men spent much of their time clear-cutting
an area northwest of Clear Lake for fuelwood and posts; they also helped man
a private mill just south of the main park gate, which was used to cut logs hauled
from the two worksites. The men at the new Norgate camp, on the other hand,
cleared the right-of-way for a new road north to Whirlpool Lake, salvaging
poles, posts, and fuelwood as they worked. The superintendent justified the
building of this road on the grounds that it was essential for fire- and game-pa-
trol purposes in the area, repeatedly ignoring requests from forestry officials to
put some of the men to work on an experimental forestry station in the park

Trench dug by hand for fish hatchery, Jasper. *National Archives of Canada, C141825*

north of Clear Lake. Somewhat curiously, though, once the men punched the road through to Whirlpool Lake, they spent several weeks removing dead or windblown timber from around the lakeshore and then laying out the site for a future campground.[80]

There was no subterfuge regarding the use of conscientious objectors at Jasper. During the improvement work on the Medicine Lake road, a heavy rock cut had absorbed most of the internees' time and effort. Since this work was still incomplete when many of the men finished their term of service, a small winter camp was set up to remove rock from a particularly nasty, nine-hundred-foot section of the road. Just over sixty of the new recruits tackled this project in late November, armed with only one tractor, one compressor, one grader, two teams of horses, and an assortment of hand implements. Some three months later, however, they had managed to remove almost all the debris. This herculean effort was rewarded with a new assignment—digging a three-foot-deep ditch from the Maligne River to the site of a new fish hatchery some seventeen hundred feet distant. It was probably no coincidence that the superintendent at Jasper, James Wood, had served at Prince Albert during the Depression and knew from experience what could be done with a captive labour force. Camp inspector George Tunstell, meanwhile, was not so much impressed with the progress of the work as he was worried that the men were not putting in an eight-hour day.[81] He seemed to think the men were little better than common criminals for their beliefs.

The winter alternative service work at Banff was also a continuation of a project that had been started earlier in the fall by the summer crews. In late August 1941, an infestation of bark beetle in the lodgepole pine stands resulted in most of the men being pulled off other projects and put to work removing and burning infected trees. Little headway was made, however, before the internees had to be released. The culling was resumed by a hundred new men divided between two tent camps: an existing one at Healy Creek and a new one at Hillsdale, about fifteen miles west of Banff along the main highway to Calgary. The internees were organized into five-man cruising squads, with one man carrying a map and compass, another serving as spotter, and the remaining three felling and burning the beetle-damaged trees. Although it was a change from previous duties, the work was no less difficult, especially since they spent most of their days tramping through snow of varying depth and climbing hills. Their return to camp at night, moreover, provided little relief; they had to cut and haul fuelwood from great distances and were constantly winterizing their sleeping tents against the cold and wind. Tunstell was dismayed by the amount of energy the men spent on camp maintenance, and wondered whether lumber bunkhouses should have been erected at the beginning.[82] These living and working conditions certainly did not encourage future recruits. In mid-February 1942, two Calgary-area conscientious objectors refused to report to Banff and were sentenced to eight months imprisonment and fined fifty dollars. As one of the men told his hearing, "I cannot and will not voluntarily agree to be isolated in a work camp."[83]

This problem also arose at Prince Albert. Although the park camps had been closed in November 1941 in accordance with Superintendent Knight's wishes, he evidently began to worry that he might lose any future claim to "conchie"

Clearing and burning infested lodgepole pine, Banff. *Courtesy A. Dick*

labour, and suggested to Ottawa in December that a new townsite breakwater be undertaken as an alternative service project. Approval was quickly secured and by early February 1942, two twenty-five-man camps were busy hauling stone, cutting timber, and installing cribbing. The men who initially worked on the 461-foot breakwater were conscientious objectors who had not yet completed their four-month term of service when the camps had closed the previous fall. The project ran into difficulty in March, however, when several of the workers' replacements, perhaps advised by earlier recruits about working and living conditions, were late reporting. Fortunately, the weather remained cold so that by the time the camps were brought up to strength again, the men were still able to complete the cribbing work before spring break-up.[84]

Logging in Kootenay National Park, March 1942. *National Archives of Canada, C141828*

Kootenay was the only other national park to operate work camps that winter. Here, about a hundred men, mostly Saskatchewan Mennonites, were enlisted to clean up a dense stand of insect-killed lodgepole pine along both sides of the Banff-Windermere highway near McLeod Meadows. This culling had been needed for some time. Remembering how the winter weather had played havoc with previous relief camps, however, a small crew erected two sets of wooden camp buildings before the bulk of the men reported in mid-November; there was even provision for a recreation hut at one of the camps. The internees were roughly divided between logging and sawmill operations. One camp cut and burned damaged trees, salvaging any sound timber; the other camp retrieved and cut the logs into lumber and then hauled the finished product to a woodyard at Kootenay Crossing. By late February 1942, the mill had produced more than two hundred and twenty-five thousand board feet of commercial lumber, and it was estimated that there was enough damaged timber in the Kootenay valley to keep the internees occupied for the duration of the war—if not longer.[85]

· · ·

While the conscientious objectors worked diligently throughout the winter of 1941-42, Parks Director Gibson began to make plans for securing access to the men for the duration of the war. The matter had first been raised by General LaFleche at the November meeting between Parks Bureau and National War Services officials, but no decision had been made. Gibson emerged from the meeting, however, tantalized by the possibility of having a steady labour force at the disposal of the parks, especially during this period of reduced budgets. And in keeping with the strategy of his predecessor, J.B. Harkin, during the first year of the Depression, he decided to put together a detailed work programme in the likely event that conscientious objectors were called up for continuous service. He also wrote General LaFleche in early December—by coincidence, the day before the Japanese bombing of Pearl Harbor—to let him know that the parks were the best place for these men and that several hundred could be employed there on a continuous basis. "The nature of the work, the surroundings, and the environment," Gibson argued, had given the men "a greater appreciation of what Canadian citizenship means." He also reminded LaFleche that "these men must be used for some good purpose," especially since military authorities were not interested in supervising them, and that a season's training in the park camps would "probably change their whole outlook, thereby making them available for combatant service." Above all, Gibson contended that the recreational value of national parks had been overlooked and that the facilities provided through alternative service labour would help relieve the stresses and strains of the war. "The first line of defence lies in the soul of a people," he observed, "and is anchored deeply in the land."[86]

Not surprisingly, Gibson never bothered to consult the men who had recently completed their term of service about how they looked upon their work in the parks. If he had, he probably would have been surprised to find that although the men deeply appreciated the alternative service option, most would have preferred more worthwhile or meaningful tasks. Anton Dyck best captured this feeling when he bluntly observed, "As a farm boy at twenty-one years of age you expect to do something more important than to pull weeds along the road."[87] Nor did the time spent in the parks change the men's attitude towards war. The forced separation from their families, menial labour, and paltry wages never shook the men of their beliefs. Dyck reported that he still felt the same way about war and its destruction after he came home from Riding Mountain.[88] So too did Art Dueck of Rosthern, who suggested that "the men at

Riding Mountain camp reunion in honour of foreman Ed Brooks's (front centre) eightieth birthday. *Courtesy H. Sawatzky*

Prince Albert were heroes of faith."[89] And Peter Unger confided that he would not have gone into the ministry if not for the experience.[90] Even crusty Ed Brooks, the foreman of Camp One at Riding Mountain, mellowed over time. At the thirtieth anniversary camp reunion in September 1971, at which he was the guest of honour, Brooks claimed that he emerged a better person because of his association with the men.[91]

Gibson's proposal to use conscientious objector labour in the parks for the duration of the war was discussed at yet another joint interdepartmental meeting on 14 January 1942. General LaFleche confessed that the constant calling up of men for four months of service was proving to be a headache, and that it would probably be easier to assign the Parks Bureau a fixed quota. At the same time, he hinted that conscientious objectors might be required for other work—now that Japan and the United States had entered the war—and all he was prepared to do for the time being was allow the Parks Bureau to requisition replacements as they were needed.[92] Although LaFleche's decision did not satisfy senior Parks officials, at least they were guaranteed a steady, if not permanent, supply of workers. This seemed to be the case, for exactly two months later, LaFleche informed the divisional registrars that Mines and Resources would need another 650 men for its summer operations.[93]

Many of these men were never sent to the parks, and the Parks Bureau was fortunate in continuing to have access to alternative service labour at all over the following months. On 30 March 1942, the King government finally issued a proclamation requiring conscientious objectors to serve for the duration of the war, an order that had been anxiously awaited by the Parks Bureau—but Ottawa had other plans for the men. The federal government had been regularly criticized for using alternative service labour in national parks, even in areas that stood to benefit from the work. A January 1942 editorial in the Minnedosa *Tribune,* for example, questioned why "so-called conscientious objectors [at Riding Mountain] . . . are not put to some useful employment—something that will . . . maintain freedom in a country that has provided it for all."[94] This same concern was raised in the House of Commons. Although W.G. Weir of Manitoba noted that the men probably did good work in the parks, he advised the members, "That kind of work . . . can wait."[95] These complaints coincided with an urgent appeal from British Columbia for additional fire-fighting personnel; provincial officials feared that the Japanese might try to set forest fires through sabotage or airborne incendiary devices. The Department of National War Services therefore decided in April 1942 to send as many as a thousand conscientious objectors to the west coast for fire protection and conservation work, and in the process, answer critics who charged that the men should be doing something essential to the national war effort. The men eventually planted over 20 million trees.

This arrangement was a severe blow to the National Parks Bureau. The British Columbia forestry project was not only given first call on the allocation of alternative service workers, but was allowed to draw 120 of its recruits from existing national park camps—70 from Riding Mountain and 25 each from Banff and Kootenay. These initial transfers were bad enough, especially when there were little more than 400 men in the park camps as of 1 April 1942. Worse still, the camps were repeatedly raided over the next two months in order to meet the manpower needs of the British Columbia programme. By early July, then, there were only 131 men left in the park camps, including a mere 4 at Kootenay and just 8 at Riding Mountain.[96] The picture was not completely bleak, though, for a new, albeit small, temporary camp was established in Glacier National Park for the summer. Waterton Lakes, on the other hand, was not so fortunate. The Parks Bureau had wanted to open a 50-man camp at Waterton as part of its January 1942 proposal, and had a number of ambitious road projects ready to be tackled. The British Columbia agreement, however, meant that this work was now placed on hold until an adequate supply of men could be secured.

The reduced numbers of men translated into a modest work programme at several of the parks that summer. Whereas the Parks Bureau would have preferred to see such projects as the Maligne Canyon–Medicine Lake road in Jasper completed, they had to settle for mostly fire trails or routine maintenance

At work on the new breakwater at Waskesiu, Prince Albert, spring 1942. *Prince Albert National Park, 049–15*

work. At the new camp at Glacier, for example, the internees performed minor improvement duties, in particular the dismantling of old snow sheds along the abandoned rail line through Rogers Pass. The men at Riding Mountain, meanwhile, restrung several miles of telephone line, as well as developing picnic facilities at the new Whirlpool Lake campground. Although a far cry from what the workers had been called upon to do the previous summer, the work was more in keeping with the expectations of the park camps. Now that the Parks Bureau did not have exclusive claim to alternative service labour, it had to walk a fine line in matters of how the men were employed. On the one hand, Parks Director Gibson was afraid that he would lose the few remaining conscientious objectors in the camps if they were seen to be doing work that had nothing to do with forest conservation. He therefore ordered all Parks officials in late June 1942 "to make it clear"—whether it was true or not—"that we are doing fire trail work rather than . . . building roads."[97] On the other hand, he was equally concerned that the various park projects be considered of national importance. When a member of Parliament suggested that conscientious objectors were doing essentially useless work in the parks, the Parks Bureau responded with an itemized list detailing the number of miles of improved fire trails and volume of salvaged timber. Not a word was said, however, about recreation improvements, such as the new breakwater at Prince Albert.[98] It seems to have miraculously risen from Lake Waskesiu.

·   ·   ·

The park camps also began to be plagued by a growing number of desertions and other violations—largely in response to the new order that required all future call-ups to serve for the duration of the war. The first hint of trouble occurred in late May 1942, when the fifty alternative service workers who were to be transferred from Banff and Kootenay to British Columbia were granted a seven-day leave of absence to return home before taking up their new posting. By 1 June, however, almost half the men had failed to report, and the British Columbia officials were livid. "This is a serious business and not a farce," a district forestry officer warned Ottawa. "If these absentees and malingerers get away with it, there will be no holding the others nor any useful work accomplished by them—they would be better weeding beets."[99]

Parks officials did not seem overly concerned with these defaulters. They resented the loss of the men to the B.C. programme anyway, and also seemed to believe that the missing workers were no longer their responsibility. They reacted much differently, however, when they began experiencing problems of their own during the spring and summer of 1942. Some of the men would obtain leave for compassionate or medical reasons and never report back. Lawrence Willems of Borden, Saskatchewan, for example, was granted leave from one of the Prince Albert camps in October 1942 to attend his father's funeral and then refused to return—this was the second time in four months that he had been absent without leave. He had not only been three weeks late reporting, but had also been retrieved by his wife from a Prince Albert hospital in late June when he was unable to obtain sick leave. At his trial in August, Willems was found guilty of leaving the park without permission—his illness was dismissed as a ruse—and fined fifty dollars and court costs; in default of

Off to town (Jasper) on a Sunday afternoon. *Courtesy A. Dick*

payment, he faced two months in gaol at hard labour.[100] A few slipped away while being transferred to another camp. John Fast of Dalmeny, Saskatchewan, disappeared from the Saskatoon railway station en route to another camp in late June 1942 and was found a few days later hiding at home; he too was fined fifty dollars and costs.[101] Still others, such as David Sawatzky of Vonda, Saskatchewan, simply left without permission after their leave applications were repeatedly turned down by the Banff superintendent.[102] And who could blame them? It did not seem fair that they had to serve for the duration of the conflict, while like-minded individuals who had completed their four-month service before 1 April 1942 were able to stay at home. One in four of the new internees, moreover, was married, and family ties tugged hard on their hearts. It might also have been a different story if they were doing something other than spending the war on park maintenance. Many questioned the value of the work and wondered whether they were simply being punished for their beliefs—a view shared by Tommy Douglas, the Co-operative Commonwealth Federation member for Weyburn, Saskatchewan. "Simply to take a young man out of university," he spoke in defence of a University of Saskatchewan chemistry student who had claimed conscientious objector status, "and send him to a labour camp where he is not needed, because he antagonizes those who do not agree with his point of view, is not fair."[103]

The park superintendents, in contrast, did not find anything trivial about their alternative service work programme or the growing number of absent-without-leave cases. They greatly valued the men and more importantly, their labour, and were worried that camp discipline would be impossible to enforce if delinquents went unpunished.[104] They also had access to fewer workers than the previous summer and could not afford to lose a single labourer. As a result, whenever one of the men failed to return on time or went missing, local RCMP were notified to issue a warrant for the man's arrest, and either escort him to camp or prosecute him for violating National War Services Regulations.[105]

The parks also took whatever men were available. In August 1942, for example, the divisional registrar asked the Prince Albert superintendent if he was interested in a man who had previously failed to report to Banff and had just completed a six-month gaol sentence. The man in question was later ordered to report to Prince Albert twice, but had still not appeared by the following spring.[106] He was not alone. As of 30 March 1943, twenty-five men were absent without leave—more than 5 percent of the total national park camp population at that time.[107]

· · ·

In an effort to secure more workers and thereby bring the camps up to more economical, fifty-man units, the Parks Bureau tried to convince the National War Services Department to recall those conscientious objectors who had completed their four-month term of service under the original regulations; after all, most of these men had worked in the park camps and had proven their worth—and then some. The King government, however, placed greater priority on agricultural production and had no desire to reduce the prairie labour force if it could be avoided. Large numbers of conscientious objectors, including those who had once served at the parks, were therefore granted farm leave; many others were not called up until late that fall. And to its discomfort, the Parks Bureau was inundated with letters in August 1942, including an appeal from the government of Alberta, to release men from its camps to help with the harvest. Although it was willing to accede to this request—albeit grudgingly—it reminded the National War Services Department that such a move would disrupt important work already underway in the parks. In the end, the men stayed.[108]

Having limped through the summer with a vastly reduced workforce, the Parks Bureau decided to try to get the alternative service camps back up to their 1941 levels for the winter months. To this end, Director Gibson put together a proposal in early September 1942 that called for doubling the camp population and concentrating the new recruits' energies on the bark beetle control operations at Banff and Kootenay. This programme was favourably received by General LaFleche—now that the harvest season was over—and the divisional registrars were instructed in early October to find the additional men.[109] One of these new call-ups was Abram Dick of Coaldale. Instead of appearing before a War Services Board, though, Dick and several others received confirmation of their status by letter, on the recommendation of B.B. Janz, an Alberta Mennonite leader.[110] The Parks Bureau's efforts to revive the sagging fortunes of its camps were also helped by the Mennonites themselves. In an article entitled "A Grave Warning" in the weekly *Die Mennonitische Rundschau,* the Mennonite Central Committee argued that a few misguided malcontents were not only jeopardizing camp leave, but severely testing the good will of Canadian authorities. It thereupon called on all communities to encourage deserters to return to camp and abide by programme regulations; otherwise, if the violations continued, new recruits might be forced to submit to military training.[111] But this public appeal did not stop the men from running; desertions continued after the appearance of the article. It did, however, demonstrate that Mennonite leaders preferred this type of alternative service work, especially when compared to combative training. The article also reinforced the reputation of Mennonite recruits as co-operative and accommodating—something the Parks Bureau would sorely miss over the next few years.

Despite the promise of additional men, there were only 191 men in four national park camps by 1 December 1942; most of the workers were stationed at Banff and Kootenay, while skeleton crews did what they could at Jasper and Prince Albert. Whether the situation would improve was uncertain, particularly since administration of the National War Services Regulations—the rules governing alternative service work—was formally assumed by the Department of Labour that day. This transfer was designed to bring about the more efficient use of manpower for the national war effort, and it was not clear if and how the national park programme would be affected. Parks officials did not want to take any chances and immediately submitted a brief account of their association with conscientious objectors—how the parks had provided work when no one else was interested—and an outline of their need for 450 men.[112] The acting Parks director described in two subsequent meetings how conscientious objectors had become indispensable to their operations because of the scarcity of regular labour, emphasizing that they performed useful and essential work—whether as reserve fire-fighters or lumbermen. He evidently made a convincing case, for according to the notes of the second meeting, the new officer in charge of the men indicated that national park requirements "should and could be met."[113]

· · ·

For the first three months of 1943, then, the park camps enjoyed something of a revitalization. The number of men more than doubled, and they returned to the wide-ranging activity that had characterized the programme during its early days. Any pretence of restricting the internees to forest conservation work was replaced by a desire to use them wherever they were needed in the parks. It was as if the National Parks Bureau had its own personal army—ready for any action. And action they saw. By the time the final tallies had been made for the fiscal year (ending 31 March 1943), alternative service work had provided more than eighty thousand man-days of labour for Parks projects.[114] Teams of men removed some eighteen thousand beetle-infested trees at Banff, while similar work at Kootenay netted almost 1 million board feet of lumber. At Prince Albert and Riding Mountain, meanwhile, where the camps numbered less than fifty each, the men attended mainly to maintenance work in the townsites and campgrounds; they removed brush and trees, built new kitchen shelters, cut firewood, and stored ice. The internees at Jasper, on the other hand, continued with various road projects, including the construction of the Rocky Canyon bridge and the installation of a guardrail along the Maligne Canyon road. They were also involved in one of the most bizarre episodes of the war.

In the fall of 1942, British inventor Geoffrey Pyke concocted a scheme to fashion a fleet of indestructible warships from "pykrete," a mixture of ice and wood chips. The idea would undoubtedly have been scorned if not for the fact that Nazi U-boats were wreaking havoc on Allied shipping. The British were desperate, and pykrete seemed to offer hope. Before construction of the bergships—code-named "Habbakuk"[115]—got underway, however, it was decided to build a small ice prototype in Canada. This work was secretly carried out in the early new year on secluded Patricia Lake in Jasper by an unsuspecting group of conscientious objectors. According to Abe Dick, who worked on the project for a few weeks, they cut blocks of ice from the lake and then fit them into a wooden-framed structure with four-foot-wide walls that the men sus-

Securing ice blocks for the "ice-ship" experiment, Patricia Lake, Jasper. *Courtesy A. Dick*

pected was a barge. The model was kept frozen over the ensuing summer, but the scheme was ultimately deemed unrealistic and quietly shelved. It was not until contacted by the author almost fifty years later, in fact, that Dick finally learned what he was doing on Patricia Lake that February—and more important, how his principles had been violated in the name of science.[116]

The rest of the work programme that winter was not without its problems. Now that they were expected to serve for the duration of the war, some of the men tried to exercise a certain control over their working lives. In January 1943, for example, the Banff superintendent reported that a group of recent arrivals from Toronto had organized the men at the Castle Mountain camp into an association with elected officials. Ottawa was horrified by this development—alternative service did not mean alternative rules—and ordered an immediate end to the new association's activities, regarding the actions as nothing less than "ganging-up on the Government."[117] The more serious issue, however, was the very employment of conscientious objectors in national parks, especially at a time when Canadians were being called upon to make every possible sacrifice to help win the war. The park maintenance and improvement work, when measured against the Axis threat, seemed a trivial use of the men. As the Prince Albert *Daily Herald* sarcastically remarked in early 1943, "References to the Conchies helping win the war by cutting bridle paths in the park always gets a laugh."[118] This kind of criticism coincided with a growing demand from agriculture and industry representatives for access to the men to meet other wartime needs. And in April 1943, the King government introduced new regulations authorizing the Department of Labour to direct conscientious objectors to essential war work in farming and other areas.

· · ·

The new alternative service policy threatened to decimate—if not end—the national park camps. Parks officials privately speculated that most of the camp inmates would choose the "selective service" option, particularly since they could earn up to twenty-five dollars per month; all earnings in excess of this amount were to be donated to the Canadian Red Cross.[119] They were also somewhat miffed that they had not been consulted about the change in policy. Instead of picking a fight with the Department of Labour, though, Parks Director Gibson set his sights on securing a minimum, fixed number of alternative service workers for each national park, on the grounds that they were required for fire prevention.[120] His Labour counterparts were not immune to this argument and agreed to leave the park camps intact until National Selective Service officers had had a chance to assess the men's qualifications for other work. They also suggested that interned enemy aliens could replace any conscientious objectors who were released. What saved the park operations, however, was the considerable number of men who refused to accept any assigned work; the park camps were designated for these cases.[121] Gibson gladly welcomed this role—as long as it meant that the national parks continued to get their share of the men. He did not seem to be concerned that he would likely inherit a troublesome workforce in the process.

The channelling of conscientious objectors to agriculture and industry did not adversely affect the park camps at first. Although the camp population would eventually drop by half by March 1944, the Department of Labour tried to provide replacements for any men that it relocated. As a result, the Parks Bureau was able to operate summer camps at six national parks, including one at Glacier for August and September. The men were stationed at the parks on the understanding that they were needed for fire protection and attended to various chores associated with this duty, such as improving trails or rebuilding telephone lines. Whenever possible, however, they also worked on tourist facilities, and did a number of special jobs, including the building of fish-rearing ponds and the culling of a herd of elk. This kind of activity served only to promote further questioning of the park alternative service programme. Future Conservative leader John Diefenbaker was the harshest critic, describing the work as "an unjustifiable waste of man-power."[122] The men themselves also questioned the wisdom of the programme. When Otto Regier of Laird, Saskatchewan, was denied leave to work on his father's farm in June 1943, he decided to go to Ontario as a farm labourer rather than report to a park camp. As he explained to the National Selective Service officer in Regina, "You must agree that the work in Prince Albert Nat. Park Alternative Service Camp is not only non-essential but even ridiculous at such a serious time as this and I consciously believe that I am carrying out the wishes of the Federal Government in relieving the farm labour shortage."[123] Other men made their feelings known by failing to report back to camp. Twenty-five-year-old Steve Swidrowich was picked up by the Mounted Police in Battleford, Saskatchewan, and hauled before a Prince Albert magistrate in mid-July 1943 when he did not return from leave.[124]

Parks officials could not afford to ignore this poor image of the camps, especially since the work programme was being financed from the special war appropriation fund and came under regular parliamentary scrutiny. They began to worry, as well, that unless they ran an extremely cost-efficient operation, they might lose whatever workers they were guaranteed by the Department of Labour.[125] Parks Controller James Smart therefore decided to reorganize the use of alternative service labour. The camps at Glacier, Jasper, and Prince Albert were closed that fall in favour of consolidating operations at Banff and to a lesser extent, Kootenay and Riding Mountain. The camp facilities were also refurbished, particularly at Banff, where the men now occupied portable, sectional bunkhouses. Finally, the superintendents were given explicit instructions that conscientious objectors were to work only on projects that directly contributed to the national war economy. Any other work was considered ill-advised. "We must get away from the idea entirely," Smart counselled the Banff superintendent, "that we are acting to take care of a number of men such as . . . with Unemployment Relief, where in many cases we had to . . . keep men busy by making them do something."[126] The new emphasis on harvesting park resources—in this case manufacturing mine pit props, lumber, and fuel-wood—was quite a change from past camp practices, where the men essentially worked on tourist facilities. It was also a violation of the spirit of the 1930 federal National Parks Act, which defined parks as inviolable wilderness reserves. But park authorities were more concerned with proving the worth of the alternative service camps to the national war effort, and the best way of doing this was by setting unofficial production quotas and ensuring that these targets were reached by encouraging intercamp competition. The results were truly astounding. By the spring of 1944, the three parks had produced nearly four thousand cords of wood, eight hundred thousand board feet of lumber, and more than 1.5 million linear feet of mine props.[127]

It was not all work though. Abe Dick, who was transferred to Banff in the back of an open truck in the dead of winter, related how the men in the Spray River camp tried to keep their spirits up by playing jokes on one another, such as blocking the chimney of a neighbouring cabin with a log, or placing a handful of pepper on a hot stove. He also described how he and his friends formed singing quartets, climbed nearby mountains, and walked to the Upper Hot Springs Bathhouse—even in -30°F weather. He also continued his schooling by taking a correspondence course. One of his most haunting experiences, however, was walking to the train station late at night to meet his mother, who was passing through Banff on her way to visit relatives in British Columbia.

Swimming in winter at the Upper Hot Springs, Banff. *Courtesy A. Dick*

When Dick retraced the five miles back to camp, he was serenaded by a pack of howling wolves or coyotes.[128]

This kind of leniency was about to end. The Department of Labour had come to regard park camps as "the official camps to which men may be ordered for refusing to accept alternative service work elsewhere."[129] This role was readily apparent in October 1943, when the minister of Labour responded to a suggestion from his colleague at Mines and Resources that camp wages be increased to bring them in line with those earned by conscientious objectors working in agriculture and industry. "The thing is," he reasoned, "if we make the Camps too attractive we will not be able to get men who are conscientious objectors to go to farms."[130] By the end of the year, the Department of Labour had assumed an even tougher stance. Fearful that there would be a shortage of experienced agricultural workers for the coming crop season, the department announced on 27 December 1943 that all alternative service workers stationed either in British Columbia or in national parks would be directed to farm employment in the early spring. Any man who refused this assignment or otherwise violated National Selective Service Regulations would be sent to one of four detention centres, including Riding Mountain and Kootenay National Parks.[131] The implications were quite clear. As the Parks controller sized up the new policy, "It looks to me as if they are simply going to consider the Alternative Service Work camps as internment or prison camps."[132]

By the end of March 1944, the camp population had once again dropped below two hundred, and it seemed only a matter of time before many of these men would be directed to farm work. The anticipated demise of the park work programme, however, never materialized, and the number of men available to the parks actually increased over the next few months. Determined to ensure that labour resources were being properly mobilized, the Department of Labour directed local magistrates to intensify their prosecution of conscientious objectors whose service had been postponed, but who refused to accept alternative service contracts in essential areas. This clampdown produced an unexpected windfall of new men for the camps; in Ontario alone there were more than a hundred prosecutions by the third week of May.[133] More significantly, it dramatically altered the composition of the camp population. Whereas Mennonites had been the dominant group since the summer of 1941, the campaign netted for the first time–in any significant number–Hutterites and Jehovah's Witnesses.

Hutterites, a small Anabaptist sect intensely committed to the principle of communal ownership, had easily secured conscientious objector status at the beginning of the war but had never been called upon to provide alternative service. This government leniency soon attracted public criticism,[134] and in 1943 the Department of Labour began to assign Hutterite men to alternative service contracts. The men either refused or abandoned these postings and were thereupon prosecuted and sentenced to alternative service camps. This punishment was accepted by Hutterite elders as the lesser of two evils, for at least the men would be kept together and thereby less subject to liberal influences, especially since they would be chaperoned by a Hutterite minister.[135]

The King administration was not so understanding of Jehovah's Witnesses. Indeed, their wartime treatment has been described as "a blot on the record of modern Canada."[136] Members of an evangelical religious group who owe their loyalty directly to God, Jehovah's Witnesses believe that the secular world is demonic and refuse to serve in the military or participate in patriotic services, whether it be saluting the flag or singing the national anthem. What got the organization into trouble at the beginning of the war, however, was its bitter denunciation of the Roman Catholic Church as Satan's instrument and its concerted attempt to win converts in Quebec. The Roman Catholic hierarchy was naturally alarmed by this activity. And in order to appease church leaders in Quebec and prevent a possible threat to national unity, the federal government in July 1940 officially outlawed Jehovah's Witnesses under the Defence of Canada Regulations. This ban was eventually lifted in October 1943–but only after many Witness men of military age were denied conscientious objector status and sent to prison–and the Department of Labour thereafter expected them to serve in some alternative service capacity. Jehovah's Witnesses, however, refused to report on the grounds that they were ministers for their faith, and were hauled before a magistrate under police escort, sentenced, and then taken against their will to a camp. Federal authorities apparently believed that it was more sensible to make these defaulters work in Canada's national parks than to fill the country's gaols with them.[137]

From April 1944 to March 1945, some 285 men were sent to park camps for alternative service duty. Although some of these new internees, together with many of those already held in the camps, decided to accept an outside assignment during the course of the year, there were still more than 300 men in national park camps by the spring of 1945—the majority being Jehovah's Witnesses.[138] These workers were something of an unexpected bonus for the National Parks Bureau, all the more so since it was agreed in May 1944 that the men could be transferred from the two park detention centres to any other park. In addition to Riding Mountain and Kootenay, then, the Banff camps were kept open, while those at Jasper and Glacier were reactivated.[139]

The conscientious objectors' official role in the parks continued to be fire suppression, and where possible, the manufacture of various wood products from fire- or insect-damaged timber. The superintendents were given a relatively free hand, however, in the deployment of the men and in keeping with past practice, had them handle a host of maintenance and small construction projects. They built, for example, a number of bridges along park roads, including a new steel structure over Sinclair Creek in Kootenay, and replaced or installed a number of culverts. They also groomed more than a hundred miles of trail, repaired fences, dug ditches, re-laid water lines, and planted one hundred thousand tree seedlings. One could easily have mistaken the men for the enemy alien workers who had laboured at many of the same park jobs during the last war.

Much of this labour was done under duress. Two Witness men the author located in the Edmonton area refused to talk about their Jasper experience, and an attempt to contact former internees through a church official involved in hosting a national convention also met with a wall of silence. What is known from the official records, though, is that the superintendents quickly began to complain that the Witness prisoners feigned illness, malingered, and accomplished about one-third of the work of the former Mennonite internees. These problems soon prompted the Parks Bureau in August 1944 to seek the replacement of the Jehovah's Witnesses by other alternative service workers. L.E. Westman, the chief alternative service officer, responded at length on behalf of the Department of Labour, and his comments betray the contempt with which the religious group was widely held at the time. He warned that Witness men were "extremely difficult to handle" because they were poorly educated, mentally unbalanced, and martyrs for their cause. "A medical officer skilled in mental

The alternative service camps meant that park development and maintenance continued through the war years. *Courtesy H. Sawatzky*

cases," he remarked, "would find them very interesting." He also explained that the government did not want to set up a special concentration camp for them, and that the Parks Bureau was doing his department a favour by holding them in park camps, especially given the public mood. He then suggested that the men be kept in relative isolation and handled firmly, using if necessary "a reasonable form of mild visible restraint"; any attempt, however, to get a specific amount of work out of the men was sheer folly.[140]

Parks officials were disturbed by this assessment but had little choice but to keep the Witness prisoners if they wanted to continue to run an alternative service programme in the western parks. They took steps, however, to ensure the smooth operation of the camps. In early September 1944, Parks Director Gibson made special arrangements for any Jehovah's Witness who refused to work to be brought before a magistrate and considered for a possible gaol sentence. He also issued instructions to superintendents that camp leave was to be granted "only in exceptional circumstances where proven compassionate grounds exist."[141] This directive was likely in response to the proselytizing efforts of the Witness men being held at Banff; their weekend door-to-door canvassing and distribution of material at street corners were not appreciated in the townsite. "On Saturday evening last on Banff Avenue there was material for a first-class young riot," the *Crag and Canyon* warned, "but it didn't just click. Next time it may!"[142]

The Jehovah's Witnesses regarded the new policy as yet another infringement of their religious rights and formally protested to the authorities. The minister of Labour, in turn, sought the advice of the Justice Department, arguing that the men could come together for private religious observances in the camps, and that freedom to worship did not mean that they should be given temporary leave to contact the public at large.[143] The deputy minister of Justice supported this position. Admitting that he had little understanding of Witness faith, he not only saw nothing wrong with the leave restrictions, but also suggested that the Jehovah's Witnesses were not being badly treated given the circumstances of their confinement. After all, they had been sent to the camps essentially as prisoners.[144]

Over the following months there was an uneasy truce between camp officers and their Witness internees. Because the men had been picked up by the police and brought directly to camp from their hearings, most were not properly clothed for outside work, especially during the coming winter. In a reversal of past policy, it was therefore decided in late October 1944 to supply essential articles to anyone in need. This generosity, however, had little to do with the welfare of the men; the Parks Bureau simply wanted to ensure that they did not have an excuse for not turning out for work. Even then, officials were generally displeased with what the men were able to do. When, for example, the Jasper superintendent was asked in early January 1945 whether he could use more men for park projects, he said that he would accept anyone, "but only if they were better workers than Jehovah's Witnesses."[145] This low regard for the men unfortunately meant that supervisory personnel were not as fastidious in ensuring that camp conditions were properly maintained. Nor did many bother to try to develop any kind of working relationship with the men. During a visit to the Banff operations in mid-January 1945, the new camp inspector found the buildings dirty and the foreman and his charges at odds. When it was suggested that the foreman dine with the men during the lunch hour in order to get acquainted with them, he bluntly told the inspector that "he saw enough of them during working hours."[146] There had been similar problems at the small Glacier camp the previous summer, when the superintendent decided to decline the services of an experienced Japanese cook in favour of hiring a local farmer for the eleven-man camp; he not only had trouble planning meals, but his bread was renowned for being "sour and most unpalatable."[147]

· · ·

This uneasy situation in the park camps seemed about to end in early May 1945 with the defeat of Nazi Germany and the surrender of Japan three months later. Alternative service officials were swamped with petitions and private requests calling for the immediate liberation of the internees. In order to avoid possible public censure and be seen to be fair, however, the King government decided that it could not release conscientious objectors until Canada's soldiers had returned from overseas and were demobilized.[148] Camp workers were officially advised, then, that the end of hostilities did not alter their status and that it was uncertain when a change in policy would be forthcoming; all officials were prepared to do was release those who were willing to abide by outside work contracts. In the meantime, magistrates continued to sentence anyone who violated National Selective Service Regulations and send them to the park camps.[149]

Although the Parks Bureau considered the Witness men of "inferior quality,"[150] it continued to operate camps at four national parks (Banff, Jasper, Kootenay, and Riding Mountain) through the summer and fall of 1945. It also temporarily dispatched in May a twenty-four-man crew from Kootenay to Yoho for a four-month period—the first time that alternative service workers had been stationed in that park. Now that the war was over, Parks officials anticipated a dramatic rise in tourist traffic and wanted to be prepared. Most of the men were therefore put to work on visitor and maintenance facilities; there was no attempt to use them in any other capacity, apart from cutting timber. The situation at Banff was a good example. Work crews repaired sidewalks in the townsite, supplied wood for all the outlying campgrounds, rebuilt fences at the animal paddocks, and cut new hiking trails near park attractions. Similar work was done at Yoho. Here, all the major roads, including the section of the Trans-Canada Highway that ran through the park, were repaired. Bridges and park buildings, especially those in the Kicking Horse campground, were also refurbished and painted.

By early October 1945, there were less than two hundred alternative service workers in detention,[151] and the number would gradually decline over the winter. Some, like the Hutterites, were simply released on the understanding that their return to their communities would not upset the postwar job market for veterans. A few—but only a surprising few—went absent without leave. The majority of the departures, however, were transfers to farm work; many internees evidently concluded that it was the only way to get out of the camps, and they finally accepted work contracts. As a result, the parks became home for the most recalcitrant—namely, Witness prisoners. Parks officials were somewhat uncomfortable with this development, but kept all the camps open through the winter and used small crews to plough roads, cut firewood, and brush campgrounds; those not needed were granted extended leave.

In the early spring of 1946, the Parks Bureau decided to consolidate all the remaining internees at Banff. Continued operation of the camps for such small numbers of men was uneconomical, and the labour of the remaining internees could best be utilized if they were concentrated in one place.[152] Privately, though, the Parks administration had several concerns. Veterans were now being hired to work in the parks, and authorities dreaded the possible consequences of contact between the two groups.[153] There were also worries about how the presence of conscientious objectors, especially Jehovah's Witnesses, might adversely affect tourism. At Yoho during the summer of 1945, for example, the alternative service camp was located next to the Kicking Horse campground, and visitors would often drive into the camp by mistake, or stroll around the buildings; the Witness workers, in turn, sought new converts.[154] The fact that the Jehovah's Witnesses constantly protested and challenged their confinement was also a factor behind the decision to relocate all the remaining men to Banff. Camp superintendents were tired of dealing with the men, and although they employed them in various capacities, they eventually decided that the extra labour was not worth the grief and were anxious to see them go.

• • •

The last park conscientious objector camp—numbering about seventy-seven men—was located at Healy Creek in Banff National Park. The camp superintendent put the men to work at a number of maintenance tasks, confining them as much as possible to the area. To prevent Witness internees from visiting Banff, he also limited camp leave to one night per month. This rule served only to aggravate the group's sense of persecution and elicited another batch of letters to government officials and politicians. Martin Widawski, for example, asked the minister of Mines and Resources why they were still being held, especially when alternative service duty was supposed to be only for the duration of the war. He also resented working as a national park lackey at what he regarded as

The last alternative service camp, at Banff, was closed in July 1946, almost a year after the war ended. *National Archives of Canada, C100699*

slave wages. Above all, he demanded to exercise his rights as a Canadian citizen and suggested that the Union Jack flying in the compound guaranteed certain basic freedoms, even in a concentration camp.[155] The chief alternative service officer, however, remained unsympathetic to Widawski's plight and dismissed his letter as "just one of a type . . . we receive dozens each week."[156]

If there was any consolation for Widawski and his fellow prisoners, it was that their alternative service days were almost over. The Parks Bureau had originally been advised that the Banff camp would likely operate until October 1946, at which time all conscientious objectors were expected to be released from their duties. The King government, however, ordered the camp closed on 15 July and repealed the alternative service regulations a month later. At the time of the camp's closure there were only forty men left, and any work was being done under protest; it made little sense to continue the charade.

There was one internee, though, who would not be going home. Stephen Kushner, a Jehovah's Witness from Burnaby, British Columbia, had been admitted to hospital in Calgary with a pulmonary infection on 23 April 1946, and died from lung cancer three days before alternative service officially ended. Kushner had been brought to Kootenay under police escort in May 1944 and had been serving as a truck driver at Banff at the time of his illness. His family wanted the young man buried near home, but the undertaker in Vancouver who handled the funeral on behalf of the Department of Mines and Resources ignored these wishes and placed him in Mountain View Cemetery; by accident, however, he mistook Kushner's call-up number for a military service designation and buried him in a soldier's plot. When the error was discovered later that fall, the Department of Veterans Affairs was mortified and launched an internal investigation, which eventually resulted in the removal and reburial of the body in March 1947 at Parks Bureau expense.[157]

In many respects, the Kushner incident was representative of the conscientious objector experience during the Second World War. Although their military training was technically postponed, the men were still expected to perform some kind of alternative service and were prosecuted if they failed to report, let alone refused to co-operate. And even though some groups, such as the Mennonites, were regarded as better workers than others, their contributions were never accorded the same respect or worth as military duty. At Banff, for example, where the park directly benefitted from their labour—for no less than five years—the local newspaper forever complained about the presence of conchies in the townsite and suggested that pacifism was "simply a cute method of saving their yellow hides."[158] Whether the men were cowards or shirkers, however, did not really matter to the National Parks Bureau. It was more interested in the men's labour and what that labour meant to continued park development and maintenance, especially during the war. Parks officials consequently fought for continued access to the men and essentially used them—if not abused them—as a captive workforce. What is often overlooked about these activities, however, is that they made little or no contribution to the national war effort. Although many conscientious objectors questioned the need for the park work, while others were there under sentence, their various jobs, however onerous or mundane, did not compromise their status or beliefs. The same could not be said of alternative service in agriculture or industry. In the late 1940s, moreover, when Canadians started to visit national parks in unprecedented numbers, trying to put behind them the dark days of the war and its many sacrifices, they enjoyed facilities that had been developed, improved, or maintained by men who had refused to take part in the military campaign. The image of Canada's national parks as sanctuaries of peace thus reflected a double—if somewhat ironic—meaning.

CHAPTER FIVE

"Japs"

H E DID NOT WANT THEM. BUT JAMES WOOD, THE SUPERINTENDENT of Jasper National Park, had to accept some of the evacuees. Since early January 1942, the Department of Mines and Resources had been pressed by federal and provincial politicians to find work for the hundreds of Japanese nationals who were to be removed from the British Columbia coast following the beginning of the Pacific War. And although the National Parks Bureau had successfully fended off suggestions that it take in some of the Japanese, the Surveys and Engineering Branch, another division of the department,[1] agreed to provide highway construction work for more than two thousand men. Three of the road camps were to be located in the western section of Jasper National Park, as part of the northern transprovincial highway project from Jasper, Alberta, through the Yellowhead Pass to Blue River, British Columbia. As far as Superintendent Wood was concerned, however, they were three camps too many, especially when they were to be populated by three hundred Japanese nationals. Although he dearly wanted to see the road completed, he feared that the presence of Japanese workers would tarnish the public image of the park; that was too high a price to pay for any new highway. Wood viewed the Japanese as unwelcome visitors, as park intruders, and wanted them gone as soon as possible. Ironically, the Japanese, separated from their families, felt much the same way and would gladly have obliged him—if only they could.

The question of what to do with the approximately twenty-three thousand Japanese living in British Columbia at the time of the December 1941 attack on Pearl Harbor was nothing new. The Japanese—all Asians for that matter—had never been welcome in Canada's Pacific province, and through a series of restrictive policies and other discriminatory measures, had been relegated to the lower rungs of British Columbia's economy and society in the early twentieth century. They were segregated in urban ghettos or rural communities, largely confined to a few labour-intensive occupations, and generally prevented from integrating with the host society in any significant way. The dominant white population regarded the Japanese as a blot on the province's character and subjected them to a pervasive racism that bordered on hatred. For most British Columbians, the Japanese were unassimilable, acquisitive, immoral, and treacherous. This anti-Oriental feeling reached new levels of intolerance in the 1930s, when a seemingly insatiable Japan invaded Manchuria and then China as part of an apparent plot to take over Greater East Asia. These actions revived white British Columbians' fear of the Japanese as a potential military threat—an advance force, poised and ready to strike.[2] It was only a matter of time.

The surprise bombing of the American fleet at Pearl Harbor seemed to confirm these suspicions and generated a new, more potent, wave of anti-Japanese hysteria. Feeling more vulnerable than ever before, the white population of British Columbia demanded nothing less than the immediate internment of *all* Japanese, including those born in Canada.[3] The King government trod more warily. In the days immediately after Canada's declaration of war against Japan, federal authorities rounded up a few dozen suspected subversives, impounded the Japanese fishing fleet, closed Japanese-language schools and newspapers, and required all Japanese nationals and those naturalized since 1922 to report to the police.[4] Beyond these steps, Ottawa counselled restraint. It did not want to provoke any Japanese retaliation against Allied captives. Nor did it believe, based on the reports of its security forces, that the Japanese in British Columbia represented a security threat. British Columbians, however, had a completely different assessment of the situation—an assessment coloured by their long-standing antipathy towards Asians. They genuinely feared that a Japanese attack somewhere along the Pacific Coast was imminent, especially in light of the successive military victories in southeast Asia. They also harboured deep-seated doubts about the loyalty of the local Japanese population, and believed that their continued presence in coastal areas greatly threatened public safety. British Columbia's political and community leaders therefore ignored federal pleas for calm and continued to agitate for the mass expulsion of the Japanese.[5]

The King government tried to defuse the growing tensions by announcing on 14 January 1942 that all male Japanese nationals (the Issei, or first generation) between eighteen and forty-five years of age were to be removed from a hundred-mile-wide coastal defence zone by 1 April. It also proposed the creation of a volunteer workforce—the Canadian Japanese Construction Corps—composed of military-age Japanese Canadians who would serve on various projects outside the protected area for the duration of the war. These measures, although appreciated, failed to satisfy British Columbians; they wanted *all* Japanese relocated as soon as possible, not the evacuation of only seventeen hundred men in ten weeks. The deteriorating military situation in

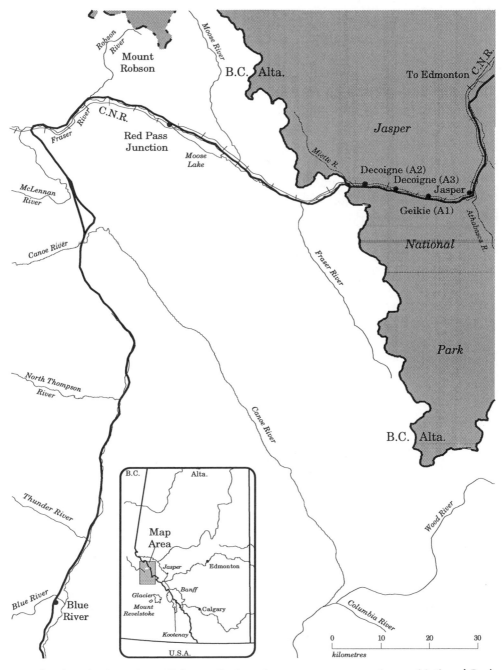

Yellowhead–Blue River Highway Project, Japanese evacuees, Jasper National Park, 1942.

the Pacific made the situation worse, not only aggravating British Columbians' already strong sense of insecurity, but also intensifying their paranoia about Japanese fifth-column activity.[6] In the face of this simmering unrest and under sustained pressure to act, the King government finally capitulated. On 24 February 1942, two months after the Christmas Day fall of Hong Kong and the death or capture of two thousand Canadian defenders, the governor general signed an order authorizing the evacuation of all remaining Japanese and Japanese Canadians, forcibly if necessary, from the coastal defence zone. A few days later the British Columbia Security Commission, the federal agency responsible for the relocation and care of the Japanese, was formally established.[7] Any personal possessions the evacuees could not take with them were to be entrusted to the federal government's Custodian of Enemy Property; beginning in January 1943, these assets were liquidated at fire-sale prices.

Prime Minister King publicly justified the evacuation on the grounds of national security. There was some truth to the statement. Defence officials had become worried about the rapid succession of Japanese victories in the Pacific and, no longer discounting an attack on the west coast, suggested that local Japanese be removed from strategically sensitive areas and that military forces be bolstered.[8] The Canadian cabinet's position was tacitly supported, if not indirectly influenced, by American policy; on 19 February 1942, the United States government took a similar step against its own Japanese population.[9] What Prime Minister King and his government privately dreaded more than anything else, however, was a major racial outburst against the Japanese. Anti-Oriental protest had been a recurrent feature of British Columbia's history, and there was every reason to believe provincial representatives who warned that if the Japanese were not removed—and soon—hostile British Columbians

On 24 February 1942, the Canadian government ordered the mass evacuation of all Japanese—including Canadian citizens—from the Pacific Coast. Several hundred Japanese nationals were sent to one of three road camps in Jasper National Park. *Confidential source*

might resort to mob violence. This prospect made the federal government extremely uneasy, for it threatened to jeopardize national unity and thereby undermine the war effort. In addition, Ottawa was about to sponsor a national plebiscite, in which Canadians would be asked to release it from its 1939 pledge not to introduce conscription for overseas service. In order to appease British Columbians, then, the government caved in to their demand and approved the mass removal of all persons of Japanese ancestry from the coastal defence zone.[10] In the process, it gave credence to the widespread belief that the Japanese were untrustworthy, when in reality they were being relocated to protect them from potentially unruly white British Columbians. Unfortunately, it was a belief that would persist until well after the war.[11]

•   •   •

It was one thing to decide to evacuate the Japanese; it was another to try to figure out what to do with them, especially when most Canadians considered them the enemy. The matter had first been bandied about for two days in early January 1942 at a special Ottawa Conference on the Japanese Problem, attended by federal and provincial politicians, military and police representatives, and senior officials from various government departments. Canadian diplomat Escott Reid from External Affairs later recalled that British Columbia representatives such as Ian Mackenzie, the federal minister of Pensions and National Health, "spoke of the Japanese-Canadians in the way that Nazis would have spoken about Jewish-Germans . . . I felt in that committee room the physical presence of evil."[12] During the conference it was suggested that all physically fit adult male Japanese nationals could work on road projects in the interior; this scheme would not only isolate the Japanese but keep them busy and thereby reduce the chance of subversive activity.[13] Little had been done about the idea, however, by the time the King government announced the partial evacuation of Japanese nationals on 14 January 1942.

Over the next few weeks the Department of Labour, the agency responsible for the camps, asked various federal and provincial bodies about possible highway projects. In particular, it came to depend heavily on the experience and assistance of its counterpart, the Department of Mines and Resources. Not only was the department currently operating camps for conscientious objectors in a number of national parks and along the Trans-Canada Highway in northern Ontario, but its predecessor, the former Department of the Interior, had employed several thousand destitute men on road work during the 1930s. Mines and Resources also had personnel with the expertise necessary to organize the highway projects, if not run them. Indeed, the new director of the Surveys and Engineering Branch was James Wardle, who, as national parks chief engineer, had supervised and coordinated all the highway construction relief work during the Depression.

Wardle interpreted the Department of Labour's request for assistance as a call to arms, and in keeping with his previous practice during the 1930s, canvassed his field officers about possible highway work. There was no shortage of projects. The Japanese could improve the eastern leg of the Big Bend Highway between Golden and Revelstoke, complete the road from Nordegg, Alberta, west to the Banff-Jasper highway, or take over construction of the Maligne Canyon road in Jasper National Park presently being cleared by alternative service workers. It was also suggested that the Japanese could widen the Golden-Leanchoil section of the Trans-Canada Highway, but only if they were well guarded since they would be working above the main line of the Canadian Pacific Railway and could easily disrupt traffic by rolling rocks down the Kicking Horse canyon. There was even a proposal to replace the alternative service crews in Kootenay National Park with Japanese workers, and have them clear and cut dead timber in winter and improve sections of the Banff-Windermere highway during the summer.[14] The most attractive project, however, was the construction of a new road from Jasper, Alberta, through the Yellowhead Pass to Blue River, British Columbia.

The Yellowhead–Blue River highway had been contemplated since the end of the Great War; not only would it provide a more direct link between the northern prairies and the Pacific Coast via Kamloops, but it promised to attract additional automobile traffic to the region, in particular to Edmonton and Jasper National Park. By the beginning of the Second World War, however, the only work that had been done on the project was a November 1936 reconnaissance survey of the proposed route, using wherever possible abandoned sections of the former Canadian Northern or Grand Trunk Pacific grades.[15] Despite this lack of progress, the highway maintained its supporters throughout the ensuing years. During the early 1930s, Charles Stewart, the former Alberta premier and federal minister of the Interior, frequently called for the construction of a highway through the Yellowhead Pass as a relief project. In April 1934, for example, he told the House of Commons that it made more economic sense to open a northern route to the coast rather than finish the Banff-Jasper highway.[16] All the Bennett administration was willing to do, though, was put relief crews on the road between Edmonton and Jasper. The project resurfaced again in the early months of the Second World War, when the King government was looking for possible projects for interned aliens and prisoners of war.[17] Nothing was done about the highway, however, until the summer of 1941, when a small force of alternative service workers began to push through a crude road from Geikie, some eight miles west of Jasper, to the western boundary of the park. Less than three miles of trail, passable by car, were cleared by 15 November 1941.

The beginning of the Pacific War less than a month later put the Yellowhead–Blue River highway in an entirely different light, and Wardle promoted it as the perfect project for the relocated Japanese. Building the road would easily absorb all the Japanese nationals who were to be evacuated, and provide enough work for them for months, if not years, especially if they were required to do as much as possible by hand. The mountain location would also serve as a kind of natural prison, keeping them away from public view in a place where they could do little or no harm—apart, perhaps, from sabotaging the Canadian National Railway main line, which ran parallel to the proposed highway in several places. But even here, security concerns were more than outweighed by the convenience of having the railway to move men, supplies, and construction materials and equipment.

The Japanese evacuees were ripped from the bosom of their families and banished from their home communities. *Vancouver Public Library, 1384*

The project enjoyed considerable public support, both in the Edmonton area and on the other side of the Cariboo Mountains in the Kamloops district.[18] This local backing was particularly important during the first few months of the Pacific War, given the general feeling that the Japanese should not simply be removed from the coast, but made to contribute in some meaningful way to the national war effort. The Yellowhead–Blue River highway was a significant project—one of the remaining gaps in a Trans-Canada Highway network. The one hitch was that the Parks Bureau was not interested in having any Japanese, whether nationals or Canadian-born, working in the national parks. Parks Director Roy Gibson did agree, however, that the Yellowhead–Blue River road was a worthwhile endeavour and had no objection to the Japanese building the park section of the highway—on the understanding that they were to be under the direct supervision of the Engineering and Construction Service of Wardle's department.[19]

Wardle made his recommendations to Labour Department officials on 24 January 1942; he also suggested sending evacuees to northern Ontario to assist conscientious objectors with highway work there.[20] These plans were immediately endorsed by the minister of Labour, Humphrey Mitchell, who was anxious to move the Japanese nationals from the coast as soon as possible, even if the work camps were not ready for occupation; according to internal meeting notes, the minister privately believed that all Japanese, regardless of citizenship, should be treated alike.[21] Mines and Resources agreed to direct the road work, provided provincial authorities in British Columbia and Ontario were willing to co-operate and the RCMP would be responsible for camp security and the conduct of the Japanese. As Wardle advised the deputy minister of Mines and Resources, "We would demand a fair day's work for the wages paid, and if this is not forthcoming, we would ask the unsatisfactory men to be removed."[22] In keeping with the concerns of the Parks Bureau, Wardle also indicated that the first shipment of Japanese nationals would be posted in Jasper National Park in order to complete that section of the highway as quickly as possible.

· · ·

The first few days of February 1942 were largely taken up with negotiations between Wardle's office and provincial authorities. The deliberations were animated by a sense of urgency, as emotions in British Columbia continued to escalate. They also had to deal with ongoing developments. Wardle had initially expected to have two thousand men at his disposal; by early February, however, Labour officials were talking in terms of more than thirty-four hundred placements.[23] Local British Columbia communities also had their own wish-lists. The Prince Rupert board of trade, for example, requested that the Japanese be used on the Prince Rupert–Terrace highway; Kamloops, on the other hand, was worried that the Valemount–Blue River section would not be built in favour of tying the new Yellowhead road into the Big Bend Highway. There was even talk of completing the road from Tête Jaune Cache to Prince George.[24] Once it was decided to remove all Japanese from the defence zone, the Surveys and Engineering Branch found itself operating three major road projects in British Columbia (Jasper to Blue River; Hope to Princeton; and Revelstoke to Sicamous) and one in northern Ontario (Schreiber to Jackfish).

While these discussions were under way, Wardle dispatched one of his engineers, J.H. Mitchell, to inspect the proposed route of the Yellowhead–Blue River road, and identify possible campsites. Mitchell travelled the 141-mile distance from Jasper to Blue River and back by train over a three-day period, performing an inspection that would normally only have been possible during the summer. But it had not been a typical winter; there were only twelve inches of snow in areas that usually averaged four feet.[25] Mitchell was therefore able to provide a detailed assessment of the route and reported on 11 February 1942 that almost thirty-three miles of the proposed right-of-way were already up to grade—seven of the eighteen miles in Jasper National Park and some twenty-six miles of the existing British Columbia provincial road that ran between McBride and Valemount. That still left more than 75 percent of the highway to construct, only nineteen miles of which would be converted from the abandoned railway grade in the area.[26] Mitchell also submitted a list of tentative campsites, located every four to five miles along the route as close as possible to existing railway sidings. In the case of the Jasper section he recommended three camps: one at Geikie and two near Decoigne.

The other urgent requirement was assembling enough camp material to accommodate and equip two thousand men. Wardle handled this aspect of the operation himself, planning to erect the same kind of frame-and-tar-paper bunkhouses that had been used to house relief workers during the 1930s. It would be several weeks, however, before these structures could be ready for occupation, since it was standard policy to have the workers build them. In the meantime, Wardle arranged with Canadian National to have two train units with bunkhouses, diners, and supply cars spotted at the desired sidings in the Yellowhead Pass to accommodate the first group of Japanese nationals.[27] As for camp equipment, he borrowed beds, stoves, and mess kits from the Department of National Defence and the British Columbia Public Works Department. He also asked the Parks Bureau for camp equipment for the Jasper section of

Bunkhouses, similar to those used during the Depression, were built at the camps located outside the park boundaries. *Canadian Parks Service, Western Regional Office, Webster Collection*

the highway, but their surplus material had last been used during the Depression and was not worth shipping.[28] Wardle planned to house the workers in shack tents, with wooden floors and walls and canvas roofs, until more permanent bunkhouses could be built.

Once the route and camp arrangements had been determined, Wardle met with Labour Department officials to work out camp policy. Although these rules and regulations had been debated for several weeks, it was not until 13 February that the two sides finally sat down face-to-face in Ottawa to hammer out the details. The Japanese were to be paid twenty-five cents per hour for an eight-hour day, forty-eight-hour week; one dollar per month would be deducted to cover possible medical care; and all earnings would be subjected to the national defence tax. At first glance, this wage compared favourably with the fifty-cents-per-day rate being paid to alternative service workers. But the Japanese labourers were expected to look after their own messing, and also assign twenty dollars per month to their wives. On questions of security and conduct, it was decided that the Japanese were not to be considered internees and that they could leave camp during daylight hours as long as they had permission. At the same time, they were not allowed to go near the tracks or any railway buildings. Any men, moreover, who failed to do a fair day's work were to be reported to the local RCMP detachment; those who refused to co-operate with camp officials could be charged and possibly have their dependants' monthly allowance withheld. Department responsibilities were also confirmed at the meeting. Mines and Resources, in particular the Engineering and Construction Service, would supervise the road work; the Department of Labour, on the other hand, would ensure that the evacuees were physically fit and properly clothed for heavy outside work, and deliver the men to their respective campsites.[29]

The decisions at this meeting formed the basis of the cabinet order five days later that formally authorized the minister of Mines and Resources "to establish work camps for male enemy aliens, including Japanese nationals, on projects located outside of protected areas."[30] There was, however, one last-minute revision. In the interests of efficiency, it was decided that it would be easier for camp officials to feed the Japanese workers at a cost of twenty-five cents per meal until the camps were fully operational.[31] This change effectively meant that almost half a man's weekly earnings—if he worked the full week—would go towards his sustenance. This was no small matter, especially if the individual also had to set aside twenty dollars for his dependants, or missed a few days of work because of illness or inclement weather. And it would later prove to be a source of grievance. Government officials were more concerned, however, with the growing urgency of getting the Japanese away from the coast, and took whatever steps were necessary to get the Yellowhead–Blue River camps up and running as quickly as possible. "This arrangement is as vital a defence action as the erection of fortifications," Wardle exhorted his engineers. "It is a war emergency and should be handled accordingly."[32]

. . .

The Japanese did not feel the same way. On 16 February 1942, in response to the first evacuation order, Japanese nationals from the coastal areas packed what belongings they could carry, said goodbye to their wives and families, and departed for Vancouver. Here, at Hastings Park, they were briefly interviewed and given a number, assigned to a particular road camp, and then temporarily housed in the stalls of the livestock building, which was normally used to showcase animals during the Pacific National Exhibition. The first shipment of a hundred road workers—men, married or single, who were Japanese nationals—were ordered to leave Vancouver by train two days later for the Yellowhead Pass. The Issei, however, refused to go voluntarily, arguing in their defence that they had until 1 April to vacate the defence zone. They also resented the fact that they did not seem to be wanted anywhere else in Canada, and apparently believed that they would be better off staying together.[33] A few were confident that Japan would eventually triumph, while many others were frightened and confused by the idea of being sent to distant mountain camps.[34] As George Funamoto and Kinzie Tanaka recounted, they had been raised as Canadians, taught to respect the government and be loyal to their new country, and now they were being told that it did not matter and they had to be ready to leave in a matter of days.[35] What was most distressing to these first evacuees, though, was the anguish and turmoil of being ripped from the bosom of their families and banished from their home communities. They had done nothing wrong. They had committed no crime. And yet they were heartlessly removed from the security of their homes and the love of their wives and children, simply because of their race. It was a grievous wound that many of "the exiles"[36] would carry with them for the duration of the war, if not forever.

Government officials, who had expected the Japanese to co-operate, were stung by their refusal to leave Vancouver. An exasperated associate deputy minister of Labour suggested advancing the evacuation date to the day the road camps were ready.[37] The situation became worse six days later, when the King government decided to uproot all Japanese from the Pacific Coast. This political act only hardened the resolve of the Issei; they had been led to believe that Canadian citizens would be left alone if they went to the road camps.[38] It now appeared that any hope of eventually being reunited with their loved ones and returning to the dear and familiar had been misplaced; their world as they knew it was to be wiped out. Federal authorities, on the other hand, were now saddled with the additional burden of trying to find placements for the thousands of Japanese who had to leave the protected area. They had been under mounting pressure since early January to do something about the so-called Japanese problem, and the mass evacuation order made their work

The Japanese evacuees were deposited at selected rail sidings along the length of the Yellowhead–Blue River road project. *Canadian Parks Service, Western Regional Office, Webster Collection*

brutally simple—round them up and ship them out as if they were cattle. Basic civil rights were expendable in wartime Canada, especially when the greater interests of the state were seen to be at risk. Judge James Hyndman of Alberta had made this perfectly clear almost a year earlier when he observed, "It is not possible to fight a war according to the principles of Magna Carta."[39] What officials did not seem to realize, though, was that many of the Japanese evacuees wanted—more than anything else—to remain together as families.[40] It was a bond that no government had the right to sever.

In the face of Issei resistance, Canadian officials resorted to heavy-handed tactics and eventually coerced several hundred nationals to "volunteer" for road work.[41] Some would later complain that the RCMP had promised they would not be required to work if they left the coastal zone.[42] Many others were threatened with internment if they continued their refusal to co-operate. All carried with them the pain of being forced from their communities against their will. It was one of the saddest moments in the lives of these men in their adopted country. The *New Canadian,* the only Japanese newspaper allowed to continue publishing, reported that up until the first group of evacuees left, "photographers were still doing an encouraging trade. The men wanted pictures of their wives, their children, their homes. They did not expect to see them for some time."[43] Some thirty-five years later, a Nisei (second generation Japanese) remembered going to the train station to see his father off. "It was the first time," he recalled, "I saw my father . . . whipped. Beaten. Not a man any more but a number on a card in a file, being sent with a bunch of other whipped men to some stretch of road up in the north to use a shovel and axe. That was part of my growing up."[44] The most poignant account was provided by nineteen-year-old Yosie Yasui, a recent high school graduate who was among the first group of nationals to be sent to the road camps. "I can clearly picture the masses of people standing on the platform that momentous Monday night, busily saying goodbye, shaking hands, bowing stiffly to those of us on the train," he reported. "Suddenly the whistle blows . . . and hundreds of voices and hundreds of hands are raised in farewell. But in a few fleeting minutes the throng is a shadowy, indistinct mass in the evening dusk, and then darkness and distance sweep them out of sight."[45]

· · ·

The first hundred evacuees left Vancouver on 23 February, and after an overnight train trip under the supervision of Mounted Police plainclothesmen, were deposited in equal numbers at Lucerne[46] and Rainbow, where they moved into the workcar units that had been placed on the sidings in anticipation of their arrival. For the next few weeks, until the camps were erected and ready for occupation, these specially fitted boxcars would serve as their new home. Another hundred Japanese, headed by Hiroshi Maruno, left Vancouver the following night—this time destined for Geikie in Jasper National Park. Ranging in age from nineteen to fifty-five, the men came from various backgrounds and professions—from farmers, mill hands, and seaman to teachers, clerks, and engineers. Two-thirds were married and half this number had at least one child. Yasutaro Sakamoto left behind a wife, six children,

The men lived in boxcars until the camps were built.
Canadian Parks Service, Western Regional Office, Webster Collection

an aged father, and one of the largest strawberry operations in the Langley district. Twenty-four-year-old Yoshimitsu Higashi, on the other hand, had been awarded the governor-general's medal upon graduation from the University of British Columbia and was serving as business manager for the *New Canadian* when he received his evacuation notice. According to one of the surviving camp lists, there were also fathers and sons, brothers, uncles and nephews, or cousins sent to the camps.[47]

As the contingent sped eastward under the cover of darkness, it was learned that workcar units were still being put together in Jasper. The men therefore had to be brought into the park townsite, and after milling around the station platform for two hours and buying some warm work clothes at local stores, were eventually placed in hurriedly fitted boxcars on a nearby siding. Late the next day, the Japanese were returned to Geikie, only to find that local supervisors were prepared for only fifty men. The excess men, in their workcar unit, were shuttled farther westward to Red Pass Junction, the divisional point for trains going to Vancouver or Prince Rupert and the new headquarters for the Yellowhead–Blue River project.[48] Those left behind on the Geikie siding settled down as best they could, beginning their new lives in exile in boxcars that had only a few days earlier been used to haul freight. One nineteen-year-old evacuee from the Fraser Valley remembers being so cold in his new home that "I had to sleep with my shoes on"; he also felt terribly alone, for his father had been one of those sent farther down the line.[49]

Senior assistant engineer Mitchell, who had been placed in charge of the road camps, was infuriated by this episode and telegraphed his Ottawa supervisor that only the co-operation of Canadian National had "prevented the men you requisitioned for Geikie from being dumped in a snow bank." In order to avoid a repeat incident, he asked for authority to alert Vancouver when the Japanese should be sent. "Don't ball things up," he bluntly told head office, "by trying to do the field work from Ottawa."[50] Wardle approved this request, on condition that Mitchell fully understood the urgency of moving the Japanese and did everything possible to rush camp construction. His "minimum objective" was to have twenty, hundred-man camps in place along the highway route by 1 April 1942.[51] This was a tremendous undertaking, given the location of the project, the time of year, and the supplies and building materials required. But Wardle looked upon the challenge as his own private war and was not prepared to lose. To this end, he arranged for Mitchell to have whatever funds were needed—there was no limit—to purchase materials from district mills and to hire labour from as far away as Edmonton and Kamloops to work ten- to twelve-hour days to put up the camp buildings. It was amazing what a difference a war could make from the penny-pinching days of the park Depression camps. Wardle also enlisted the aid of the British Columbia Department of Public Works to build several camps along the Tête Jaune Cache–Blue River section. He even investi-

The Japanese spent their first few weeks in the park building twenty-man shack tents.
Canadian Parks Service, Western Regional Office, Webster Collection

gated using abandoned relief camps as temporary detention quarters until the Yellowhead–Blue River facilities were ready.

For their part, the Japanese generally accepted their fate in a spirit of resignation ("shi-kata-ga-nai")[52]–and some relief. Takeo Nakano, formerly of Woodfibre, was glad to escape the stench and confinement of Hastings Park and looked upon his new life in the shadow of Mount Robson as something of an adventure. He found his boxcar home crowded but cosy and the food palatable. He also enjoyed his days in the bush, swinging an axe when not marvelling at the raw, natural features of the land and the local wildlife.[53] There was no denying, however, in the words of Nakano, that the men "had fallen from a better state and had lost some of their human dignity by the fall."[54] They were the people British Columbia did not want, and the mountain setting compounded their sense of emptiness and helplessness. "At those times when my loneliness was particularly acute, I went to stand under the night sky," Nakano recounted some forty years later, "and it seemed to rain something sympathetic upon me."[55] Not even their nightly routine of card-playing and storytelling could dull the pain of separation from their families. They were there for as long as the war lasted–or until the road was completed–and did not want to think about the future and what it might hold for them. "All this is still a dream," wrote Yosie Yasui from the camp at nearby Rainbow. "I still have the feeling that at any moment I'll wake up to all the hustle and bustle of Vancouver . . . my home my 'bunch' and everything that we did. But as the days go by . . . the never dreamed of experiences [are] becoming more and more real."[56]

Hiking in the mountains was a popular pastime for many of the evacuees. *University of British Columbia Library, Special Collections and University Archives Division, Japanese Canadian Photograph Collection*

While people like Nakano and Yasui were busy felling trees along the right-of-way or erecting tent houses at the campsites, Parks Director Gibson began to question his earlier decision to allow the Japanese nationals to work within Jasper National Park. In an obtrusive memo dated 24 February—the same day the Issei left Vancouver for Geikie—Gibson reminded Wardle of his promise that the Japanese would not be brought into the townsite and that project headquarters would be located on the other side of the provincial border in British Columbia. He also insisted that the families of the men never be allowed to live with them in the park, and that all park regulations be strictly observed at the three proposed road camps.[57] Gibson would actually have preferred to use alternative service workers on the park section of the new highway. He was worried that the Japanese would need constant supervision—if not guarding—and that they would be poor workers, especially in comparison to the conscientious objector crews. He also suggested, aping the racial stereotypes of the time, that the Japanese looked different, were unsuited to the climate, might not understand English, and were used to a different standard of living. They were also unwelcome. "Residents of the parks, and tourists," he observed, "might resent the presence of Japs in the National Parks."[58] For Gibson, then, conscientious objectors, who refused to fight on principle, were fine as park workers, while the Japanese, who had yet to be identified with a single act of sabotage, were not.

. . .

By the middle of March 1942, some three weeks after the first consignment of Japanese had left Vancouver for the Yellowhead, camp construction was progressing so well that accommodation for eighteen hundred men was expected to be available by the end of the month. In the meantime, well over a thousand evacuees were living fourteen men to a bunk-car—the official regulation was ten—in Canadian National workcar units, which had been spotted up and down the length of the proposed route. Even at Geikie, the only camp that was complete and fully occupied, the men were living in eighteen-by-eighteen-foot shack tents, not bunkhouses.[59] Despite the conditions, the evacuees did what they could to make themselves comfortable, trying to add an element of the familiar whenever possible. They collected rocks and wood for the gardens that they expected to cultivate as soon as the ground thawed out. They also insisted on the construction of traditional bathhouses with large soaking tubs.[60] The men at Decoigne, some three miles from the interprovincial border, tried to leave as many trees as possible around their tents to create a parklike setting. They also planned a large garden on the east side of the camp and laid out a baseball diamond to the west. At night they were comforted by the sounds of a violin and bamboo flute and the verses of a haiku poet:[61]

(At the discarded railway tracks)

Tetsudo-towa nanominokorite tsutsumigusa
Shinryoku-wo irodoru asagi tento-kana

(railway tracks remain in name only covered in grass
newly opened green leaves reflect the light blue tent)[62]

But they could not forget where they were. "Even in this bed believe it or not," wrote a *New Canadian* correspondent from Red Pass in a sarcastic vein, "I can still dream of the wife and children I left behind."[63]

Mitchell directed much of the camp construction from Jasper, when not in the field, and on 11 March formally asked that the townsite be designated the administrative headquarters for the project because of the presence of telephone and telegraph facilities. Wardle, however, was not about to break his

One of the first buildings to go up in each camp was a traditional bathhouse with a large soaking tub. *University of British Columbia Library, Special Collections and University Archives Division, Japanese Canadian Photograph Collection*

pledge to the Parks Bureau, especially since Canadian National Railways was also uncomfortable about its role in the project. The day before the first group of Issei were originally scheduled to leave for the Yellowhead, R.C. Vaughan, president of CN, had complained to the minister of Transport about the placement of enemy aliens along the railway's main line; if the Japanese were such a threat, he seemed to be asking between the lines, then why were they not being kept away from such a vital transportation link?[64] By early March, the railway's concerns had shifted slightly. It was now worried that the use of CN facilities might have cost it tourist traffic, particularly in the Jasper area, and indirectly helped its competitor.[65] Not wanting to alienate Parks and railway officials any further, Wardle therefore ordered his engineer to move his offices immediately to Red Pass, British Columbia, which was closer to the middle of the project.

This directive did not come soon enough, for the next day, a delegation from the Jasper branch of the Canadian Legion visited Superintendent Wood to complain about the presence of the Japanese in the townsite and the potential threat of sabotage. They were deathly afraid that the Japanese would poison the water supply and take over the village, particularly when there were only two guards for the one hundred men at the Geikie camp. Where and how these law-abiding men might find the opportunity to obtain the poison and weapons, let alone summon the inclination to do so, was a moot point. But Wood did nothing to ease these concerns and forwarded to Ottawa a list of recommendations calling for the establishment of restricted areas, an increase in the number of camp guards, and the arming of the Veterans Volunteer Reserve Company.[66] Parks Director Gibson was furious when he received the superintendent's letter, believing that his understanding with Wardle had been broken. "This matter should be straightened out promptly," he urged, "before the Japanese think that they have established any rights to privileges that would not be in the best interests of the National Park."[67] Wardle regarded Gibson's request as "most reasonable" and forwarded the problem to the RCMP for action. As he explained to the commissioner, S.T. Wood, "a town in a National park depending largely on tourist traffic for its existence, is in a different category than the average town."[68]

Decoigne 2A, one of the three road camps in the park, May 1942. *National Archives of Canada, C100701*

Commissioner Wood's response to the Jasper complaints was totally at odds with the feeling in the community. He was one of the few senior government officials who seemed to have sympathized with the plight of the Japanese from the beginning; he also came to believe that the breakup of families was a terrible mistake and would "lead to increasing unrest, if not trouble, in the camps already established."[69] His handling of the Jasper protest was consequently circumspect and sensible. Wood explained that the two guards in each camp had been placed there at the request of Canadian National to protect railway property and were not in any strict sense responsible for watching the Japanese. He also suggested that the Japanese were "well disciplined" and should simply be told not to enter the townsite. There was no need for drastic action, especially the arming of a group of local citizens already nervous about the Japanese being in the park, let alone the townsite. Finally, he said there was a simple reason behind the Japanese visits to Jasper. In keeping with their status as enemy aliens, they were required to report monthly to the nearest RCMP detachment–in Jasper–and secure formal permission if they wished to move elsewhere. According to the police commissioner, then, the problem of the townsite visits could easily be remedied by having the Japanese report to the camp guards.[70]

Jasper residents were not so easily pacified. Although Superintendent Wood announced that the Japanese would not be able to move about so freely, the townspeople began to question why they were even placed in the park when they had been evacuated from the coast for security reasons, and demanded at the very least that they be placed under a heavily armed guard behind barbed wire enclosures. There was also a fear that Jasper would become known as a "Jap town," and that potential tourists would take their business to long-time rival Banff.[71] The Edmonton *Bulletin* probably spoke for many park residents when it claimed "that many Canadians and their visitors will regard this intrusion as not unlike allowing dogs in the drawing room . . . we cannot escape the conviction that somewhere in the Japanese race is a barbaric strain that makes them loathsome animals in the fever of conflict."[72]

While these feelings ran rampant in Jasper, engineer Mitchell was trying to overcome a serious shortage of trucks. Although horse teams were to be used

Many of the evacuees were unprepared for the heavy, manual labour—especially given their age. *Confidential source*

Project officials wanted to use impounded Japanese trucks on the Yellowhead road.
Vancouver Public Library, 1358

as much as possible to haul supplies, trucks were needed to remove debris or carry gravel. In what can only be described as a heartless move, the Engineering and Construction Service contacted the Custodian of Enemy Property in Vancouver to see whether impounded Japanese vehicles could be turned over to the project and used by the same men who might once have owned them.[73] There were also problems with the labour force. Many evacuees could perform only light chores because of old injuries, chronic conditions, or their age—some were in their seventies[74]—and should never have been sent to the camps; one man at Lempriere camp had just been released from a psychiatric institution. There were eventually so many Japanese patients being treated at Seton Hospital in Jasper for strains and other construction-related injuries that hospital officials asked Mines and Resources to absorb the costs of adding a second floor.[75] At least half the men, moreover, had never used picks and shovels and were unprepared for the heavy manual labour that was expected of them.[76] By early April 1942, a few simply refused to work, while others did so at such an infuriatingly slow pace that camp foremen began to bitch. Mitchell wanted the worst malingerers removed; otherwise, enforcing camp discipline would be difficult, if not impossible, and little work would be accomplished. As for the rest of the men, he did not know what to do. The threat of "no work, no pay" had little impact, since the monthly deductions, especially for meals and dependants, left the Japanese with only a few dollars; the worried wife of one worker, for example, complained to the *New Canadian* that her husband had only $5.62 to show for working twenty-five days in April, and that he would have been in debt if he had been sick for more than two days.[77] And many evacuees quickly realized that they would be financially better off in an internment camp, where at least they would get 20¢ a day.[78]

· · ·

The tensions continued through the spring, but never escalated into a major work stoppage. A rumoured sit-down strike at Decoigne over crowded conditions turned out to be just that—a rumour. Similar stories about the raising of a Japanese flag, men getting drunk in camp, and a worker being killed in a landslide also proved to be products of overactive Jasper imaginations.[79] In reality, camp officials carefully monitored and regulated the activities of the Japanese. The workers could not be absent from camp from one hour after dusk until dawn, and were allowed to visit Jasper only in small groups on an infrequent basis—usually to purchase clothes or other personal goods. They also had to stay away from the rail line and other sensitive areas at all times. And they had to obey the instructions of their supervisors or be reported. Nothing was left to chance. As a precautionary measure, for example, dynamite was transported to the Jasper camps on the day it was needed; unused material had to be returned to the townsite that night.[80]

The Japanese, in turn, generally co-operated, if not passively resisted. When Peter Elliott, an Edmonton reporter, visited Geikie and Decoigne in early April, several of the older men told him that they preferred internment to road work. Many others claimed that it was "next to impossible" to live on their monthly wages after deductions. The most persistent complaint, however, was the separation from their families. "The last time I saw my wife and children they were at Hastings Park," volunteered Yasutaro Sakamoto, the Japanese headman. "I'm worried about them . . . I haven't heard how they're getting along or how my old father is."[81] This sense of helplessness gnawed away at the men's insides, and they craved any news about their loved ones and the world they had left behind.[82] The most anticipated part of each day was the distribution of mail at suppertime, when the men would gather anxiously in the hope of hearing their names called; but even here, their privacy had been violated by government censors who had carefully cut out sections of the letters.[83] And whenever a train carrying a new batch of evacuees passed Geikie, the men would instinctively drop their tools and wave at their compatriots. On one occasion, when a train stopped to pick up a passenger, the workers rushed forward—stopping at the edge of the rail bed as if there were an imaginary line they could not cross—and shouted back and forth to the men on the coach. James Baker, the foreman at Geikie, sloughed off the men's concerns about their families, telling them that they were lucky to be living in a "white man's country . . . at least we won't let people starve here."[84] He was also confident that the Japanese would settle down and find their place once actual road work

Foreman Jim Baker (front centre) and the rest of the supervisory personnel at Geikie.
Confidential source

got underway. "This whole business is not a picnic," he admonished the reporter. "It's a tough proposition any way you look at it. The Japs don't like being here any more than we like looking after them."[85]

This understanding had its limits, however, and some of the project supervisors were easily provoked. On the morning of 7 April 1942, for example, Baker telephoned Mitchell that two Japanese had thrown their breakfast rations on the floor, started a fight in the dining room, and demanded to go to an internment camp. By the time a local RCMP constable arrived the next day, the Japanese had quietly resolved the matter—they denied anything serious had happened—and all was running smoothly; it seems they had been feuding among themselves over camp privileges and work assignments. The investigating officer chided Baker for his handling of the incident and told him to try to solve problems himself before calling the police.[86] But Baker could not really be blamed for his reaction, especially given the uncertain status of the Japanese. The veteran foreman had been hired to build a camp and then start clearing and levelling the highway right-of-way. And as far as Baker was concerned, the Japanese under his supervision were there to work or face possible internment. They were the enemy—or at least sympathetic to Japan's cause—and had been assigned to the Yellowhead project to keep them busy. It was not unusual for project supervisors to adopt an aggressive attitude to breaches of discipline. And most of the railway guards stationed on the bridges and the RCMP "special" constables posted outside the camps were locally hired ex-servicemen who shared similar views. "Brother, when I tell 'em to halt," boasted a guard brandishing his loaded rifle, "they better halt."[87]

Trying to find an effective way of dealing with the Japanese nationals preoccupied the Engineering and Construction Service for much of April. C.M. Walker, supervising engineer at Banff, encouraged camp foremen to be tactful when dealing with the Issei and to avoid foul or abusive language or any physical coercion. "The Japanese in our camps are not there as internees in an internment camp," he remarked, "but must be considered as voluntary workers, and as such they must be accorded decent treatment at all times."[88] H.A. Dixon of the British Columbia Department of Public Works, on the other hand, was considerably less constrained in his advice, warning that the "Jap . . . crafty and suspicious" would do anything "to save his face," exploiting at the same time any "outward sign of disagreement among those in charge."[89] Wardle, for his part, did not seem to be interested in understanding Japanese values, particularly their sense of honour and respect. Nor was he willing to grant them any concessions, however small or trivial, unless they earned them. Drawing upon his experience running the national park relief projects, he believed that the Japanese should be handled firmly or they "will be in effect running the camps instead of ourselves."[90] He also recommended that the British Columbia commission ask newspapers to refrain from publicizing Japanese complaints and carry only "good news" stories about life in the camps.[91]

There was little good news, however, in the camps in May. Although the Japanese had organized themselves and settled into a regular routine, including

Lucerne, 1 July 1942. Authorities believed that the Japanese used camp baseball games to plot strike strategy. *Courtesy G. Funamoto*

highly competitive, intercamp baseball games,[92] they continually tested their supervisors. They defied, for example, the camp regulation that lights were to be put out at ten o'clock. Wardle's handling of the matter only made things worse. Worried that the Japanese would be unable to put in a full day's work, he ordered lights to be removed from the bunkhouses for a day or so. If the problem continued, the violators were to be charged by the RCMP.[93] Other difficulties with overzealous supervisors also carried on. At Lucerne, on the British Columbia side of the project, the Japanese refused to work one day when foreman Mustard tried to remove seven young, well-educated men for questioning his running of the camp. When every one of their complaints was confirmed by the special police constable on duty—"he was a dictator and treated them like dogs"—Mustard turned down a transfer and quit on the spot.[94] In addition, there were unfortunate foul-ups that served only to aggravate the mood in the camps. The April paycheques, which were already small to begin with, were not received until the third week of May. An intercepted letter from A. Takagi at Geikie to his wife in Haney, British Columbia, captured the sense of frustration among the men: "Everybody is now kicking. Our foreman JIM BAKER here used to say to us 'No Work No Pay' now everybody saying to him 'No Pay No Work' to get even with him."[95]

The project itself also encountered problems, both real and potential. Although all but one bunk-car unit had been returned to Canadian National by the end of May, there were only seventeen camps in operation and just over thirteen hundred men occupying them. The three Jasper camps, for example, had eighty-five (Geikie 1A), twenty-nine (Decoigne 2A), and sixty-three (Decoigne 3A) men on the May pay list.[96] This number was well below what the project was supposed to accommodate, even more so after fifty men had been recalled from the camps in late April to work on sugar beet farms on the prairies.[97] This smaller workforce meant that the completion of the highway might be delayed, especially since there were plans to do most of the finishing work by hand. The spring run-off presented problems as well, when the rising waters of the Miette River forced the evacuation of Decoigne 2A camp in late May. Although the few men affected were easily absorbed by the other two Jasper camps, work on that section of the highway had to be postponed until the flood waters retreated.[98] There was also the possibility that work on the road might be suspended. The Joint Chiefs of Staff began to question whether it was such a good idea to trust Japanese working alongside a major transportation link. Wardle dismissed this concern as "rather late and out of order," particularly when the Department of National Defence had endorsed the project several months earlier.[99]

· · ·

June brought new troubles. Up until then, the Japanese had generally pursued a strategy of passive resistance; they did what was asked, but did not exert

The flooding of the Miette River forced the evacuation of Decoigne 2A in late May 1942. *University of British Columbia Library, Special Collections and University Archives Division, Japanese Canadian Photograph Collection*

themselves.[100] Once it became apparent, however, that they might be separated from their families for several months, if not the next few years, and that they were to be used on the highway project essentially as drudges, they decided to disrupt the work and force the British Columbia Security Commission to do something about their situation.[101] This turn of events should not have surprised government officials. There had been numerous public demonstrations of how the Japanese struggled daily with the pain of separation. At Geikie, for example, the farewell banquet in honour of the twenty men who were to be reunited with their families on sugar beet farms was tempered by a general "feeling of homesickness."[102] At another camp, fifteen minutes of each working day had been negotiated to allow the men to talk openly about their wives.[103] Recent developments in Vancouver also undoubtedly hardened attitudes on the project. In the early spring, a group of second generation Japanese steadfastly refused to be separated from their families and formed the Nisei Mass Evacuation Group. Although several hundred men were subsequently sent to northern Ontario internment camps for failing to leave for road work, their resistance spilled over into the Yellowhead–Blue River camps in the form of pamphlets exhorting the workers to join their struggle and fight for reunification with their families.[104]

The security commission had also been warned by one of the Japanese

The evacuees decided to withhold their labour in order to bring about reunification with their families. *University of British Columbia Library, Special Collections and University Archives Division, Japanese Canadian Photograph Collection*

office workers at Red Pass Junction about "the rising tide of trouble that is bound to burst."[105] On 26 May 1942, Kinzie Tanaka, former first vice-president of the Japanese Canadian Citizens' League, wrote a lengthy, private letter to evacuation authorities, detailing how morale in the camps was virtually nonexistent and how the men interpreted any grievance as a personal affront and were ready to revolt. "You who are in authority must realize that men without spirit cannot work effectively, you must realize that men without spirit are always discontented," he argued passionately. "All they see ahead is this hard work which looms in their minds as lifeless drudgery," he continued. "They see several months of lifeless living with very little to distract their minds, no entertainment, no travelling, no wife or children, no happiness."[106] Tanaka's solution was twofold. He suggested that the married men be reunited with their families in small communities outside the defence zone, and that their places on the road project be assumed by young, single men who would not only be given supervisory positions but also paid a decent wage.[107]

Tanaka's letter received a sympathetic response from the commission–the chairman allowed that it was an "unfortunate situation"–and was forwarded to the Department of Labour, along with the recommendation that the married men be reunited with their families over the winter months, if necessary in

Kinzie Tanaka warned authorities in a private letter dated 26 May 1942 about "the rising tide of trouble that is bound to burst." *Courtesy K. Tanaka*

vacant Indian residential schools; otherwise, trouble would likely arise in the camps once the cold weather arrived, if not sooner.[108] The letter was also brought to the attention of the RCMP commissioner, who had recently been asked by the federal minister of Justice whether the location of the Yellowhead–Blue River camps constituted a threat. Although he was not surprised by the growing restlessness described in Tanaka's letter, Commissioner Wood continued to insist that the evacuees were not a menace, and suggested that the danger of subversive activity would be effectively removed if families were allowed to join the men. The only other possible guarantee against sabotage, he told the Justice minister, was the closure of the camps along the Canadian National line.[109]

Before any action could be taken, the Japanese at Gosnell (camp B18) evidently decided to force the issue and went on strike the first week of June. Immediately investigating the work stoppage, supervising engineer Mitchell wired Ottawa that the reasons for the dispute were "trivial and unjustified" and called for the removal of the agitators. "If these people are allowed to continue refusing to give a fair day's work," he reasoned, "it would be more economical for the Government to confine one and all to an internment camp and supply the project with power machinery."[110] Mitchell's frustration was shared by the Ottawa office. Wardle, for example, believed that the Japanese were finally showing their true nature, and felt the time had come to take "a very firm and definite stand" against them. He consequently requested permission to do a thorough housecleaning of suspected troublemakers, and suggested as well that they stop serving meals to men who would not work. If these steps were not taken, he warned the Labour Department, "all the camps can only be regarded as concentration camps, not work camps."[111] While appreciating Wardle's argument about the need to remove agitators from the camps, the associate deputy minister of Labour regretted that nothing could be done at the moment because of the lack of available space at internment facilities. He simply suggested that the striking men be given two meals a day until they returned to work. Wardle was disappointed with this response and asked Mitchell whether it would be possible to "designate one of our less comfortable camps as a camp for nonworkers and strikers."[112] He also decided to write the security commission directly about the need for "proper corrective action," lest the success of the camps be jeopardized.[113]

While government officials were trying to decide what to do about the steadily deteriorating situation in the camps, project officials announced the new two-meal-a-day policy at Gosnell on 12 June 1942. An attempt to remove the strike leader the next day, however, nearly precipitated a riot, when the entire camp chased after the man and his armed escort, encircling them before they could reach the local station. Unable to convince the mob to disperse, the supervising foreman wisely decided to return the man to camp when the Japanese vowed to resume work if no one was taken away. But the rescue was short-lived. An RCMP detachment arrived the next day from Vancouver, quickly rounded up all the members of the camp committee, and took them away in a boxcar to a temporary detention centre—the Blue River Ski Club clubhouse. The police commander then ordered the rest of the men back to work, letting it be known that the detachment would remain on the scene if they failed to

Lempriere camp, 1 July 1942. *Courtesy G. Funamoto*

co-operate.[114] The strike was barely over, however, when another flare-up occurred. This time, the men at Grantbrook (B5) struck work on 17 June, and in a scene reminiscent of the 1935 On-to-Ottawa Trek, set off for project headquarters at Red Pass Junction to complain about their situation. Along the way they induced the men at Rainbow camp (B6) to join them, bringing the total number of marchers to two hundred. Mitchell personally intercepted the marchers along the shore of Moose Lake and promised to relay their grievances—in particular the restrictions on travel to other camps—to the appropriate officials. Although the men voted to return to their respective camps, they decided to remain on strike until some action was forthcoming.[115]

These incidents prompted another round of questioning by government officials about the operation of the camps and the behaviour of the Japanese. There was, in fact, growing public criticism of camp management. On 4 June 1942, the Kamloops *Sentinel* charged that the foremen were flunkies for the Japanese nationals, that the Japanese controlled rations, and that the guards were laughed at and had no backing.[116] These accusations were repeated in the House of Commons by T.J. O'Neill, the Liberal member for Kamloops, and when the minister of Labour attempted to respond a few weeks later, O'Neill shot back, "How much longer are we going to pussyfoot with those yellow devils in the West?"[117] This kind of censure wounded project engineers, but in many respects, as far as they were concerned, it was true. J.H. Mitchell was clearly annoyed that the Japanese could malinger on the job or flout camp regulations and not be punished accordingly. His immediate supervisor, C.M. Walker, agreed, suggesting that the project officers had been "placed in the position of 'foster mother' to the Japanese."[118] They not only had to listen to their every complaint, no matter how trivial, but were forever coaxing, if not begging, them to get on with their jobs. What was most galling for Walker and other supervisory officials, however, was that the Japanese knew that camp officials could do little to make them work. They also assumed that the Japanese had an attitude problem and simply wanted special privileges—why else would they complain when regular "white" workers lived and worked under the same camp conditions without complaint?[119]

Distressed by this assessment and what it ultimately meant for highway construction, Wardle strongly urged the deputy minister of Mines and Resources to see that project foremen were given the authority to remove immediately anyone who refused to do a fair day's work. "If they are at fault," he argued in defence of his demoralized men, "it is that they are too lenient."[120] There were also a number of other, less draconian, ideas put forward to break the deadlock in the camps. Mitchell suggested that the Japanese might be more manageable if they were segregated by religion, rather than nationality.[121] The associate deputy minister of Labour, on the other hand, naively wondered whether the presence of men from the YMCA or Frontier College might "bring about a better feeling?"[122] Project officials also quietly investigated the practicality of having the men's families join them in the camps.[123]

. . .

The news from the camps, in the meantime, continued to be bad. On 22 June 1942, R.M. Corning, one of the resident engineers, reported that the Japanese, believing that the highway was to be a military road, were prepared to do their best to forestall its completion. Recent construction statistics bore this out; the work was not only costing three to four times what it normally did, but was alternating between two speeds: stop and go-slow. Corning also expressed concern about the Japanese exploiting every opportunity to undermine operations, and commented that their use on the project was turning out to be a miserable failure. "Kindness on the part of the staff," he remarked, "is looked upon as weakness; tolerance as fear; and appeasement with contempt."[124] Camp administrators were also in a quandary about how to deal with the constant work stoppages. Since men were paid only when they worked, strikers could not afford to pay for their meals. But if they fed these men free of charge, then the entire camp could walk off the job, knowing that rations would still be provided. And if food supplies were curtailed, neutral countries monitoring the camps might complain. Walker nicely summed up the thinking of his colleagues when he observed, "The Japanese are very much under the impression they have the white man on the run and need only to threaten to go on strike in order to gain any concession which they may desire."[125] Wardle, by this point, was thoroughly exasperated. He had handled similar situations in the past with an iron hand, and he was not about to change his style. The evacuees' antics had to be crushed. To this end, he cautioned his minister that unless "prompt and firm action" was taken, "the Japanese will become insolent and rebellious to the point where they can only be checked with violence, with the possible loss of life."[126] Essentially, Wardle was advocating the transformation of the road camps into internment centres, similar to those that had existed in the national parks during the last war.

It was around this time that the Jasper camps came to a standstill. The first inkling of trouble was 11 June 1942, when one of the project engineers recommended the removal of eight men from Geikie for disciplinary problems.[127] Four days later, after a meeting in the mess hall, the Japanese put forward a petition for the dismissal of the camp subforeman for being drunk and abusive on the job.[128] An internal investigation confirmed the substance of this complaint; the Jasper superintendent had also reported that the foreman and his assistants were bringing booze into camp. But before the men could be replaced, tensions finally erupted. On the afternoon of 22 June, a teamster carrying a partial load of dynamite would not allow a small group of Japanese, who were smoking, to hitch a ride back to work on his wagon. One individual, M. Inouye, apparently refused to get off and was yelled at by the driver. Shamed

The men at Geikie constantly complained about the separation from their families. The camp was raided on 25 June 1942 by the RCMP and park wardens in an effort to remove men who refused to work. *National Archives of Canada, PA118000*

by the incident, Inouye visited the man's tent after supper and challenged him to a fight with sticks. When the teamster refused, Inouye struck the man on one of his legs.[129] A sergeant from the Jasper RCMP detachment visited the camp the next day and tried to get the two sides to forget about the incident. But when the Japanese refused to load the teamster's wagon, the policeman wired Edmonton for reinforcements and returned the next day with a heavily armed truck caravan, including park wardens, to remove Inouye and the other agitators. A search of the camp also uncovered a number of tools—mostly axes and hammers—as well as a camera and bottle of brandy. The police detail then continued down the line to Decoigne, where it picked up a handful of troublemakers and posted extra guards in an apparent effort to prevent communication between the two camps. Decoigne responded by going on strike.[130]

Mitchell spent the last week of June trying to get the Jasper camps back to work, and the Japanese at Decoigne evidently shared this desire. On 26 June 1942, one day after the police raid, they informed Mitchell that they would end their strike if the arrested men were returned and two camp foremen were replaced. "Ever since five men been arrested, we are in despair, very unpeaceful, we are unable to carry on as usual," their letter read.[131] Mitchell replied in an open letter to the workers three days later, regretting that the arrest of the men had caused them grief, but claiming that it was strictly a police matter beyond his control. He also balked at getting rid of any supervisory personnel, but promised to send to Decoigne in a few days a man who would try to resolve their grievances. Finally, he encouraged the men to pick up their tools and not let recent events bother them. "Your going on strike does not meet with my approval," he scolded them, "and as a friend who is always trying to better your condition, let me say that a strike is only an injury to yourselves."[132] This paternalistic tone would have shocked Jasper residents. Word about the assault at Geikie, followed by the strikes there and at Decoigne, had them up in arms. They felt vulnerable and were worried that their three-man police detachment would be no match for the Japanese if they ever decided to march on the townsite. The Jasper Women's Institute petitioned the Department of National Defence to establish a military camp in the park–a request seconded by Superintendent Wood in a confidential memo about recent events to his superiors. "It appears that the Japanese are pretty much out of hand," he cautioned Ottawa, "and do practically what they please."[133]

. . .

By early July 1942, both Geikie and Decoigne had resumed work on the road. Project officials were under no illusion, though, that the situation was back to normal–if it ever had been. The men at Decoigne seemed determined to foil project officials and were threatening to strike again on 15 July if the hard-nosed foreman was not removed. These continuing tensions coincided with a number of reports on the state of the highway project and the problems with the workers. By the end of June, Mitchell reported that a crude, driveable tote trail existed between Geikie and Albreda–a distance of 103 miles–and that the Japanese between Jasper and Tête Jaune Cache would be building the actual road grade for the rest of the summer. Progress was soured by the fact that the workers were giving only 40 percent value for their wages, and over half a million dollars had already been spent on the highway.[134]

The Engineering and Construction Service completed its investigation of the idea of having families join the men on the project, and flatly refused to be responsible for the camps if the scheme ever went ahead. It was argued that there was no room at the existing camps for additional accommodation, that the families would have to be evacuated during the winter months anyway, and that the presence of children would create unwanted burdens, such as schooling. "It appears to me that there would be so many conflicting interests between the Japanese themselves, and so many intricate problems to look after," Walker warned, "that the engineer in charge of such projects would be absolutely unable to handle the situation."[135]

There were also two independent, external reviews of the Yellowhead–Blue River project at this time. In late June, the RCMP commissioner dispatched Detective Sergeant W.J. Woods to determine whether the Japanese located along the major rail lines constituted a threat. Visiting all fifteen Yellowhead camps, he found that "the fundamental cause of discontent" among the Japanese was not the food, the accommodation, nor the work, but the separation from their families. He was also informed by the guards that men from neighbouring camps were secretly meeting in the bush at night to plot strategy, and that foremen generally had no control or influence over their charges. As a result, Woods recommended that all the Japanese be removed from the region, and suggested that if the highway was considered a military necessity, then it should be constructed by regular labour with proper equipment.[136]

Mess hall and kitchen staff at Albreda road camp. *Courtesy C.J. Okawara*

The other assessment was made by Ernest Trueman, Japanese placement officer for the Department of Labour in Toronto. Trueman would create something of a small storm in January 1943, when he publicly claimed that the Japanese had been evacuated from British Columbia to satisfy white residents.[137] His June 1942 report to the British Columbia Security Commission on the conditions in the work camps was equally hard-hitting. He too visited most of the Yellowhead camps, but unlike Detective Sergeant Woods, he found the men to be "grievously misused." He described inexplicable delays in mail, pathetic monthly earnings, "monotonous and meaningless" work, arrest and internment for minor complaints, lack of recreation, low morale, and an overwhelming sense of emptiness. In the end, though, his conclusion was the same: the men should be reunited with their families. Otherwise, Trueman counselled, "when feelings are as intense as they are at present, the slightest spark may set off a conflagration that might have consequences of an international nature."[138]

These reports were damning in their own right; taken together, they were impossible to ignore, especially since they suggested that sabotage might become a real possibility the longer that family reunification was delayed. And on 3 July 1942, the associate deputy minister of Labour privately advised Wardle that the married men on the project would soon join their families in new housing settlements in the British Columbia interior.[139] In the interim, the Department of Labour believed that attaching at least one uniformed RCMP constable to each camp and establishing a military training camp near Jasper would have a calming–if not intimidating–effect on the road camps.[140] One week later, the question of what to do with the Japanese working on the Yellowhead–Blue River highway was formally decided at a special cabinet subcommittee meeting. After reviewing the history of strife in the camps and the present situation, the minister of Labour recommended that work on the project be suspended; married men would be united with their families as soon as accommodation was available, while the single Japanese would be sent to highway camps in northern Ontario. Wardle was to be given one week's notice before the first batch of men was removed sometime in August.[141] The evacuees had apparently won.

· · ·

The decision to close the camps could not have come soon enough for the residents of Jasper. Believing that British Columbia had simply handed them its problem, they had resented the mere presence of the Japanese in the park. They also continued to fear that the Japanese would rise up one day and overrun the townsite–a feeling that festered with each passing week and every unfounded rumour. But the Department of Labour, in co-operation with the BC Security Commission, evidently decided to wait until the evacuation plans were more advanced before announcing the closure of the camps. And emotions in Jasper continued to escalate through July, so much so that seven of the townsite's organizations banded together with the chamber of commerce and sent a joint three-page resolution to the minister of National Defence on 13 July 1942. Pleading with the minister to take action before a repeat of Hong Kong was played out on Canadian soil, they called for the establishment of armed units at strategic points along the highway project. If the government was not prepared to protect its citizens, they requested permission to arm themselves and form their own defence corps. Tired of being treated with indifference and

Ornamental gardens were erected at some road camps. *University of British Columbia Library, Special Collections and University Archives Division, Japanese Canadian Photograph Collection*

complacency by Ottawa, they demanded "action now, *not* after the Japanese have invaded our shores, when it is too late."[142]

While Jasper remained ignorant of the government's decision about the future of the Yellowhead road camps, the BC Security Commission lost no time in informing the Japanese of its new reunification policy—and for good reason. A representative of Spain, which served as the protecting power for Japanese interests in Canada, was scheduled to inspect the road camps in late July, and the security commission wanted to avoid any suggestion that the Japanese were being mistreated. The commission was also worried that the men at Decoigne might follow through on their threat to strike and possibly set off another round of work stoppages around the time of the international inspection.[143] Before the fate of the project had been officially decided by the cabinet subcommittee, then, two leaders of the Vancouver Japanese community, Ippei Nishio and Toshi Tanaka, arrived in Jasper on 8 July to visit the road camps and explain that married men would soon be joining their families. Over the next few days, with C.M. Walker as their personal guide, they slowly worked their way from camp to camp, announcing the new policy and then listening to any complaints or concerns. Between camp visits, the two Japanese leaders and Walker politely argued about the reasons for the problems in the camps. Nishio and Tanaka tried to impress upon the engineer the need for camp foremen to be more understanding and sensitive; Walker, in turn, took every opportunity to point out men sitting along the banks of the right-of-way frittering away the working day.[144] As with the situation on the project, they were worlds apart.

Representatives of the protecting power arrived to inspect the project on 18 July 1942. The delegation included two members of the Spanish consulate in Vancouver, an International Red Cross official, Frederick Mead of the security commission, and a senior bureaucrat from External Affairs; Walker once again represented the Engineering and Construction Service. Travelling by private railway car along the Yellowhead route, they visited only three of fifteen camps–Red Pass, Rainbow, and Geikie–before taking refuge from the constant rain at Jasper Park Lodge. Curiously, the only complaints about working conditions were heard at Geikie, where the Japanese grumbled about leaky tents, as well as the shortage of green vegetables.[145] Otherwise, all was well–or at least the delegates seemed to think so. It is possible that the delegation might have spent more time visiting the camps and the Japanese might have been more forthcoming about their lives there, were it not for the fact that the days of the project were apparently numbered. Revisiting all the Yellowhead camps on the heels of the delegation, RCMP Detective Sergeant Woods reported similar findings and confidently reported that the new reunification policy "has certainly eliminated all the former tension and hostility."[146]

Once his duties with the protecting power had been fulfilled, Walker left for Vancouver to confer with the commission regarding the evacuation of the men. It had been three weeks since they had decided to reunite the workers

Washday at Rainbow camp. *Courtesy G. Funamoto*

with their families, and the commission was ready to move. Between 500 and 600 married men were to be placed on the Hope-Princeton highway as soon as possible, and the rest of the approximately 1,260 Japanese would be moved shortly thereafter. Walker was surprised at the speed with which the commission intended to shut down the road camps, and suggested that a man be immediately dispatched to Red Pass Junction to make the necessary arrangements for the transfer of the men.[147] Little did he realize, though, that by the time he returned to Banff on the evening of Friday 24 July, he would have a telegram waiting for him advising that the three most easterly camps—Geikie, Decoigne, and Yellowhead (B1)—were to be closed the following Tuesday. The move was officially confirmed by the Department of Labour in a brief memo three days later stating simply that the work of the Japanese had been "entirely unsatisfactory," and that construction would be discontinued pending an assessment of the military significance of the highway.[148]

Jasper residents greeted the news of the impending closures with relief and a sense of vindication. The Edson-Jasper *Signal* suggested that using Japanese aliens on the road had been a serious error. "It soon became a question of which was the most objectionable—the Japs or the blockade to the Coast," the newspaper contended. "Now the Japs themselves have settled the question."[149] Other organizations and individuals undoubtedly had less charitable things to say. Nor did the rumours subside. While camping in the park in late July, E.T. Love, chairman of the Jasper Park Development Committee, was told that one of the last defiant acts of the Japanese was to throw a beer bottle through the window of a speeding passenger train.[150] Many hoped that the rest of the tourist season might be salvaged following the departure of the Japanese from Geikie and Decoigne. As Love told the development committee in the late spring, "Tourists who can travel this year will not care to go to any place where there are Japs, and if tourists do visit Jasper, they will certainly not enjoy seeing the Japs."[151]

There were other groups and individuals, however, who regretted the suspension of work on the Yellowhead–Blue River highway. Both the Alberta Motor Association and the National Parks Highway Association formally protested the government's plan; there was even speculation that the agitation against the Japanese had been deliberately fomented by other localities who wanted work done on their roads.[152] T.J. O'Neill, the Kamloops MP, also wanted to see the road completed—by forced labour, if necessary—and questioned the reasons behind the closure of the camps. "Really no argument or excuse can be offered," he scolded the deputy minister of Labour, "except that the Japanese did not wish to be separated from their wives and families. I am afraid the Government adopting such a policy will be well-nigh inexplainable."[153] Evidently, a road through the mountains was more important than the personal lives of several hundred evacuees.

Project authorities were also upset with the way in which the removal of the Japanese was being handled. On 21 July, after being advised by Ottawa that the project was to be shut down, RCMP Detective Sergeant Woods took it upon himself to travel from Jasper to Red Pass, announcing the imminent closure of the camps. This news not only had an unsettling effect on the Japanese—they were apparently overwhelmed by the prospect of seeing their families again—but was extremely disconcerting to supervisory personnel, who had yet to receive any official confirmation.[154] Then, while Chief Engineer Mitchell was visiting Prince Rupert on business, an official from the security commission arrived at Red Pass on 24 July and told project officers that all the Japanese were to be removed without delay. Four days later, with Mitchell still away, the 176 Japanese at Geikie, Decoigne, and Yellowhead were evacuated, leaving the camps virtually abandoned, with only the dazed local foremen to clean up the sites and attend to the equipment and tools. There were problems at the other end as well. The settlements established in the BC interior to accommodate evacuated Japanese were not prepared for the sudden arrival of so many men, and despite earlier promises, some of the Issei could not be reunited with their families.[155] So the commission ordered its overly efficient man at Red Pass to slow down his operations and not ship any unmarried Japanese until at least the middle of September.[156]

This slowdown worked to the benefit of the project. In early August, the British Columbia minister of Public Works asked the federal minister of Labour if it would be possible to leave enough single men in the camps to complete a crude road from Jasper to Blue River, a request that was seconded by the Department of Mines and Resources. J.M. Wardle inspected the route from Geikie to Red Pass later in the month and was "agreeably surprised" by what had been accomplished, particularly in light of the negative reports emanating from the camps in May and June. "The strikes and other troubles with the Japanese," he confessed to the chairman of the commission, "no doubt diverted everyone's mind . . . from the fact that a good deal of useful work was being done."[157] Wardle later argued with Labour officials that if the single Japanese could continue to work satisfactorily—as they were doing at the time of his visit—then there was no reason to move them, especially when there was a good chance of having a passable road in place by late fall. He maintained as well that the remaining 296 men would be less of a threat, not only because of their reduced numbers and markedly improved behaviour, but also because the bulk of the heavy work yet to be done, between Gosnell and Thunder River, was on the opposite side of the Thompson River from the Canadian National main line. These representations carried the day, and on 15 September, at roughly the time that the single Japanese were scheduled to be evacuated, Mitchell was advised by Ottawa that the men would remain at work on the highway as long as progress was being made.[158] The news must have come as a cruel joke.

· · ·

The continuation of the project did not mean that Japanese would be brought back into Jasper National Park, even though there was a swampy section of road requiring fill near Decoigne. Mines and Resources officials were not that stupid. Instead, Superintendent Wood gladly lent the services of ten conscientious objectors who had been engaged on other park work. Armed with two bulldozers, this small crew reopened the camp in mid-September and spent the next few weeks doing what one hundred Japanese had been expected to do with shovels and wheelbarrows.[159] The other workers, in the meantime, were consolidated in four camps along the Thompson River, where the highway had yet to be cleared. Because this area was not subject to the same amount of snowfall as the pass, it was also decided to transfer project headquarters to Blue River.

By the following summer, fewer than two hundred Japanese were working on the project in the Thunder River area; the rest of the road received little, if any, attention. While visiting Jasper in September 1943, C.M. Walker inspected the grade west from Geikie to Yellowhead and found the route extremely rough, somewhat narrow in places, and generally wet; the Miette River had washed over the road in two places, and a huge boulder had rolled down from Yellowhead Summit and come to rest squarely in the middle of the road.[160] These conditions prompted a probing letter from the Jasper Chamber of Commerce decrying the fact that the highway could not be used by park visitors. Wardle probably shook his head over the note, but simply chose to remind the Jasper group that his department had been obliged to remove the Japanese from the area before they were able to bring the road up to standard; he did, however, likely create something of a stir in the townsite by suggesting that the camps might be re-established the following summer.[161]

This never actually happened, and although there was talk each year of removing the remaining Japanese and putting them on other work, the project limped along as best it could with a steadily declining workforce. By July 1944, there were only about eighty-five mainly elderly Japanese still assigned to the camps; almost two years later, the number had dropped to thirty-five. Fortunately, more of the work was done by heavy equipment, particularly on a bad stretch near Thunder River, and by October 1944, a pioneer road was finally punched through to Blue River. It was little better than a tote trail, though, and by the time the project was officially closed on 31 May 1946, the highway had still not been opened to the public because of slides, washouts, and the generally poor condition of the grade. Project engineers doubted whether it would be ready for several more years.[162]

The project would also come back to haunt many of the Japanese. In August 1944, Prime Minister King announced that his government would establish a special commission to determine which persons of Japanese ancestry would

Single Japanese males laboured on the road project for the duration of the war.
Confidential source

be allowed to remain in Canada after the war; those considered disloyal would be deported to Japan. Gathering evidence for these hearings, Norman Robertson, the undersecretary of state for External Affairs, asked Mines and Resources to provide a list of all Japanese who had caused trouble on any highway or construction project. This request provided the Engineering and Construction Service with a perfect opportunity to secure a measure of revenge. During the spring and summer of 1942, project officials had been thoroughly frustrated in their attempts to get the Japanese to work on the Yellowhead–Blue River highway. Now they were being asked to identify individuals for possible deportation, and they welcomed the chance, combing through back files, as well as consulting with men who had been in charge of the camps.[163] In the end, a list of seventy-five men was submitted, including those from Geikie and Decoigne who had been forcibly removed by the RCMP in late June 1942.[164] And the reprisals did not stop there. In January 1946, T.B. Pickersgill, the commissioner of Japanese placement, informed C.M. Walker that the few remaining nationals on the Yellowhead project might be removed and repatriated the following month.[165] Although the camps continued to operate until the end of May, it is not clear—in either case—how many of the Japanese were eventually deported. It is also not known whether any of the men were given the choice of repatriation or staying in Canada, but moving east of the Rockies.

This outcome was hardly surprising. Although the Yellowhead–Blue River highway would have greatly benefitted Jasper National Park and its desire for more tourists, park residents were not prepared to accept Japanese nationals within park boundaries. It did not matter that the evacuees would be working on a road that would finally open the Yellowhead Pass to automobile traffic. Their very presence constituted a threat not only to the park's image but to the townsite itself, and local residents wanted them gone. Project officials and foremen also had a difficult time with the Japanese. They could not understand why the men refused to render a full day's labour, let alone appreciate the underlying cause of their unrest. All they knew was that their workforce not only refused to co-operate, but could not be dismissed or disciplined. Having never encountered such a frustrating situation, their patience was quickly exhausted.

As for the Japanese, their stint on the Yellowhead–Blue River project was equivalent to a prison term. Taken from their wives and children, dispossessed of their property, and sent to toil in isolated road camps, their confusion and disillusionment quickly turned to bitterness, and they used the only weapon they had to fight back—the withdrawal of their labour. In the end, the Japanese forced the Canadian government to recognize a fundamental fact about human behaviour that transcends all races and circumstances—it is "impossible to separate men from their families."[166]

CHAPTER SIX

Nazis

I**T WAS ONE OF THE DECISIVE BATTLES OF THE SECOND WORLD WAR.** In late October 1942, Allied forces under the command of the diminutive British General Bernard Montgomery routed the well-fortified German Afrika Korps at el Alamein and sent Field Marshall Erwin Rommel, the so-called desert fox, fleeing back to Berlin. In the days that followed, several thousand stranded German soldiers, including twenty-four-year-old George Foerster, surrendered to Australian troops and were temporarily held in Egypt. They were then transported by boat first to South Africa, then Uruguay, and finally, Liverpool, England. Here, they boarded the *Queen Mary* and travelled back across the Atlantic, this time with a special passenger—British Prime Minister Winston Churchill, who was on his way to confer with American President Franklin Roosevelt. Landing at New York, Foerster and his fellow Germans were taken by train across Canada to a large, new prisoner-of-war camp in Medicine Hat, Alberta. He did not stay long, for in the early fall of 1943, he volunteered to serve in a woodcutting camp at Riding Mountain National Park in westcentral Manitoba. And on the morning of 26 October, exactly a year after the North Africa campaign, Foerster climbed into the back of a waiting truck at the Dauphin railway station and was whisked away to his new winter home on the shores of Whitewater Lake.[1]

That prisoners such as George Foerster would come to be interned in Canada was entirely unexpected at the beginning of the Second World War. The King government was prepared to act against suspected enemy aliens and did so, beginning 3 September 1939, under the new Defence of Canada Regulations.[2] But guarding soldiers captured in foreign lands was another matter. Wishing to fight a "limited liability" war, Prime Minister King deliberately tried to avoid major commitments in the interests of national unity. The one exception was the British Commonwealth Air Training Plan (BCATP), a December 1939 agreement between Great Britain and its Commonwealth partners to train air crews on Canadian soil for the Allied war effort. But even here, it was a contribution that did not involve sending large numbers of Canadian men and women overseas. And during the negotiations, King insisted that the plan take precedence over all other forms of military assistance.[3] He was determined that conscription would not rack the country as it had done during the Great War.

The government's war strategy was perfectly suited for the opening months of the conflict—what was known as the Phoney War. But following the spring 1940 German offensive, the evacuation from Dunkirk, and the fall of France, Britain came back knocking on Canada's door. Fearing a possible German invasion, the British government asked Ottawa to provide detention facilities for several thousand civilian internees and prisoners of war. The Canadian government initially balked at the request; it was busy rounding up its own suspected enemy aliens and trying to calm public fears about fifth column activity.[4] But when the British persisted, the King administration reluctantly agreed to serve as one of the official gaolers for the Allied war effort. During the winter of 1940-41, Great Britain and the dominion governments formalized the arrangements under which prisoners of war would be held.[5] Britain agreed to cover the costs of transporting and maintaining the men, including the construction of new camp facilities; the holding country, on the other hand, would pay for work performed by the prisoners. These financial and administrative agreements eventually resulted in more than thirty-four thousand German prisoners of war being housed at some twenty-five different sites across Canada by 1946.[6]

· · ·

The National Parks Bureau had first been contacted about providing detention stations in June 1940, one of the bleakest months of the European campaign. Normally, this kind of free labour would have been fought over by the various parks, especially since the war had brought about another period of retrenchment and consolidation in park funding. Many Parks officers, however, remembered the sorry experience with enemy aliens in national parks during the Great War—how the men could not be compelled to work under international regulations—and believed that any new attempt to establish similar camps for civilian internees or prisoners of war would likely have the same result. They were also concerned that the costs of guarding German combatants would far outweigh the value of their labour, especially when internment officials indicated that each camp would need to hold a minimum five hundred men.[7] "The real Nazi is a wolf to handle," warned a department official, "and the amount of work obtained from such prisoners would depend entirely on the degree and kind of discipline maintained with such prisoners."[8] Anticipating problems, the Department of Mines and Resources proceeded carefully and in mid-July 1940, agreed to employ only a few hundred civilian internees on a stretch of the Trans-Canada Highway between Schreiber and White River in northwestern

George Foerster was one of more than four hundred German prisoners transferred from Medicine Hat to Riding Mountain in October 1943. *Riding Mountain National Park Collection*

Ontario. It had no interest, however, in babysitting a nest of Nazis.

The matter resurfaced in December 1941, when the King government agreed to accept four thousand German prisoners from the North Africa campaign. This time, internment officials proposed to build three permanent, ten-thousand-man camps and thereby solve their accommodation woes with one stroke. They had to hurry, though—the men were scheduled to arrive within four months. In late January 1942, two Defence Department officers called upon Roy Gibson, the director of Lands, Parks, and Forests Branch, for a list of sites where holding pens might be erected; they were looking for federal lands that were open and level, relatively accessible, and easily serviced. They also warned that the camps would be first and foremost detention centres—the prisoners were not expected to perform any useful work. Although Gibson was lukewarm to the idea of becoming involved in internment operations, particularly when the camps would be little more than prisons, he identified several national parks, forest experimental stations, and Indian reserves where the men could be placed.[9] By the spring, however, Ottawa decided to build two large, identical camps in southern Alberta—one at Lethbridge, the other at Medicine Hat. It also took steps to consolidate the administration of internment operations under the Department of National Defence; as of January 1943, it would have sole responsibility for the maintenance and care of all prisoners of war and internees.[10] The camps would be guarded by a special Veterans Guard, created in May 1940 and made up of ex-servicemen considered too old for combat duty.

By November 1942, more than sixteen thousand prisoners of war were held in Canada.[11] This number would jump by almost a third in 1943, when Canada agreed to accept another large batch of Germans from North Africa, including George Foerster. The presence of so much idle labour soon proved too much of a temptation for the King government. Although Ottawa had initially doubted whether these men could be expected to do much work, the situation by 1943 was entirely different. The strains of war had taken their toll, and there was a growing demand for the better allocation of human resources on the home front. Ottawa responded in April 1943 by giving the Department of Labour the power to direct several thousand conscientious objectors to essential war work in agriculture or industry. That still left many areas of the economy, such as the harvesting of natural resources, facing a serious shortage of workers. And the pool of German prisoners could nicely fill this role—as long as their labour did not make a direct contribution to the Canadian war effort. On 10 May 1943, then, the King administration introduced new regulations authorizing the Departments of Labour and National Defence to employ volunteer prisoners of war on essential work projects across the country.[12] A few weeks later, a Directorate of Labour Projects for prisoners of war was formally established to supervise and coordinate the new programme. Work got under way in early August in the fields and forests, on the docks, and in the factories. By the end of the war, almost sixteen thousand prisoners of war had been involved in 169 different projects.[13]

According to the regulations, the Department of Labour could make an arrangement with any other federal department or provincial government for access to the men. And the department lost little time finding potential jobs or customers for the prisoners' labour. Just three days after the work scheme had been approved, the associate deputy minister contacted Roy Gibson and asked if there were any isolated places under his branch's jurisdiction where interned Germans could be used to cut fuelwood. The firewood situation had been particularly acute during the winter of 1942-43, and it was predicted that there would be a shortfall of 1.3 million cords (or 12 percent of the normal consumption) for the coming winter. This was a serious challenge to the domestic war effort; almost half the households in Canada at the time still depended on wood as a source of heat.[14] The King government did not want Canadians worrying about keeping warm, especially when the war was far from won. The Department of Munitions and Supply, which was responsible for fuelwood production and consumption, was so concerned about the impending fuel shortage that it established in late May the new position of Wood Fuel Controller, with special responsibility for purchasing supplies, setting up reserve stockpiles, and organizing special production projects.[15]

Gibson, in the meantime, had not changed his mind about getting the parks involved with prisoner labour again, and tried to discourage the establishment of a woodcutting camp. Given his department's disappointing experience with enemy aliens during the last war, he remained leery of the value of this labour,

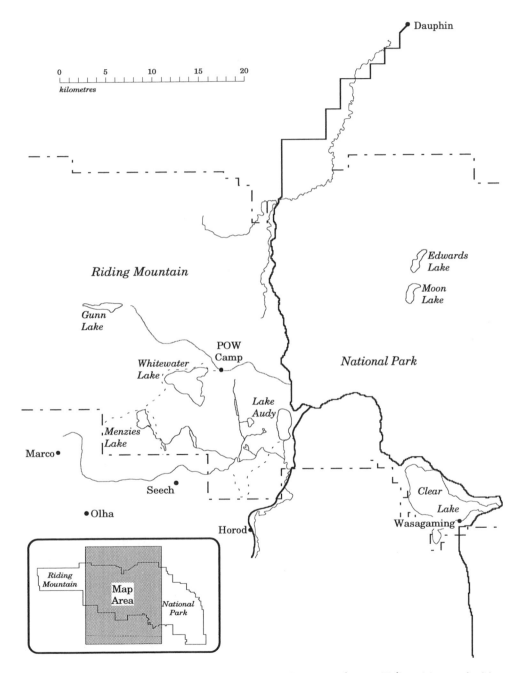

Whitewater Woodcutting Project, German prisoners of war, Riding Mountain National Park, 1943–45.

particularly in light of the recent problems with Japanese evacuees on the Yellowhead project.[16] He also reported that Canadian civilian internees, now being held at several forest experiment stations, "were not even cutting enough wood to keep themselves warm";[17] alternative service workers were supplying the fuel for these camps, as well as their own. He even suggested that individuals or small companies could be granted special permits to cut timber on federal park lands and forest reserves. But the fuel shortage problem would not go away, and in early June 1943, C.D. Howe of Munitions and Supply formally asked his counterpart at Mines and Resources about the possibility of using four hundred German prisoners of war to cut ten thousand cords from a fire-killed area near Lake Audy in Riding Mountain National Park.

The National Parks Bureau, privately warned that such a request would be forthcoming, continued to have mixed feelings about the proposal. It was not clear, for example, who would be responsible for the camp and the supervision of the men—Mines and Resources, Labour, Defence, or Munitions and Supply? The problem of conflicting jurisdictions had plagued the enemy alien work camps during the Great War. Parks officials were also uncertain about what their exact role should be; although they did not want to be directly involved in the project, they were equally worried that park interests might be sacrificed if they did not have a voice in the running of the camp. In addition, there were fears that the presence of Nazis in the park would not only frighten off summer campers, but pose a security threat both to the visiting public and the forest. The matter was further complicated by the fact that many of the immigrants living around the park were from continental Europe—would they be sympathetic to the Germans and possibly aid their escape? These were sticky questions, and as far as the Parks Bureau was concerned, the easiest solution would be to give Riding Mountain an extra two hundred alternative service workers and have them do the job without the accompanying grief.[18]

These men were not available, however, and the Parks Bureau had no choice but to enter into negotiations with the other concerned departments. By mid-June, it had been agreed that Munitions and Supply—in particular the Wood Fuel Controller's office—would operate the camp; it would attend to the general care of the men and direct the woodcutting work. The other departments would play lesser, but no less significant, roles. Labour would retain responsibility for camp security, while Defence would oversee the movement of prisoners, project censorship, and mail. Mines and Resources would be restricted to selecting the campsite and locating roads, identifying the timber to be cut, and enforcing national park regulations. This bureaucratic tangle of split responsibility promised only confusion, if not trouble. The arrangements also went against the way in which relief and alternative service camps had previously been organized in the parks. But as the short-lived Japanese road camps in Jasper National Park had shown, there were limits to the kinds of workers that were welcome in Canada's national playgrounds. And if they could not be kept out, the Parks Bureau wished to restrict its involvement as much as possible.

. . .

Originally, the German prisoners were to have been placed along the south shore of Lake Audy at the site of a former National Forestry Programme camp. But after investigating a number of possibilities, the park superintendent pointed out that there would be more work for the men—and for several years after the war—if the camp was built along the north shore of Whitewater Lake near a fire-damaged stand of poplar, which was likely to yield two hundred thousand cords of fuelwood. Although this site was more isolated and would present access problems, especially during the winter, it was quickly approved by an inspector from Wartime Housing Limited, the federal crown corporation created in 1941 to provide accommodation for persons engaged in war work in areas where there was a housing shortage.[19] The Carter-Halls-Aldinger Construction Company of Winnipeg was then engaged to begin work immediately on the camp. But because of the unusually wet spring, the trail leading to the campsite from Lake Audy was too soft for heavy traffic, so the contractor was forced to spend several frustrating weeks, beginning in late June, filling and corduroying the trail to the worksite. This delay threatened to set back completion of the camp until the fall, and to speed up the work, both on the road and at the campsite, the Riding Mountain superintendent secured permission to use the small park crew of alternative service workers on the job. The irony of this activity—using conscientious objectors to build a prisoner-of-war camp—seems to have been lost on the various officials. But they had a camp to build and little time in which to do it.[20]

The Whitewater camp was built with the help of conscientious objectors from the alternative service programme. *Riding Mountain National Park Collection*

Despite the extra manpower and the commandeering of park road equipment, work on the camp trail continued to be hampered by heavy rains, and it was not until early August that the contractor finally began work on the actual camp buildings. J.S. Whalley, the Wood Fuel Controller, used the intervening time to finalize camp arrangements and try to find a project foreman. He repeatedly tried to foist this job on the park superintendent, Otto Heaslip, but in late July Gibson finally stepped in and politely but firmly reminded him that there was a "definite understanding" that Parks personnel were to provide only support and advice.[21] He repeated this warning about a month later when it became apparent that Whalley's office was still being dogged by organizational difficulties. No arrangements had been made, for example, to line up truckers to bring in supplies or haul the wood, and even if they had, the park roads in the area would not be able to withstand the continuous traffic unless they were upgraded.[22] These and other problems were also identified by the general manager of Wartime Housing, who visited the site in mid-August following formal approval of the project[23] and came away thoroughly discouraged. In the face of this criticism, Whalley withdrew his office from supervising the project in favour of handing over the job to Wartime Housing, a curious development, since the corporation's activities during the war were largely confined to providing or acquiring housing in urban areas. Operating a four-hundred-man prisoner-of-war camp in the heart of Riding Mountain National Park did not seem at first glance to fit its mandate. But the firewood was needed and Munitions and Supply was committed to the project. And besides, Wartime Housing was technically responsible for constructing and managing accommodation for workers engaged in the production of essential supplies.[24] Why not a labour camp? The change in management, however, did nothing to alter the park's relationship with the project. "This operation is to be carried on," Gibson instructed Superintendent Heaslip, "as though it were a private enterprise under park regulations."[25]

One of Wartime Housing's first jobs was to secure a supply of woodcutters. And on 6 August 1943, around the time that the camp buildings had finally started to go up, R.S. Fordham, the director of Labour Projects, asked the Department of National Defence for several hundred noncombatant prisoners, preferably from the same service, for Riding Mountain.[26] Nothing was done about the request—probably because camp construction was behind schedule—until mid-September, when the call for men was forwarded to the new Medicine Hat facility. Wartime Housing wanted a minimum of four hundred men who were fit enough to cut and stack three-quarters of a cord of wood per man per working day. If possible, it was also interested in securing skilled tradesmen, cooks, clerks, and service and health care specialists, who could attend to the daily operation and maintenance of the camp. Finding this number of workers would not be difficult. The leader of the German prisoners

Most of the Riding Mountain prisoners had been captured in North Africa in the fall of 1942. The bearcub in the foreground, taken from its mother as a baby, was led around on a leash and became good friends with the camp dog. *Riding Mountain National Park Collection*

at Medicine Hat, or camp spokesman as he was called,[27] expected to be flooded with volunteers once the details of the project were circulated among the prisoners. George Foerster, for example, was bored at the large camp and jumped at the chance to work outdoors in the forest. Josef Gabski, another former prisoner now living in Chico, California, felt much the same way; the Medicine Hat camp was crowded—in his words, it was like being "locked up like a wild beast"—and he wanted to do something useful, especially if it meant an end to his close confinement.[28]

The ease with which the men were secured undoubtedly pleased project officials, particularly after all the setbacks in getting the camp established. Wartime Housing, however, got more than it expected. Most of the German prisoners at Medicine Hat had not only seen extensive combat duty in North Africa, but a good number were also hard-core Nazis blindly committed to Adolf Hitler and his National Socialist Party. By September 1943, in fact, a camp Gestapo was effectively governing Medicine Hat through a mixture of intimidation and terror, and had already executed a prisoner who had questioned its leadership.[29] This same virus would soon infect Riding Mountain, especially since the camp leader played a direct role in selecting volunteers for the new camp; he probably tried to ensure that the Nazi element would flourish there as well. It was not clear at the time, however, how many of the Riding Mountain recruits actually shared these convictions. The Department of National Defence had only recently established a Psychological Warfare Committee and begun to classify and segregate prisoners according to colour: black (ardent Nazi), grey (in-between), and white (anti-Nazi). This process was so incredibly slow that by war's end, almost two-thirds of the German prisoners held in Canada had yet to be classified.[30] As a result, the twenty-five Veterans Guards assigned to Riding Mountain had little warning about the type of men they would be watching. Nor did the larger group of civilian guards—around forty local men—who would supervise the prisoners in the camp and at the woodcutting sites.[31]

· · ·

Four hundred and forty Germans[32] arrived at the new Whitewater camp on Tuesday, 26 October. It was an impressive facility—not at all like the camps the Parks Bureau had operated for other groups over the past quarter century. Constructed at an estimated cost of a third of a million dollars, it featured six large bunkhouses, each with its own washroom and shower facilities; a large cookhouse and dining room; an administration office; staff quarters; a separate bunkhouse for the kitchen staff; a large commissary store; a combination garage and workshop; a hospital; and a barn. There was even a camp powerplant.[33] What probably surprised the prisoners most was that there was no enclosed compound or guard towers. Instead, the boundaries of the camp were designated by red blazes on a ring of outlying trees; beyond that, there was nothing but mile after mile of wilderness. Project officials believed that the lack of fencing would serve as an inducement to the men to work.[34] To help the Veterans Guard keep track of their charges, however, the prisoners wore blue denim work clothes with a red stripe down the outer leg of the trousers and a large red circle on the back of the shirt and jacket. This outfit was not only resented by prisoners, but made them uneasy—it was as if they were carrying targets on their backs. Internment authorities, however, had steadfastly refused to budge on the matter since 1941, and had even threatened at one time to change the circle to yellow, the colour used in Nazi Germany to identify Jews.[35]

Despite these precautions, it did not take the prisoners long to embarrass their guards and call camp security into question. On their first Sunday afternoon in the park, nineteen men, including George Foerster, decided to go for a long hike in the woods and became disoriented when a snowstorm blew up. It was not until late that evening—coincidentally, Halloween—that the prisoners were reported missing to the local RCMP detachment, and a manhunt organized for the next morning. Shortly after sunrise, Foerster and another of the lost men, cold and hungry, wandered into camp; the rest straggled back in small groups throughout the day.[36] Although irritated by the episode, camp authorities accepted the prisoners' explanation and publicly denied that there had been an escape attempt.[37] The police staff sergeant who investigated the

The Whitewater camp had no fence or guard towers. Authorities believed that the camp's location in the heart of the park would discourage the prisoners from trying to escape. *National Archives of Canada PA178642*

incident suspected otherwise. In his report he claimed that "the prisoners were out exploring the country around the camp and if some escape was anticipated at a future date they would know which direction to take."[38] Only time would tell.

The rest of November, not as exciting, was generally a period of adjustment for both the Germans and the other 175 military or civilian personnel associated with the project. In the interests of prisoner morale, the new camp leader, Leo Manuel, wrote both the World Council of the YMCA and the International Red Cross representative for books, games, musical instruments, and sports equipment. A piano, card- and writing-tables, dartboards, and ping-pong tables had already been assembled by Wartime Housing in an entertainment room adjoining the dining facilities.[39] The officer in charge of the Veterans Guard, on the other hand, was more concerned about prisoner rights and privileges and had requested a copy of the Geneva Convention, which arrived the day after the men got lost. Park authorities, meanwhile, secured permission to conscript prisoners to do maintenance work on the Strathclair road, the camp's only direct link to Dauphin. They also arranged for park warden Dave Binkley, who was stationed at nearby Lake Audy, to direct the woodcutting operation on the understanding that his meals and accommodation would be supplied by Wartime Housing.[40] Despite its earlier reservations, the Parks Bureau was gradually drawn into the project, partly because it had no faith in Captain Knuth, the new camp administrator. Fortunately, he was replaced by Colonel R.H. James the second week of November.

Working in crews, the prisoners were expected to cut and stack fuelwood for fifty cents per eight-hour-day. Initially, it was hoped that they would be able to average three-quarters of a cord per man per day. But after two weeks on the job, production averaged only half a cord per man-day.[41] Although Superintendent Heaslip was generally pleased with this output and expected it to rise, the woodcutting never came close to the camp quota over the following weeks. Part of the problem was that the prisoners were cutting in a fire-damaged area and not all the wood was salvageable. They were also relatively inexperienced, and minor accidents were not uncommon; it did not help, either, that one of the prisoners serving as saw sharpener was still waiting for the set of eyeglasses that had been ordered for him at Medicine Hat. The biggest obstacle to higher production, however, was an ongoing feud over canteen privileges. According to the Geneva Convention, prisoners were permitted to operate their own canteen and collectively benefit from any profit. But in the case of the Riding Mountain camp, Wartime Housing not only refused to establish a separate canteen for the Germans, but pocketed the revenue from the sale of such things as clothing, tobacco, and personal items at the company store. This issue proved such a sore point with the prisoners that they deliberately refused to meet the proposed cordwood quota,[42] and after less than a month on the job, the men were apparently ready to give up on the project. In the words of camp leader Manuel, the situation was close to the point "where the success of this enterprise is in danger."[43]

·   ·   ·

More serious problems surfaced in December. Near the beginning of the month, the officer in charge of the Veterans Guard recommended the return to Medicine Hat of a handful of agitators who were intimidating the other prisoners and trying to prevent them from working. This was not an unusual development; every camp normally went through a shaking-down period. What project authorities were soon to learn, though, was that some of the men were being terrorized by a well-entrenched camp Gestapo. In the early evening of 15 December, Frits Dornseif and Otto Ecker walked up to the guard at the camp entrance and asked to be taken into protective custody. Around the same time, Peter Fergen and Paul Nowack slipped away from camp and were discovered by two farmers the next morning, hiding in a haystack some seventeen miles away. During their subsequent interrogations, the four men told much the same story. All former German-born French Legionnaires, they had been drafted into a special unit (the 361) after the beginning of the war and were serving under Rommel in North Africa at the time of their capture. Since being interned in Canada, their lives had been a miserable lot; not only were they blamed for the German defeats, but they were also generally suspected of being traitors to the Nazi cause. These tensions were now being played out at Riding Mountain. The men were treated as outcasts at the best of times and were frequently threatened with the crude dirks some of the prisoners had fashioned from table knives and the elk and deer horns they had collected around the camp. A rope was even placed around Fergen's neck in one of the sleeping huts, and the men were told that it was time for another hanging—an obvious reference to the July murder of another former legionnaire at Medicine Hat. With the expectation of being transferred elsewhere, Dornseif and Fergen had earlier tried to escape the persecution by being found medically unfit for outside work; when it was suggested that they simply be assigned other duties, they, along with the two other escapees, decided to try to secure "protected personnel" status.[44]

Josef Gabski (far left) welcomed the opportunity to work outdoors at Riding Mountain. He returned to the campsite almost fifty years later. *Courtesy Josef Gabski*

When Manuel was interviewed by Colonel James, the camp commandant, about the men's complaints, he coolly maintained that they should have come to him for advice and that he did not care what happened to them—the men had effectively deserted.[45] This attitude placed the commandant in an extremely awkward position. Without the co-operation of the prisoners and their leaders, the woodcutting operation would be a dismal failure; the kitchen staff was already refusing to cook for the so-called deserters. Realizing that it would be easier to transfer the four men than try to expunge the Nazi element within the camp, Colonel James recommended that the prisoners be removed from camp on the grounds that he was unable to guarantee their safety. Senior internment authorities initially seemed to believe, however, that the four men were paranoid, and it took several weeks and several letters, including a report from the Winnipeg-based Swiss Consul, who visited the camp on 10 January 1944, before Defence officials moved on the matter.[46] Even then, the real reason for their eventual transfer to Hull, Quebec, on 21 January was that no one wanted to jeopardize the project.

Before the four men were moved, Defence authorities wanted to know whether there were any other prisoners who should be relocated because they were likely to seek protective custody. There was one such individual—William Schnackenberg, another former legionnaire—who fled from camp four days before Christmas and when found, some twenty miles away, asked to speak to the police. He told the same story—that he was constantly watched, repeatedly threatened, and feared for his life. In contrast to his attitude towards the other four men, however, the camp leader told Schnackenberg that the younger men were only kidding him, that he needed a rest in the camp hospital, and that if he returned to work he would be protected. This assurance seemed to resolve the matter, and Schnackenberg agreed to stay.[47] Project administrators were apparently willing to allow the Germans to sort out their own problems as long as the success of the operation was guaranteed.

In an effort to resolve the outstanding canteen problem and get the men working up to their potential, Colonel James met with Manuel and the visiting Swiss Consul in early January 1944. It was decided that canteen profits would accrue to the German prisoners once the camp's daily output reached three-quarters of a cord per man.[48] Manuel agreed to this deal on the understanding that twenty-seven men be replaced (in addition to the four deserters), that the amount of marching to the worksite be reduced through the use of some form of transport, and that the prisoners be supplied with more tools.[49] Trying to be as accommodating as possible, Colonel James was rewarded for his efforts when the camp quota was finally met for the first time on 21 January, the day the four deserters were removed. But all was not well. Although the prisoners started receiving their share of the canteen profits on 1 February, Manuel expected to secure all the monies dating back to their arrival at Riding Mountain; when this request was rebuffed, he submitted another formal protest to the Swiss Consul. One prisoner, meanwhile, quietly took matters into his own hands and would later be investigated for embezzling canteen funds.[50]

Curiously, internment authorities failed to take advantage of this ideal opportunity to remove some of the troublemakers from camp. During his January negotiations with Manuel, Colonel James approved the return to Medicine Hat of only thirteen men—less than half of what the camp leader had requested. By this time, however, camp administrators and senior military officials knew the identity of the men who had terrorized the former legionnaires; Dornseif and Ecker had provided five names during their interrogation in mid-December.[51] But project officials evidently decided that the welfare of the woodcutting operations took precedence, and that the removal of these men might create more problems than it solved. In the end, only one known agitator, Walter Wolf, was transferred. And he was removed with Manuel's blessing because he was trying to take over leadership of the camp and set up his own Gestapolike network.[52] Howard Kelly, a former truck driver at the camp, remembered "old Wolf" as a sinister figure who skulked around the camp spying on the other men.[53] Wolf was later involved in the murder of a second prisoner at Medicine Hat—this time, a doctor—in September 1944 and was executed, along with three others, in the Lethbridge gaol just over two years later.[54]

· · ·

While James and Manuel were locked in a war of wills over the canteen, the prisoners quickly adapted to camp life and generally did as they were told by their hut and bush leaders. The same military discipline that had governed their behaviour on the field of battle was now in place at Whitewater. Wartime Housing, in turn, placed considerable trust in the prisoners. The Germans operated the camp power-plant, had regular access to horses and trucks, and often went to town to help pick up supplies. It is doubtful whether national park authorities would have allowed the men to do some of these things—they took Canada's enemies seriously — but Wartime Housing seemed pre-

This cub was captured by some of the prisoners and became the camp mascot. *Riding Mountain National Park Collection*

pared to let the prisoners help run the camp as long as the wood was cut. Joe Gabski maintains to this day that "the operation could not have run without German inner control."[55] The prisoners also enjoyed special privileges, such as being allowed to keep stray dogs or cats that wandered into camp. They even had a camp mascot. During a hike along the lakeshore in late spring, about forty prisoners came across a black bear and her two cubs. Chasing away the mother, the men captured one of the cubs and spirited it back to camp. The captive animal became close friends with one of the camp dogs and was led around on a lease. It was still a bear, though, and when it did not get its morning porridge one day, the cub ransacked the kitchen. Come fall, it hibernated under one of the barrack buildings.[56]

When not cutting wood, the men spent their evenings in idle conversation—usually talking about things that were out of reach[57]—reading, playing games, or listening to the camp radio and the latest news about the war. Some of the men had theatrical or musical talents and staged regular performances. Others were fascinated with the forest setting and would often sit up for hours at night to listen to the elk bugling or the wolves howling.[58] A good many also turned their hands to crafts, an activity that became something of a cottage industry, using the readily available wood to create a number of elaborate models, including ships in bottles. It was as if they did not see enough wood during the day. "When inspecting the POWs huts, I am constantly amazed at the . . . junk, ranging from dog houses and wooden suitcases to works of art," Colonel James reported in late March. "When moving time comes, no railroad will find transportation for half of it."[59] Several of the prisoners applied their skills to boat making, carving dugout canoes from some of the large spruce along the lakeshore, which they then used to paddle to an island on the lake, where they often had a bonfire. They also formed the boats into a small flotilla one day and launched a mock invasion of the camp; it is not known whether the commandant was given any advance warning.[60] Today, the remains of the dugouts lie rotting in the mouth of a creek near the site of the former camp.

Both Foerster and Gabski found camp conditions comfortable. The men were well clothed for outside work and were never cold in their sleeping huts. They also had plenty to eat. Not only were fresh meat and groceries trucked from Dauphin on almost a daily basis, but the prisoners also had their own cook, Albert Simon, who prepared mainly German food.[61] Former civilian personnel who were interviewed about the camp seemed somewhat resentful that the prison kitchen was not subject to the same rationing as the Canadian public. The men varied their diet by raising pigs in a small enclosure and catching fish in the nearby lake. They may also have grown vegetables in the small flower-beds outside their bunkhouses; some perennials were still blooming when the author visited the campsite almost fifty years later. For those with a sweet tooth, candy, chocolate, cookies, and soft drinks were available on a

Several of the prisoners made dugout canoes from some of the large spruce trees along the lakeshore. *Courtesy Josef Gabski*

credit basis at the company store. The prisoners could also place special mail orders there from Eaton's catalogue and then patiently wait, like the thousands of other customers across the prairies, for their parcels to arrive. Ironically, this service caused the first serious labour dispute, when the pyjamas that the entire camp had ordered and paid for failed to be delivered. Believing that they had been literally fleeced, the men refused to turn out for work one morning and were thereupon confined to their barracks and denied food. The pyjama strike ended two days later when Colonel James personally pledged to look into the matter; the sleep-wear finally arrived about a month later.[62]

There was one thing, however, that the men were forced to do without at camp—and that was the company of women. Thousands of miles from home and waiting for the war to end, the prisoners knew only an all-male world at Whitewater. There were no wives or girlfriends, no mothers, no sisters, no daughters. Whatever the camp comforts, it was first and foremost a "city without women."[63] And the absence weighed heavily on the men's minds. They talked about women throughout the day at the jobsite and in their huts at night. They looked forward to the next letter from home and perhaps a picture, and made plans for when they returned to Germany after the war. As an almost unbearably moving indication of his desperate loneliness, Foerster even bought wedding bands for himself and his as-yet-unknown future bride. Gabski, on the other hand, wondered whether something was being placed in the food to curb the prisoners' sexual drives. He also suggested that many of the men, after several months in captivity, were "pretty much ground down."[64] Several of the prisoners likely consoled themselves with booze. It turns out that the camp dentist also doubled as a distiller, using small crates of specially ordered dried grapes to make hooch in the infirmary. Gabski suspects, since the still was not confiscated, that some of the camp administrators were also being secretly supplied.[65]

. . .

Unlike the situation in the national park camps during the First World War, escapes were never a serious problem at Riding Mountain. It appears that the Germans were under strict orders from Manuel not to run. And the men agreed, fully realizing that any mass breakout would mean the end of their Whitewater days and their immediate shipment to a maximum security facility.[66] Hans Weis, however, had a mind of his own—George Foerster considered him deranged[67]—and repeatedly tried to escape in an apparent effort to reach relatives in New York. After an unsuccessful attempt in November 1943, he stole a truck early in the new year and was captured on his way to the nearest rail line. Upon his return to camp, he vowed to try again at the earliest opportunity.[68] And he would keep his pledge.

Other prisoners were allowed to leave camp on road detail or for the daily supply run to Dauphin. There were limits, however, to what the town would tolerate. When the camp doctor, Medical Officer Frits Gress, was spotted on the streets of Dauphin accompanied by a single guard for the second time in as many months, there were howls of protest in the local newspaper. The *Herald and Press* wondered why "an enemy of the country" was able to walk around Dauphin as if he were "on a sight seeing tour." Nor could it understand why he was allowed to visit the local BCATP Flying School, especially when local boys were overseas trying to hold Nazi Germany at bay. "Some of these prisoners may be wiser and more familiar with the country than they appear to be," the editorial concluded, "and may have already established contacts outside the 'walls' of the prison camp in Riding Mountain National Park."[69]

Little did the newspaper know how close it was to the truth. Lieutenant Mann, the new officer in charge of the Veterans Guard, first became suspicious when two prisoners went missing on 14 January and were picked up the next day walking along the road back to camp. During their subsequent interview, the two lightly dressed men claimed that they had simply gone for a hike and become lost. When pressed about their whereabouts, however, the pair stuck to their story, but conceded that other prisoners from the camp had been visiting the communities along the southern boundary of the park. Rumours circulating in the Horod, Seech, Olha, and Marco districts seemed to confirm their story.[70] And over the next few weeks, Mann learned that Germans were favoured guests at local dances and parties—largely because they carried with them rationed goods, in particular, sugar for the local stills. The men would evidently slip away Saturday night after roll-call and be back the next morning in time for the first count of the day. Once his suspicions were confirmed, Mann alerted the local Dauphin RCMP detachment, which eventually contacted the commissioner's office in mid-February. The police could not get involved, however, unless the prisoners were officially reported missing, and merely expressed concern that the men might be tempted to use their local contacts to escape once spring arrived. They also noted that the local immigrant farm population was likely sympathetic to the prisoners, and that some must be picking the men up at the camp boundaries, since it was too far to walk there and back in one night.[71]

Prisoners and horse teams readying for work outside camp stable. *Riding Mountain National Park Collection*

With the RCMP unable to help, Mann decided to take matters into his own hands and planned a late-night visit to the communities on Saturday, 19 February. The detail first raided a farmhouse in the Olha district, where they found two prisoners and the local schoolteacher working over jigsaw puzzles; the young woman admitted that she had met them previously at a dance and that they had also visited her at the schoolhouse. Acting on a telephone tip, the patrol then proceeded to Marco, where they rounded up five more prisoners kicking up their heels at a community dance. The seven men were placed under guard back at camp, and the question now became what to do with them. The camp leader tried lamely to defend them, arguing that the camp boundaries were constantly changing because of the woodcutting operations, and that the prisoners did not know that they were out-of-bounds. Colonel James, for his part, wanted them transferred back to their base camp, believing it was the only way to end their wandering habits.[72] And internment authorities did not even regard the men as escapees, since they always returned to camp. It was also apparent from police reports that the local population, who made the prisoners welcome, was as much to blame as anyone. In the end, then, little was done, apart from imploring the guards to keep the men on a shorter leash.

·   ·   ·

By this time, the director of Labour Projects had begun to regret the decision to establish such a large, elaborate facility at Whitewater Lake. At a meeting in Port Arthur on 7 February 1944, including Commandant James and other representatives from more than twenty different projects, Colonel Fordham hinted that Riding Mountain's continued usefulness as a labour camp was in doubt. Although the prisoners were cutting wood farther and farther into the bush each day, it was impossible to relocate the camp. And the problem would only get worse.[73] This pessimistic assessment was confirmed by the chief production officer for the Wood Fuel Controller's office, who visited the camp for several days in mid-February. He complained that it was a waste of man-power—and the guards' time—to have small crews cutting and stacking cord-wood in scattered piles throughout the woods, and then later having it hauled to the roadside for pickup. It made more sense to skid the logs to a central depot, where the bulk of the cutting could be done. He also warned that a section of timber had to be set aside near the camp for the following winter, or the operation might as well be shut down; the men were already working an hour's marching distance from camp and being served their noon meal in tents pitched at the cutting site.[74] These recommendations received a favourable response from the Parks Bureau; its only other suggestion was that the prison-ers clear-cut areas and not worry about selecting only dry timber. At the same time, Gibson and his officers began to worry about the possible shutdown of the operations, especially since the fuelwood shortage was apparently over because of the unseasonably warm winter.[75] And if the men no longer cut wood—for whatever reason—they faced the prospect of the camp carrying on simply as a detention centre for several hundred Germans for the remainder of the war.

In mid-March 1944, Colonel Fordham visited Riding Mountain and toured the operations. It was not a good time for an inspection. The Germans were in an ugly mood, and Fordham's presence did nothing to cheer them up. Although the men earned fifty cents per day, they were given only thirty cents in chits for the camp canteen; the remainder was to be credited to their accounts in Medicine Hat. This arrangement led to considerable griping by the prisoners— even more so once they began to meet the daily quota—and Manuel was seriously contemplating some kind of work stoppage at the time of Fordham's visit.[76] The men were also upset that their mail was not only being screened and censored, but was inexplicably delayed by several months; they had yet to receive, for example, their Christmas parcels. Into this setting came Fordham, a gung-ho administrator who scorned the idea of conferring with the camp spokesman and believed that prisoners were placed in work camps "to do what they are told."[77] It was not long before he clashed with the camp leader.

On 13 March, Manuel instructed his men not to start work until 11:30 because of the cold, blustery weather. Fordham was alarmed by this order—even more so because Colonel James was not even consulted about the matter—and told the prisoners that unless cutting started by 10:00, he would close the camp canteen, impound the new movie projector, and cancel dessert. He even threatened to dismiss the camp leader when it appeared that the men might go on strike. "Had . . . the aforesaid measures not been taken," he later told internment authorities, "the prisoners would virtually have been running the camp themselves on that day and probably subsequent days."[78] This incident, by itself, was bad enough for prisoner morale; not only had Manuel been overruled, but the men had been forced to work against their will. What happened later that afternoon, however, made their sense of grievance even worse. Max Neugebauer was struck on the head while felling a tree and rushed unconscious to the Dauphin hospital, where he died three days later.[79] Seizing upon the accident, Manuel complained to the Swiss Consul that too many

Prisoner Max Neugebauer was killed while felling a tree during a windstorm. *National Archives of Canada 178663*

prisoners were being injured because of the obsession with meeting the daily quota. There was some truth to this claim; another prisoner, Hans Aulenbacher, was hurt later that month and had to be hospitalized for a week; other men sustained injuries as well. These injuries may well have occurred during the normal course of events; it is also possible, however, that the prisoners were becoming careless through boredom or were not being properly supervised in the bush. During his visit to the woodcutting sites in mid-February, the chief production officer found that the civilian guards did little more than sit around a fire all day, fostering "a general atmosphere of indolence."[80]

Taking full advantage of this laxity, the prisoners continued their weekend visits to outlying immigrant communities in March and April. The camp commandant was now resigned to these nocturnal outings. On Sunday, 5 March, for example, Colonel James informed the Wasagaming RCMP detachment that two men were missing during the evening roll-call, but that no action was to be taken unless they failed to show up the following day. He was confident that it was not a serious escape attempt—they were probably away at Seech—and when the pair returned the next morning, they recited what had now become the standard excuse for the absences—they had become lost while walking. The police were puzzled by James's tolerant attitude and worried that it might encourage a real escape.[81] Local government officials were equally concerned. The secretary of the Shoal Lake rural municipality complained to the minister of National Defence that prisoners were visiting local homes in the area and that authorities seemed unable or unwilling to do much about it. "There is too much liberty given these prisoners," the letter warned, "and when summer comes and cars are available they will be able to travel much greater distances."[82]

The Parks Bureau was also becoming increasingly worried about the freedom enjoyed by the prisoners, especially with the approach of the tourist season. And at the urging of his staff, T.A. Crerar, the minister of Mines and Resources, wrote his cabinet colleague at Labour in late March 1944, impressing upon him the need to keep the men away from the park townsite and other recreational areas in Riding Mountain. Most visitors would already be nervous about the presence of Germans in the park and did not need the men standing in line for an ice-cream cone in Wasagaming or sharing a favourite picnic spot. Crerar also promised that local park officers would do their best to keep curious tourists away from the camp.[83] Acknowledging Crerar's concerns, the minister of Labour suggested that the camp commandant, park superintendent, and officer in charge of the Veterans Guard get together to devise some way of restricting the men's movements. Little did the politicians and government officials seem to realize, though, that until the camp was fenced, the men could not be controlled. Project administrators could post warning signs. They could also put up and man roadblocks around the clock. And they could increase the guard, as well as vary the frequency and timing of the roll-calls. But until the

The Neugebauer funeral, Dauphin, March 1944. *National Archives of Canada 173664*

prisoners were physically prevented from leaving the camp compound—in other words, until the facility became a true concentration camp—they would continue to slink away to the edge of the park and be picked up and entertained by their new settler friends.

The antics of 16 April, four days before Hitler's birthday, were a good example. On that Sunday evening, no less than eleven men were reported missing by the guard. Eight had returned by the following morning. Another prisoner, Herbert Lopens, telephoned the camp from Gilbert Plains, several miles northwest of the camp, and asked to be picked up—he evidently had become lost. When the remaining two men, Felix Boettger and Walter Koerber, failed to return to work by 10:30 the next morning, Colonel James notified the Rossburn police detachment that the pair had escaped from camp. The Mounties searched the Marco district all day—apparently chasing the men from farmhouse to farmhouse—and finally called off the search early the next morning, by which time the two fugitives had been spirited back to camp by their immigrant friends.[84] This latest episode proved too much for military officials, and Boettger, Koerber, and Lopens[85] were returned to Medicine Hat for disciplinary action. The Defence Department had also lost patience with the camp guards and demanded an investigation of their behaviour, especially the rumours that the civilian personnel were fraternizing with the prisoners and even attending local social functions with them.[86] Finally, new camp boundaries were officially posted on 24 April 1944, and a request forwarded to Ottawa for a patrol vehicle; inquiries were also made as to whether the provincial gaol or the military facilities at Shilo, Manitoba, could be used for detention purposes. Defence officials were determined to tighten camp security and keep the prisoners at home—or at least try to.

· · ·

Getting the men to work, however, became the main challenge in May. Part of the problem was the working conditions; the spring melt made it difficult if not impossible to reach the cutting areas, and if they did manage to get there, the worksites were a muddy mess. The prisoners also got their first taste of fire-fighting for three days in late April, and even though they performed admirably, many probably recoiled at the prospect of spending a summer in the heart of the mosquito-infested forest during fire season. The greatest obstacle, however, was the simple fact that several of the prisoners believed they had volunteered for only a six-month term of service and wanted to be relieved of their woodcutting duties. This misunderstanding might have been resolved had the camp leader and the project administrators been on good terms, but their relationship had turned sour. Throughout March and April, Manuel had recommended the transfer of a number of men for medical or other various reasons. Fordham ignored these requests, on the grounds that prisoners with health problems could always attend to light duties; he also suggested that the camp leader was really trying to tighten his control over the camp by removing anyone who questioned his authority.[87] These repeated rebuffs only further alienated Manuel—and lessened his credibility with the prisoners—and he finally resigned on 11 May. But the situation in camp did not improve. The very next day, the new camp spokesman, Gustav Treiber, reported that eighty men had asked to return to base camp,[88] and there was nothing Fordham or anyone else could do about it. "As they volunteered for work," the director of prisoners of war reasoned, "they cannot be compelled to stay if they are unwilling."[89]

This new development proved too much for Wartime Housing, and it decided to withdraw from the woodcutting project. It had been a constant struggle to try to get the prisoners to meet the camp quota, and the future seemed even bleaker now that the men were refusing to work. Following a series of interdepartmental meetings in late May, then, Munitions and Supply gladly agreed to turn over control of the project to the Department of Labour, effective 15 June 1944.[90] In the interests of reducing operating costs, it was also decided to downsize the camp to 200 men by transferring 118 prisoners to other work projects in northern Ontario[91] and returning another 100 to Medicine Hat. Lists were drawn up, and the evacuation date set for 14 June. When it came time to remove the first batch of prisoners, however, three were missing. When the count was next taken, another seven were gone. With the help of the Mounties, some of the men were eventually found just north of the park, near Keld, and others turned up close to the park townsite. It is not clear whether the men were trying to escape, did not want to leave, or were simply saying goodbye to friends. It did not matter—they were all subsequently sent to Medicine Hat for a disciplinary hearing.[92] Colonel James was probably relieved that his term as project administrator was over; his successor, Major J.H. Keane, likely wondered what lay ahead.

The reorganization of the camp was expected to inject new life into the project and its woodcutting operations. But production remained around one-half cord per man per day. When George Tunstell, a district forest officer and inspector of alternative service work camps, visited the operations for the first time in late June, he was amazed by the luxuriousness of the accommodation, especially in comparison to that of other park labourers, such as conscientious objectors and the Japanese. The camp not only had its own electric lighting, but it was using thirty thousand gallons of water a day. Tunstell was not as impressed with the work in the bush, finding the prisoners truculent, poorly disciplined, and lacking in incentive. Like many before him, he also questioned the need for the civilian guards and concluded that they were partly

Some of the prisoners had musical or theatrical talents and staged regular performances in the camp. *Riding Mountain National Park Collection*

responsible for the attitude of the workforce. If the situation was going to be salvaged, Tunstell reported, the men should be paid for what they produced and not for putting in a day's work, no matter what they did.[93]

Although Major Keane, the new commandant, agreed, he could do nothing to change the rate of remuneration for prisoner labour—it was set by government order. He did, however, believe that the woodcutting operations could be made more productive if he could cultivate a stronger sense of devotion to the project. He was particularly determined to stamp out the visits to nearby settlements. This would be no easy task, though, according to the information contained in a diary that had been smuggled back to the Medicine Hat camp after its author, Konstantin Schwarz, was transferred from Riding Mountain to the Ontario-Minnesota Pulp and Paper company. Schwarz explained how prisoners were virtually free to come and go at night because the Veterans Guard were illiterate "old daddies" who had been threatened with hanging if they ever shot at a German soldier. He then outlined how the prisoners had built crude compasses—ironically from watches that they had ordered from the catalogue—and spent their first few weeks in camp reconnoitring the countryside, even climbing fire lookout towers, before they chanced upon Seech and other small immigrant communities along the southern and northern boundaries of the park. Here, he and his buddy K. Schuster were welcomed as liberators by the local Ukrainian farmers, and treated like family. "We kept their convictions alive with tales of our front line exploits," Schwarz boasted. "They are all convinced that we will win. . . . This is soothing to my old Nazi heart." During their visits, the Germans were able to get anything they wanted: newspapers, radios, civilian clothes—they even "had a nice time with women." They also exchanged camp handicrafts or the hides and skins of animals poached from the park for small amounts of money, which they used to purchase goods and supplies in Oakburn while disguised as farmers. Schwarz also described how the police had repeatedly failed to recognize the pair at community dances—they would always yell out the loudest during raids, "No Germans here!"—and how local farmers were not only prepared to defend the men, but helped them return to camp in time for roll-call. Nor were they safe once they were back in their hut. The camp leader frowned upon these visits and meted out punishment "ruthlessly" if they were late returning to camp. But these excursions brightened an otherwise dull existence, and Schwarz vowed to continue his nightly forays. "Our leadership should be glad to see us in a good mood and that we dare to do something which is against the regulations of our enemies," he wrote. "That is the German way."[94]

Military officials discounted large parts of the diary as "obviously untrue."[95] But when the RCMP checked Schwarz's story against local police records, they found to their horror that "there is a good deal more truth than fiction"[96] in what he claimed. The police also feared that the amount of outside contact was probably much higher because Colonel James had not bothered to report absences unless the men missed the morning count. Schwarz's diary also raised questions about contraband material in camp. And in mid-July, a prisoner informant revealed that there were two cameras in the camp and that the owners had fashioned makeshift developing units under the floor near their bunks. The local military district dispatched an officer to investigate the report, but his surprise search of the huts turned up no photographic equipment—only a picture that a prisoner claimed had been taken by one of the civilian staff. The officer did, however, catch another prisoner trying to hide a radio in a woodpile—again, an apparent gift from one of the staff in exchange for a boat model. He also noticed the dugout canoes the men had built—Schwarz's diary revealed that prisoners were using boats to get across the lake at night. He even found Germans driving trucks on the provincial highways, hauling the cordwood to local storage depots. It was enough to make him wonder who was running the project. "It would appear that a tremendous amount of slackness has crept in the handling of the POWs in this camp," he cautioned, "no doubt, due to the fact that there have been many opportunities for contact between the POWs and civilian workmen."[97]

Major Keane flatly rejected these stinging remarks, claiming that the guards were making every effort to keep the prisoners under careful watch and that there had been no temporary absences, let alone escapes—or at least he thought so. As part of his plan to improve camp morale, however, he believed that the prisoners would work harder and be less likely to wander at night if they were kept happy and amused at camp. He consequently

The remains of the dugout canoes lie rotting in a creek along Whitewater Lake. *Collection of the author* allowed them considerable latitude, even though some of the activities went against prisoner-of-war regulations. He did nothing, for example, to stop the Germans and the civilian staff from playing baseball together. Nor did he see anything wrong with using German truck drivers, especially when it saved money. He also permitted a photograph of the camp bear cub to be reproduced and distributed without proper authorization to all the prisoners. Keane even ordered several pairs of eyeglasses for the camp from a private firm.[98]

The strategy did not seem to work though. In early August 1944, the prisoners started doing as little as possible at the woodcutting sites. With their education and training, the Germans tended to look down on their guards as country bumpkins and tried to embarrass them at every opportunity, including tactics such as sneaking back to camp unescorted. Keane believed that the slowdown had been ordered by the base camp at Medicine Hat; the heat and the mosquitoes probably did not help matters. Then, at the end of the month, Treiber and his hut leaders demanded that they and all the other men be returned to Medicine Hat; he warned that any prisoner who refused to return to base camp would be branded a traitor and that his family would suffer the consequences.[99] Fordham had no intention of shutting down the camp and made arrangements with internment officials to transfer some nineteen men, including Treiber, to Medicine Hat on 1 October 1944. Major Keane used the opportunity to send another six, including one who supposedly had a camera, to the camp reserved exclusively for ardent Nazis at Neys, Ontario.[100] Although this weeding out left the camp with a reduced workforce, production could not get much worse. By the end of October, some four and a half months after the camp had come under the direct control of the Department of Labour, the men had cut and stacked just slightly more than thirty-three hundred cords of wood.[101]

· · ·

In October 1944, the Department of Labour signed a contract with Munitions and Supply to provide ten thousand cords of fuelwood from its Riding Mountain operation by the following spring. This was a large order, but the new director of Labour Projects, R.H. Davidson, was confident that with the return of cold weather and the recent removal of troublemakers, the camp would be able to fulfil the request. He also believed that he could count on the passive co-operation of the prisoners, now that they were being more closely supervised and faced the prospect of punishment if they misbehaved.[102] Three men known to frequent the outlying communities had been sentenced to twenty-eight days' discipline at Port Arthur in the early fall, a dramatic turnaround from the way camp violations had been handled in the past under Wartime Housing. Instead of closing his eyes to illegal activity, the project supervisor was now expected to take immediate action against infractions. But it was still not enough for Major Keane, who argued that it would be difficult to prevent prisoners from absconding to Seech or other villages as long as these three men were in camp. Describing them as a bad influence, Keane felt the three prisoners should be returned to Medicine Hat at the end of their disciplinary period. Defence officials, in contrast, were concerned that other prisoners might take advantage of the situation in order to have themselves removed from the project, and felt it was in the Department of Labour's best interests and their own to punish the men accordingly, but then return them to camp.[103] On the surface, this position made sense—if projects like Riding Mountain were to continue—and Keane grudgingly had to accept the return of the three men. But the policy flatly contradicted what internment officials had argued only a few months earlier, when they reminded Wartime Housing that the prisoners were volunteer labourers and could not be forced to work. Nor did it stop the prisoners from continuing to visit the local settlers. In fact, the policy of returning men to camp after they served their sentences seemed to have the opposite effect. They became bolder. Such was the remarkable case of Hans Weis.

Missing at morning roll-call on Friday, 6 October, Weis was placed under arrest when he returned to camp at noon. He explained that he had been caught in the bush the night before during a heavy rainfall and sought temporary shelter until the storm cleared off. While in confinement, his personal belongings were searched by a guard, who found two letters from residents of the Seech area: one promised Weis a radio; the other, from a young woman, told the soldier that she already had a boyfriend and that they could only be friends. While Weis was away in Port Arthur for disciplinary action, the police tracked down the two correspondents; one was charged and fined twenty-five dollars for transmitting a letter to a prisoner of war, while the other was simply issued a stern warning about fraternizing with the enemy.[104] But the episode did not end there. After Weis returned to Riding Mountain, he sold several model ships to camp personnel, including some of the guards. Slipping away from camp one night, he used the money to buy a train ticket from Elphinstone to Winnipeg, where he was eventually apprehended on 26 November 1944.[105] While Weis was at large, the local police searched the nearby communities and found what they believed to be the missing prisoner's camp uniform in the possession of a farmer from the Seech area; the man was actually wearing the red-striped pants under his overalls while the police were interviewing him. But he claimed that the uniform had been secured from another prisoner—not Weis—earlier in the summer. This made no difference to the police, however, and the farmer was taken to Minnedosa the next day, where he was found guilty of unlawful possession of government property and sentenced to six months in gaol.[106] Weis, in the meantime, completed another twenty-eight days' detention at Port Arthur and was once again returned to camp. But he was far from cured of his bad habits, and on 1 January 1945 borrowed one of the large camp trucks—for the second time in the past year—and drove to Dauphin, where he celebrated the new year with the other patrons of the Hostess Club. This time, Weis was charged with stealing a vehicle and eventually sentenced to fourteen days in the Dauphin gaol before being finally returned to Medicine Hat—but only after he had made a mockery of the policy of keeping problem prisoners in labour camps.[107]

. . .

Weis was not the only prisoner to leave Whitewater in the new year. On 5 January, three men stopped for a meal in the Keld district and were picked up without incident an hour later, after the farmer telephoned the police. One puzzling aspect of these "escapes" was the fact that none of the three had ever been in trouble before. The investigating officer surmised by the men's behaviour that they had fled from camp with the deliberate intention of being caught—and for good reason. The camp had been on strike since the beginning of the new year—on the grounds that it was too cold to work—and the three escapees sensed that there might be trouble. They were not far off the mark. When the striking prisoners attempted to thwart the calling of the roll, the Veterans Guard called for the assistance of fifteen armed airborne personnel from the nearby Dauphin training school. The entire prisoner population was then rounded up and crammed into one hut, with the count being taken as the men were released. At this point, the guards discovered that another man was missing. The fugitive was spotted the next day walking along the road to Dauphin, and calmly surrendered to the police when they drove up to him; he had spent the night in a haystack in a futile attempt to keep warm, and was trying to reach the rail line at the time of his capture.[108]

All this trouble occurred while Major Keane was away on holiday, and upon his return to camp he traced the unrest to the new camp leader, Heinrich Weiler. According to the Schwarz diary, Weiler was a regular visitor to the outlying communities, and had nothing but contempt for his keepers. Emboldened by his promotion to the camp leadership, he decided to exercise his new clout and bring the operations to a virtual standstill. Keane immediately placed Weiler and four other men in confinement and arranged for their transfer to Neys; the rest of the prisoners returned to work the next day.[109] Although applauded by the director of Labour Projects, this decisive action did little towards solving the camp's long-term problems. Keane was fed up with the continuing turmoil—not to mention overnight absences—at Riding Mountain, and worried what the future held for the operation. One of the first acts of the new camp leader, Wilhelm Schmidt, was to demand a copy of the Geneva Convention—in German. Director Davidson therefore recommended to internment officials that the remaining 160 men be placed on individual farms as labourers.[110] Before they could be sent out, however, they had to be screened for their suitability, and more importantly, reliability, for this kind of work.

Birch-bark photograph album made by one of the prisoners. Unfortunately the pictures have since been destroyed. Prisoners did a lot of handicrafts, sometimes exchanging them for favours from the guards. *Courtesy Bob Henderson*

This classification process was carried out at Riding Mountain during the first two weeks of February 1945 by two officers from military intelligence in Ottawa. Although they were ostensibly there to identify what men could be released on farm duty, they were really trying to determine the strength of their Nazi beliefs.[111] Arriving at camp on 30 January, the officers made a brief inspection of the facilities before meeting at length with Schmidt and Medical Officer Gress to explain the purpose of their visit. The interrogations commenced the next morning and immediately raised concerns. Schmidt could not understand what some of the questions had to do with determining a man's usefulness for farm labour. The examiners, in response, bluntly told him that they had no intention of allowing devout Nazis to engage in outside agricultural work, and that no prisoners would be recommended for this duty unless they had first been questioned about their political leanings. Schmidt agreed to co-operate—he even provided a list of those he regarded as the more rabid Nazis—and the interviews proceeded without incident. The intelligence officers also held clandestine meetings with several informants, including one of the Catholic priests, who gladly pointed out undesirable characters. They also assured the investigators that the Gestapo element had effectively been eliminated through periodic transfers, and that the camp no longer received secret instructions from Medicine Hat.

With interrogations completed by mid-February, the intelligence officers submitted a detailed report on camp operations and the disposition of the prisoners. They identified only sixteen men as "black" Nazis and recommended that they be removed to Neys. Some seventy-one others designated as "white" prisoners, including the camp leader and doctor, were deemed eligible for parole on special work projects, such as farm labour. Joe Gabski was classified a "white" Nazi, while George Foerster was evidently a "grey." The most telling observation was that all the men had clearly spent enough time in the bush—no matter how luxurious the facilities—and would welcome a change.[112]

While internment authorities debated the fate of the men, there was also the question of what to do with the camp. Davidson initially backed the idea of using the facility as a central clothing depot for the various work projects in the park; he also considered its use as a clearing-house for prisoners on individual assignments, as well as a hospital for injured or sick workers. The isolation of the camp, however, soon proved a serious handicap to any of these possibilities, and by mid-April, Davidson was ready to evacuate the facility on twenty-four hours' notice. "Personally, I would not recommend that the Department of Labour buy the camp under any circumstances," he told the associate deputy minister, "as I doubt if it was scrapped that you would get $321.00 for it, instead of $321,371.74."[113]

During the first week of April, the camp population was reduced by half, when sixty-eight prisoners, including Gabski, were sent to work for the Abitibi Power and Paper Company in Minnipuka, Ontario, and the sixteen black Nazis moved to Neys. That still left some seventy-six men at Whitewater, and Labour officials tried to fob them off on the park superintendent. It is not clear how much Parks Bureau authorities actually knew about the project or the troubles it had experienced over the past year. They did know, from George Tunstell's June 1944 report, that the prisoners were unhappy workers and that they were unlikely to get a good return for the expenditure involved[114]—particularly when the Germans were being made available at the rate of $1.50 per day. They also remained uneasy about using prisoners of war in Riding Mountain—any park for that matter—and politely turned down the offer. Heaslip was instructed to continue to rely on alternative service workers for maintenance work.[115]

Labour officials, in response, lost little time finding other customers for the prisoners' muscle, and made arrangements for the transfer of forty men to another Abitibi work camp, this time at Magpie, Ontario, about a month later; Foerster was apparently in this group. The removal of this last batch of prisoners coincided with the end of the war in Europe,[116] and it was decided to use the remaining men at Whitewater to clean up the woodcutting sites and close the camp. In late spring, however, a last-minute deal was struck with the Department of National Defence to hire twenty prisoners to build a cadet camp north of Clear Lake along the Dauphin road.[117] This work delayed the decommissioning of the camp until late August, when all salvageable material was removed and stored at the Dauphin air training school for future auction

In the fall of 1945, the Whitewater camp was razed and the site cleared. These concrete supports from the powerhouse are all that remain of the camp structures. *Collection of the author*

by the federal War Assets Corporation. The buildings, in the meantime, were purchased through public tender by Billingkoff Wreckers of Winnipeg, and as soon as the last of the prisoners were removed in early October, the structures started to come down. But because of the early arrival of winter, the company had to return the next spring, at the park's insistence, to ensure that any remaining signs of the camp were cleared away.[118]

·   ·   ·

The cleanup of the Whitewater site was symbolic of the National Parks Bureau's relationship with the Riding Mountain woodcutting operation. Parks officials had wanted nothing to do with prisoner-of-war labour, and agreed to provide a home and little else for the Germans. The project was consequently unlike any other labour camp in a national park setting over the past quarter century. In contrast to its intense involvement in past projects, the Parks Bureau in this case played a largely advisory role—even though the camp was located within Riding Mountain—and the work itself was quite different from the usual park development and maintenance performed by various groups since 1915. Even the camp facilities were unprecedented. At the same time, Riding Mountain served as the setting for one of the most unusual dramas on the Canadian home front during the Second World War. Battle-hardened

German soldiers, plucked from North Africa, were sent to the park to cut firewood for the duration of the war. It was a naive hope that members of the much-dreaded Nazi fighting machine would settle down to a quiet life in rural Manitoba. And, not surprisingly, problems quickly developed. The prisoners were willing to meet the woodcutting quota only if they could participate in running the camp and enjoy certain privileges; but the sheer drudgery of the job eventually discouraged even the most co-operative volunteers. Threats, slowdowns, and work stoppages came to characterize the woodcutting operation and ultimately forced the closure of the camp.

The project also witnessed the development of unique human relationships with the enemy during the war—within the camp itself, but more particularly in the outlying immigrant communities. Although the Germans had been placed in the heart of Riding Mountain for security reasons, their forest prison had no walls, and despite increasing efforts to keep them in the camp, they were generally able to move in and out of the park with relative impunity. And even though the Parks Bureau was determined to wipe out any vestiges of the camp once it was closed—as if it never existed—it could not destroy the fact that for a few brief months during the Second World War, animosities were set aside and Riding Mountain's Nazis found a home-away-from-home in the farm communities beyond the park's boundaries. The dances at Seech were never quite the same again.

*O*N PIERRE TRUDEAU'S LAST DAY IN THE HOUSE OF COMMONS, 29 June 1984, opposition leader Brian Mulroney implored the prime minister to seize the moment and formally apologize to Japanese Canadians for their treatment during the Second World War. In his characteristic philosopher-king style, Trudeau replied, "I do not think it is the purpose of a Government to right the past. It cannot rewrite history. It is our purpose to be just in our time."[1] This is not a book about guilt. Nor is it about redress. Nor, for that matter, is it about rewriting history. It deals, instead, with a little-known and poorly understood chapter of twentieth-century Canadian history that has never been told before in any comprehensive manner.

Between 1915 and 1946, more than ten thousand men—enemy aliens, relief workers, conscientious objectors, Japanese nationals, and German prisoners of war—spent months, sometimes years, in labour camps in western Canada's prairie and mountain national parks. Apart from the German prisoners of war, who were there for entirely different reasons, these men had done nothing wrong; they had committed no crimes against the state. But they were seen as a threat to the peace and stability of Canada at a time when the country faced some of its greatest challenges. And the Canadian government exiled them to places like Banff, Waterton Lakes, and Riding Mountain to be held until they were once again accepted, if not welcome, in Canadian society.

The internees paid great dividends. While regular Parks funding was being reduced in response to war and depression, several western national parks were more than compensated by the ready availability of these large pools of men. And thanks to their muscle, the national parks experienced one of the most intensive development periods in their history. The men built a number of structures, facilities, and roads, as well as performing a wide range of maintenance duties. They tackled specific projects that had a clear purpose— they were not simply marking time. Indeed, many of the roads, such as the Banff-Jasper highway, have since become popular scenic routes, while several of the fine stone buildings have been recognized today as heritage structures.

The story of national park development in Canada has a vital, sometimes tragic, human side, a fact that is often overlooked or simply not recognized.

Little is known today about the thousands of men who were interned in the parks and built many of the park facilities. Nor is it generally realized how much of this labour was done by hand under demanding, often wretched, conditions. The story also has a sadly ironic dimension. Although the men were busy developing the parks for the future enjoyment of all Canadians, they were not even welcome in the places that directly benefitted from their labour. The same special areas, moreover, that are synonymous today with holiday escape and outdoor activity for people across the country were used at one time to intern other, less fortunate groups. For thousands of men, the parks meant confinement, isolation, and toil.

Looking back over the park prisoner experience, it is apparent that the two world wars and the Depression unleashed some deep-seated fears and tensions—some real, some imagined—among Canadians, whose sense of justice, toleration, and compassion had finite limits. It is also clear that the history of Canada's national parks is about more than wildlife preservation and outdoor recreation, and that places like Yoho, Jasper, and Prince Albert were intimately involved in national developments during the first half of this century.

The story ultimately comes back, however, to individuals such as John Kondro, Ed Turner, Peter Unger, George Funamoto, and thousands of other forgotten "park prisoners." They were the ones who were forced to spend part of their lives in the parks, who worked in relative isolation and anonymity, who gave meaning to the term national playgrounds. Parks Commissioner J.B. Harkin said as much in his 1934 annual report, when he commented about relief workers, "The amount of valuable construction work which has been carried out by the men . . . is a remarkable and a lasting monument to the character and good will of the men themselves during a very dispiriting time of their lives."[2] These words could be applied to all the groups who laboured in Canada's national parks between 1915 and 1946. Unfortunately, the spirit behind them seems to have been forgotten. Little, if anything, has been done to commemorate the camps, the labourers, and their activities. Such recognition—if only the plaquing of a site or structure—is long overdue. These men deserve better.

Aliens (pages 3–47)

1 *National Archives of Canada* [*NAC*], Manuscript Division, William Dillon Otter Papers, Otter Diaries, v. 4, f. 12, 12 March 1915; Government Archives Division, Parks Canada, RG 84, v. 45, f. Bennett, v. 3; D. Morton, "Sir William Otter and Internment Operations in Canada during the First World War," *Canadian Historical Review*, v. 55, n. 1, March 1974, 45.

2 Almost 7 percent of the Canadian population was German or Austro-Hungarian in origin. J. Thompson, *Ethnic Minorities During Two World Wars* (Ottawa 1991), 4.

3 The opposite situation existed in Australia. Since the war was being waged halfway around the world, the Australian government needed an internal enemy to justify the total war effort, and quietly countenanced anti-German hysteria. G. Fischer, *Enemy Aliens: Internment and Homefront Experience in Australia, 1914–20* (St. Lucia, Queensland 1989).

4 For a history of the British wartime experience in this area, see P. Panayi, *The Enemy in Our Midst: Germans in Britain During the First World War* (Oxford 1991).

5 *NAC*, Government Archives Division, Privy Council Office, RG 2, PC 2721, 28 October 1914.

6 During the course of the war, 8,579 men were interned, as well as 81 women and 156 children who voluntarily accompanied them. Only 3,138 internees were military reservists (eligible for military duty if they returned to their home country). J.A. Boudreau, "The Enemy Alien Problem in Canada, 1914–1921," unpublished Ph.D. dissertation (history), University of California, 1965, 34.

7 Within six months of the outbreak of war, 28,420 aliens had registered, while another 1,904 had been interned. Canada, House of Commons, *Debates*, 10 February 1915, 48.

8 See, for example, Canada, *Annual Report of the Department of the Interior*, 1914, pt. v, "Dominion Parks," 3–4.

9 Harkin was obsessed with highways during his early years as dominion parks commissioner, and there are boxes of files from this era dealing with roads and construction techniques. See, for example, *NAC*, Government Archives

Division, Parks Canada, RG 84, v. 104, f. U60, v. 1.

10 The names "Galician" and "Ruthenian" were used interchangeably to identify Ukrainians in early twentieth-century Canada.

11 In 1907, 31 percent of the immigrants entering Canada were classified as unskilled workers (38 percent were farmers). By 1913-14, the proportion of unskilled workers had climbed to 43 percent; almost half of these men were from central and southern Europe. D. Avery, *'Dangerous Foreigners': European Immigrant Workers and Labour Radicalism in Canada* (Toronto 1979), 37.

12 For a firsthand description of these immigrant ghettos, see E.B. Mitchell, *In Western Canada Before the War: Impressions of Early Twentieth Century Prairie Communities* (Saskatoon 1981).

13 J. Petryshyn, *Peasants in the Promised Land: Canada and the Ukrainians, 1891-1914* (Toronto 1985), 94-113.

14 Avery, *'Dangerous Foreigners'*, 65.

15 Of the approximately seventy thousand Ukrainians who entered Canada between 1910 and 1914, 70 percent were unattached males here as guest workers. O. Martynowych, *Ukrainians in Canada: The Formative Years, 1891-1924* (Edmonton 1991), 323.

16 There was a widespread belief at the beginning of the war that enemy agents were busy in Canada and the United States waiting for the right moment to strike. M. Kitchen, "The German Invasion of Canada," *International History Review*, v. 8, n. 2, May 1985, 245-60; J. Keshen, "All the News That Was Fit to Print: Ernest J. Chambers and Information Control in Canada, 1914-19," *Canadian Historical Review*, v. 73, n. 3, September 1992, 319-20.

17 *NAC*, Government Archives Division, Office of the Governor General, RG 7, v. 547, f. 14071C, pt. 2, A.B. Perry to L. Fortesque, 25 February 1915.

18 *Debates*, 10 February 1916, 692.

19 *NAC*, Government Archives Division, Royal Canadian Mounted Police, RG 18, v. 469, f. RCMP 1914 case n. 456, M. Donaldson to A.B. Perry, 21 August 1914.

20 Edmonton *Journal*, 26 February 1916.

21 Quoted in J.H. Thompson, *The Harvests of War: The Prairie West, 1914-1918* (Toronto 1978), 94.

22 B.S. Kordan and P. Melnycky, eds., *In the Shadow of the Rockies: Diary of the Castle Mountain Internment Camp, 1915-1917* (Edmonton 1991), 7.

23 Martynowych, *Ukrainians in Canada*, 325-26.

24 *Ibid.*, 325.

25 *Ibid.* See also Morton, "Sir William Otter and Internment Operations in Canada," 33-58.

26 Boudreau, "The Enemy Alien Problem," 34.

27 Avery, *'Dangerous Foreigners'*, 68.

28 *NAC*, RG 2, PC 2721, 28 October 1914.

29 *Debates*, 22 April 1918, 1021.

30 Calgary *Herald*, 26 August 1915.

31 Martynowych, *Ukrainians in Canada*, 327, 339; Kordan and Melnycky, eds., *In the Shadow of the Rockies*, 15.

32 *Debates*, 24 March 1919, 756.

33 *Ibid.*, 30 March 1915, 1735. Doherty would claim three years later that the men were not compelled to work and that their labour was strictly voluntary. *Debates*, 22 April 1918, 1021.

34 *Ibid.*, 15 February 1916, 850.

35 Boudreau, "The Enemy Alien Problem," 33; Morton, "Sir William Otter and Internment Operations," 41–42.

36 *NAC*, RG 84, v. 45, f. Bennett, v. 3, F.H. Williamson to J.B. Harkin, 19 May 1915.

37 O.T. Martynowych, "The Ukrainian Socialist Movement in Canada, 1900–1918," *Journal of Ukrainian Graduate Studies*, v. 1, n. 1, fall 1976, 30.

38 For a listing of these items, see *NAC*, Government Archives Division, Office of the Custodian of Enemy Property, RG 117, v. 19, f. 224, "Prisoners of War Effects."

39 Canada, *Annual Report of the Department of the Interior*, 1914, pt. v, "Dominion Parks," 5.

40 *NAC*, RG 84, v. 45, f. Bennett, v. 3, R.B. Bennett to J.B. Harkin, 24 May 1915.

41 *Ibid.*, J.B. Harkin to R.B. Bennett, 22 May 1915.

42 Calgary *Daily Herald*, 10 June 1915.

43 Banff *Crag and Canyon*, 12 June 1915.

44 *Ibid.*, 19 June 1915.

45 According to Internment records, these first Banff prisoners were classified as exclusively Austrian; a review of their names, however, suggests that many were Ukrainian.

46 C. Hopkins, ed., *Canadian Annual Review of Public Affairs*, 1915, "Condition and Treatment of Enemy Aliens in Canada," 355.

47 The individual examples are from *NAC*, Government Archives Division, Secretary of State, RG 6, v. 755, f. 3326, pt. 3; and RG 18, v. 1770.

48 *NAC*, RG 6, v. 755, f. 3326, pt. 1, A.B. Perry to Chief Commissioner of Police, 7 July 1916.

49 *NAC*, RG 2, PC 1501, 26 June 1915.

50 Kordan and Melnycky, eds., *In the Shadow of the Rockies*, 10.

51 *NAC*, Government Archives Division, National Defence, RG 24, v. 4721, f. 448-14-173, v. 2, J. Kondro to E.A. Cruikshank, 8 February 1916.

52 The camp diary, held by the Glenbow Museum Archives, has been published with an introduction and explanatory notes by Kordan and Melnycky, eds., *In the Shadow of the Rockies*.

53 *NAC*, RG 84, v. 104, f. U60, v. 1, J.M. Wardle to J.B. Harkin, 17 April 1915.

54 *Ibid.*, J.M. Wardle to J.B. Harkin, 31 August 1915.

55 Kordan and Melnycky, eds., *In the Shadow of the Rockies*, 35.

56 Quoted in *Ibid.*, 49.

57 *Ibid.*, 29, 30–31.

58 *Ibid.*, 30–31.

59 Banff *Crag and Canyon*, 21 August 1915.

60 Otter Papers, Diaries, v. 4, f. 12, 24 August 1915.

61 Revelstoke *Mail Gazette*, 17 July 1915.

62 *Ibid.*, 28 July 1915.

63 *Ibid.*, 31 July 1915.

64 Otter Papers, Diaries, v. 4, f. 12, 20 August 1915.

65 *NAC*, RG 117, v. 20, f. Prisoners of 1914–18 War Repatriation List. This file lists the movement of alien prisoners between 22 May 1914 and 13 August 1918; it includes the date of transfer, the locations involved, and the number and nationality of the men.

66 *NAC*, RG 84, v. 190, f. MR176, J.H. Williamson to W.D. Otter, 6 October 1915; F.E. Maunder to J.B. Harkin, 5 November 1915.

67 *Ibid.*, W.D. Otter to Officer Commanding, 11th District, 15 December 1915.

68 *Ibid.*, W.D. Otter to J.B. Harkin, 4 October 1915.

69 Banff *Crag and Canyon*, 25 September 1915.

70 *NAC*, RG 24, v. 4729, f. 3, D. Stuart to E.A. Cruikshank, 4 November 1915.

71 Quoted in Kordan and Melnycky, eds., *In the Shadow of the Rockies*, 50.

72 *NAC*, RG 24, v. 4721, f. 448–14–173, v. 1, E.A Cruikshank to W.D. Otter, 16 November 1915.

73 *Ibid.*, W.D. Otter to E.A. Cruikshank, 16 December 1915.

74 *Ibid.*, E.A. Cruikshank to W.D. Otter, 2 December 1915.

75 Otter Papers, Diaries, v. 4, f. 12, 1913–25, 23 November 1915.

76 *NAC*, RG 24, v. 4721, f. 448–14–173, v. 1, W.D. Otter to E.A. Cruikshank, 15 December 1915.

77 *NAC*, RG 84, v. 124, f. Y176, v. 1, E.N. Russell to J.B. Harkin, 12 August 1915.

78 *Ibid.*, Palmer to J.B. Harkin, 28 October 1915.

79 Thirty years earlier, during the 1885 North-West Rebellion, the Battleford Indian Industrial School was taken over by Canadian forces under Otter's command, temporarily renamed Fort Otter, and used as headquarters and prison during the troubles in the area.

80 *NAC*, RG 117, v. 20, f. Prisoners of 1914–18 Repatriation Lists. The file lists the death of Anton Marcela (Revelstoke prisoner 191; Brandon 271) on 6 November 1915; it does not provide a cause of death, but simply notes that he was buried in Calgary.

81 *NAC*, RG 84, v. 190, f. MR176, F.E. Maunder to J.B. Harkin, 31 December 1915.

82 *Ibid.*, v. 124, f. Y176, v. 1, E.N. Russell to J.B. Harkin, 24 December 1915.

83 Calgary *Daily Herald*, 10 December 1915.

84 *NAC*, RG 84, v. 124, f. Y176, v. 1, E.N. Russell to J.B. Harkin, 10 November 1915.

85 *Ibid.*, v. 104, f. U60, v. 1, J.M. Wardle to J.B. Harkin, 24 November 1915.

86 *Ibid.*, J.B. Harkin to W.D. Otter, 28 September 1915.

87 It is quite likely that many of the men had worked on the Edmonton-Yellowhead section of one of the two new transcontinental railways, the Canadian Northern and the Grand Trunk Pacific, before the war.

88 Canada, *Annual Report of the Department of the Interior*, 1915, pt. v, "Dominion Parks," 55.

89 Edmonton *Journal*, 19 February 1916.

90 *NAC*, RG 24, v. 4744, f. 448-14-298, v. 1, A.E. Hopkins to E.A. Cruikshank, 19 February 1916.

91 *Ibid.*, A.E. Hopkins to E.A. Cruikshank, 25 February 1916.

92 *Ibid.*, v. 4721, f. 448-14-173, v. 2, A.E. Hopkins to P.M. Spence, 5 January 1916.

93 *Ibid.*, A.E. Cruikshank to W.D. Otter, 28 February 1916.

94 *Ibid.*, H.D. Clum to A.E. Cruikshank, 25 May 1916.

95 This phrase is taken from P. Cohen-Portheim, *Time Stood Still: My Internment in England, 1914–1918* (London 1931).

96 *Ibid.*, 77.

97 Kordan and Melnycky, eds., *In the Shadow of the Rockies*, 58, 60.

98 *NAC*, RG 24, v. 4721, f. 448-14-173, v. 2, W.D. Otter to P.M. Spence, 22 June 1916.

99 *Ibid.*, E.A. Cruikshank to W.D. Otter, 28 February 1916.

100 *Ibid.*, R.H. Brett to E.A. Cruikshank, 16 March 1916; Kordan and Melnycky, eds., *In the Shadow of the Rockies*, 54, 59, 67.

101 *Edmonton Federal Records Centre [EFRC]*, Parks Canada, W85-86/147, v. 35, f. E-1-9, Proceedings of a Court of Inquiry, 10 July 1916.

102 Banff *Crag and Canyon*, 1 July 1916.

103 Calgary *Herald*, 4 March 1916.

104 *NAC*, RG 84, v. 45, f. Bennett, v. 5, R.B. Bennett to J.B. Harkin, 15 March 1916.

105 Bankhead was established in 1902, when the Canadian Pacific Railway found a workable coal seam some four miles outside the Banff townsite and within the park's boundaries.

106 *NAC*, RG 84, v. 45, f. Bennett, v. 5, J.B. Harkin to R.B. Bennett, 2 May 1916.

107 *NAC*, RG 24, v. 4721, f. 448-14-173, v. 2, "Proceedings of a Board of Officers," 13 June 1916; 14 June 1916; 20 June 1916.

108 *NAC*, RG 84, v. 124, f. Y176, E.N. Russell to J.B. Harkin, 7 January 1916.

109 *Ibid.*, J.N. Stinson to J.B. Harkin, 7 February 1916.

110 *NAC*, W85-86/148, Box 3, W.G. Jackson to E.N. Russell, 15 January 1916. This box contains previously unknown weekly work reports for Camp Otter for the winter of 1915-16.

111 *NAC*, RG 84, v. 124, f. Y176, E.N. Russell to J.B. Harkin, 5 February 1916.

112 During his inspection of Camp Otter on 24 November 1915, General Otter noted in his diary that boots were "badly needed." He penned "still in need of boots" during a subsequent inspection of the camp some five months later. Otter Papers, Diaries, v. 4, f. 12, 24 November 1915; 15 April 1916.

113 *NAC*, RG 84, v. 124, f. Y176, E.N. Russell to J.B. Harkin, 5 June 1915.

114 *Ibid.*, E.N. Russell to J.B. Harkin, 29 April 1916.

115 *NAC*, W85-86/148, v. 26, f. 16, pt. 3, W.J. Oke to E.N. Russell, 19 July 1916.

116 There were three possible road projects at Jasper: a road from the townsite down the west side of the Athabasca River to the Hardisty Falls region (today, part of the Icefields Parkway); a road from Pocahontas to the Miette Hot Springs; and finally, a road from Jasper to Maligne Lake.

117 Great Plains Consultants, *Jasper Park: A Social and Economic History* (Ottawa 1985), 288.

118 *NAC*, RG 6-B-1, v. 752, f. 3130, W.D. Otter to Commandant, Edgewood Internment Camp, 17 May 1916.

119 *NAC*, RG 24, v. 4744, f. 448-14-298, v. 4, A.E. Hopkins to E.A. Cruikshank, 8 August 1916.

120 *Ibid.*, v. 3, A.E. Hopkins to E.A. Cruikshank, 16 June 1916.

121 *NAC*, RG 6-B-1, v. 754, f. 3312, A.E. Hopkins to W.D. Otter, 23 May 1916; A.E. Hopkins to W.D. Otter, 30 May 1916; "Court of Enquiry," 8 June 1916; Great Plains Consultants, *Jasper Park*, 228.

122 *NAC*, RG 24, v. 4744, f. 448-14-298, v. 4, A.C. Bury to E.A. Cruikshank, 2 August 1916.

123 Morton, "Sir William Otter and Internment Operations," 55-56; Boudreau, "The Enemy Alien Problem," 35. For a list of the companies that received former prisoners of war, see *NAC*, Government Archives Division, RG 117, Office of the Custodian of Enemy Property, v. 20, POW 1914-18 Repatriation Lists. Several commentators have argued that the 1916 release of Austro-Hungarians confirms that unemployment was the real cause of internment. See Martynowych, *Ukrainians in Canada*, 330, and M. Minenko, "Without Just Cause: Canada's First National Internment Operations" in L. Luciuk and S. Hryniuk, eds., *Canada's Ukrainians: Negotiating an Identity* (Toronto 1991), 295-97.

124 *NAC*, RG 6, v. 752, f. 3130, W.D. Otter to W. Ridgway Wilson, 26 June 1916.

125 *Ibid.*, v. 755, f. 3326, pt. 3, List of Banff undesirables, 23 April 1917.

126 Upon a prisoner's release, the following forms were sent to Ottawa: medical history sheet, conduct sheet, statement of account, and release undertaking. Most of these records were considered expendable and were subsequently destroyed.

127 *NAC*, RG 6, v. 755, f. 3326, pt. 1, D.W. Coleman to W.D. Otter, 22 June 1916; f. 3326, pt. 2, Staff Officer, Internment Operations to Chief Commissioner of Dominion Police, 27 September 1916.

128 Canada, *Annual Report of the Department of the Interior*, 1917, pt. v, "Dominion Parks," 54.

129 *NAC*, RG 6, v. 754, f. 3219, pt. 1, G.H. Brock to W.D. Otter, 17 July 1916.

130 *NAC*, RG 84, v. 124, f. Y176, E.N. Russell to J.B. Harkin, 9 August 1916.

131 *Ibid.*, 12 August 1916.

132 *Ibid.*, G.H. Brock to W.D. Otter, 23 August 1916.

133 *Ibid.*

134 *Ibid.*, E.N. Russell to J.B. Harkin, 28 August 1916.

135 *Ibid.*, J.B. Harkin to W.D. Otter, 30 August 1916.

136 *Ibid.*, E.N. Russell to J.B. Harkin, 25 September 1916.

137 *Golden Star*, 5 October 1916.

138 *NAC*, RG 84, v. 124, f. Y176, E.N. Russell to J.B. Harkin, 8 October 1916.

139 *Golden Star*, 5 October 1916.

140 *NAC*, W85-86/148, v. 1, f. 201, E.N. Russell to J.B. Harkin, 24 October 1916.

141 Kordan and Melnycky, eds., *In the Shadow of the Rockies*, 104.

142 *NAC*, RG 6, v. 755, f. 3326, pt. 3, W.D. Otter to A.D. MacTier, 8 May 1917; Avery, *'Dangerous Foreigners,'* 69–70.

143 Kordan and Melnycky, eds., *In the Shadow of the Rockies*, 71.

144 *NAC*, RG 84, v. 104, f. U60, v. 1, J.M. Wardle to J.B. Harkin, 29 April 1916.

145 *Whyte Museum of the Canadian Rockies*, NT 91, Acc. 1838, Colonel J. Anderson-Wilson interview, 4 May 1973.

146 Banff *Crag and Canyon*, 19 August 1916.

147 Calgary *Herald*, 17 November 1916.

148 *Ibid.*, 28 September 1916.

149 *NAC*, RG 24, v. 4721, F. 448-14-173, v. 2, E.A. Cruikshank to W.D. Otter, 11 December 1916. At the time of the inspection, there were 210 prisoners and 129 military personnel in the camp.

150 Banff *Crag and Canyon*, 25 November 1916.

151 Kordan and Melnycky, eds., *In the Shadow of the Rockies*, 104.

152 Banff *Crag and Canyon*, 21 February 1916.

153 *Ibid.*, 30 December 1916.

154 *NAC*, W85-86/147, v. 34, f. B-2-8, J.B. Harkin to S.J. Clarke, 28 December 1916; f. C-2-1, S.J. Clarke to J.B. Harkin, 29 December 1916. In July 1917, the camp commandant asked permission to erect railings around the three graves.

155 *NAC*, RG 84, v. 70, f. R313-1, S.J. Clarke to J.B. Harkin, 20 June 1917.

156 On 5 May 1994, the Saskatoon *StarPhoenix* reported that the Siksika Indian band of Alberta was claiming more than a hundred acres in the Castle Mountain area and was proposing to build a casino near the old internment site.

157 Canada, *Annual Report of the Department of the Interior*, 1919, pt. ii, "Dominion Parks," 24.

158 *Debates*, 22 April 1918, 974–75. When the war was over, Clements's attitude towards enemy aliens remained bitter. He declared in the House, "I say unhesitantly that every enemy alien who was interned during the war is today just as much an enemy as he was during the war, and I demand of this Government that each and every alien in this dominion should be deported at the earliest opportunity . . . Cattle ships are good enough for them." *Ibid.*, 24 March 1919, 753–54.

159 *Ibid.*, 997.

160 *Golden Star*, 23 May 1918.

161 *Debates*, 22 April 1918, 1020.

162 Canada, *Annual Report of the Department of the Interior*, 1919, pt. ii, "Dominion Parks," 6–10.

163 Eight hundred of the interned Germans had been transferred from the West Indies and held in Canada at the request of the British government. *NAC*, RG 6, v. 770, f. 6712, v. 1, W.D. Otter to Deputy Minister of Justice, 19 December 1918.

164 For an examination of how the Borden government used internment and censorship to deal with the so-called Bolshevik threat, see G.S. Kealey, "State Repression of Labour and the Left in Canada, 1914–20: The Impact of

the First World War," *Canadian Historical Review*, v. 73, n. 3, September 1992, 292–94.

165 *NAC*, RG 2, PC 158, 23 January 1920.

166 W.D. Otter, *Internment Operations 1914–1920* (Ottawa 1921), 14.

167 General Otter estimated that the prisoners provided 640,000 man-days of work and were thereby eligible to receive $160,000. *NAC*, RG 2, PC 574, 17 March 1920.

168 As of 30 June 1926, the unclaimed balance for the Banff operations was $4,188.57; Jasper, $966.78; and Otter, $220.73. The Otter figure probably excludes the men who were transferred to Kapuskasing. *NAC*, RG 6, v. 819, f. Special Accounts and Records, 1914–1918, WWI, A.H. Mathieu to Deputy Custodian, 16 May 1951. The fate of the records is explained in G. Wright, "Destruction of First World War Internment Records," unpublished *NAC* report, February 1990.

169 Canada, *Annual Report of the Department of the Interior*, 1919, pt. ii, "Dominion Parks," 6.

170 *Ibid.*, 4.

Relief Workers *(pages 48–84)*

1 *National Archives of Canada [NAC]*, Government Archives Division, Indian and Northern Affairs, RG 22, v. 589, f. U121–3, v. 3, J.B. Harkin to W.W. Cory, 3 September 1930.

2 *Canadian Parks Service [CPS]*, Western Regional Office, Webster Collection, J.M. Wardle to J.B. Harkin, 29 April 1918.

3 *NAC*, RG 22, v. 589, f. U121–3, v. 3, J.B. Harkin to W.W. Cory, 13 December 1930.

4 See, for example, Canada, House of Commons, *Debates*, 14 June 1923, 3942.

5 Although Harkin wanted a national park in Saskatchewan, the creation of Prince Albert was done at Prime Minister Mackenzie King's insistence, as a political reward to his new constituency. See B. Waiser, *Saskatchewan's Playground: A History of Prince Albert National Park* (Saskatoon 1989), 25–35.

6 L. Alderson and J. Marsh, "J.B. Harkin, National Parks and Roads," *Park News*, XV, 2, summer 1979, 9–16.

7 Canada, *Annual Report of the Department of the Interior*, 1925, pt. iii, "Dominion Parks," 90.

8 L. Bella, *Parks for Profit* (Montreal 1987), 59–87.

9 In 1914, the federal government spent .5% of its total budget on national parks; between 1914 and 1947, this amount averaged .28%. *Ibid.*, 79.

10 *NAC*, RG 22, v. 589, f. U121–3, v. 3, J.B. Harkin to W.W. Cory, 3 September 1930.

11 See D. De Brou and B. Waiser, eds., *Documenting Canada: A History of Modern Canada in Documents* (Saskatoon 1992), 304.

12 For a discussion of how the federal government effectively used the British North America Act as a shield to prevent it from assuming direct responsi-

bility for unemployment during the Depression, see J. Struthers, *No Fault of Their Own: Unemployment and the Canadian Welfare State, 1914–1941* (Toronto 1983), 44–70.

13 Bennett was determined to preserve the notion that relief was primarily a local responsibility and that the grant was specifically designed to help the provinces discharge their constitutional obligations; he did not want the principle muddied by allowing government departments to have direct access to the fund. *NAC*, Government Archives Division, Labour, RG 27, v. 2264, f. Relief Works Correspondence 1930-31, T.G. Murphy to H.H. Stevens, 24 October 1930.

14 *NAC*, RG 22, v. 589, f. U121-3, v. 3, H.H. Stevens to J.B. Harkin, 22 August 1930.

15 L. Glassford, *Reaction and Reform: The Politics of the Conservative Party under R.B. Bennett 1927–1938* (Toronto 1992), 102.

16 Prince Albert *Daily Herald*, 17 January 1931; see also 21 January 1931.

17 *Ibid.*, 24 January 1931.

18 *NAC*, RG 22, v. 589, f. U121-3, v. 3, J.B. Harkin to W.W. Cory, 13 October 1930.

19 *Ibid.*, 12 January 1931.

20 The disbursement was justified on the grounds that a similar amount was omitted from the 1930-31 supplementary estimates for the Parks Department. The funds were to be divided: Banff, $16,000; Jasper, $15,000; Waterton Lakes, $2,000.

21 Struthers, *No Fault of Their Own*, 12–43.

22 J.H. Gray, *The Winter Years* (Toronto 1966), 8.

23 B. Broadfoot, *Ten Lost Years 1929–1939: Memories of Canadians Who Survived the Depression* (Toronto 1973), 72; see also L.M. Grayson and M. Bliss, eds., *The Wretched of Canada: Letters to R.B. Bennett, 1930–1935* (Toronto 1971).

24 *Ibid.*, 70.

25 *Debates*, 3 July 1931, 3368.

26 *Ibid.*, 3376.

27 *Statutes of Canada*, 21-22 George V, chap. 58, "The Unemployment and Farm Relief Act," assented to 3 August 1931.

28 *NAC*, RG 27, v. 2264, f. Relief Works Correspondence 1930-31, Calgary Board of Trade to T.G. Murphy, 2 October 1930; Edmonton *Journal*, 26 September 1930; Calgary *Daily Herald*, 26 September 1930.

29 Struthers, *No Fault of Their Own*, 53.

30 Bennett's Calgary West riding included Banff National Park, while that of H.H. Stevens, the minister of Trade and Commerce, contained Yoho and Kootenay National Parks. T.G. Murphy's Neepawa constituency bordered Riding Mountain; the only national park in the province, it was a kind of regional playground for central Manitoba. Waterton Lakes and Elk Island National Parks were represented by Tory backbenchers J.S Stewart and Ambrose Bury, respectively.

31 J.H. Thompson and A. Seager, *Canada 1922-1939: Decades of Discord* (Toronto 1985), 213-14, 216.

32 *NAC*, Government Archives Division, Civil Service, RG 32, v. 250, f. J.M. Wardle.

33 *NAC*, RG 2, PC 2721, 2 November 1931. This amount is even more remarkable when it is realized that Riding Mountain's regular annual grant, unlike all other national parks, also more than doubled for the 1931–32 fiscal year (from $67,583 to $155,457). More than half of the $200,000 relief grant was spent on "clearing and brushing"—this exceeded the grant allotted to any of the other national parks for 1931–32.

34 *NAC*, RG 22, v. 588, f. RM2, J. Smart to J.M. Wardle, 25 August 1930.

35 Minnedosa *Tribune*, 17 December 1931.

36 Jimmy Brown interview, 14 August 1991.

37 Confidential interview with former Riding Mountain relief worker, 14 March 1994; 14 April 1994.

38 Ed Turner interview, 21 May 1991.

39 Minnedosa *Tribune*, 7 January 1932.

40 Victor Creed interview, 9 March 1994.

41 Minnedosa *Tribune*, 7 April 1932.

42 "Riding Mountain National Park Building Report," 56–65 (this in-house report contains several previously prepared Federal Heritage Buildings Review Office reports); L. Dick, "Forgotten Roots: The Gardens of Wasagaming," *NeWest Review*, November 1986, 10–11.

43 Victor Creed interview, 9 March 1994.

44 *NAC*, RG 22, v. 588, f. RM2, J.M. Wardle to J.B. Harkin, 29 March 1932.

45 F. Goble, "The 20-Cent Men," unpublished manuscript, 302.

46 Confidential interview with former Riding Mountain relief worker, 14 April 1994.

47 Jimmy Brown interview, 14 August 1991.

48 Confidential interview with former Riding Mountain relief worker, 14 April 1994.

49 Goble, "The 20-Cent Men," 306.

50 Confidential interview with former Riding Mountain relief worker, 14 March 1994.

51 Minnedosa *Tribune*, 18 February 1932; *NAC*, RG 22, v. 588, f. RM2, J.M. Wardle to J.B. Harkin, 29 March 1932.

52 Throughout the Depression, Prince Albert authorities were forever comparing their budget with that of Riding Mountain; by November 1935, the date the Liberals returned to office, Riding Mountain expenditures over the five years of Conservative rule outstripped those of Prince Albert by more than $600,000.

53 The Bennett government might also have been trying to help the perennially unsuccessful Conservative candidate for Prince Albert, future prime minister John Diefenbaker, who had been defeated by King in the 1926 federal election and had just lost in the 1929 provincial election.

54 In the early 1930s, there was an intense debate over the carrying capacity of Elk Island and whether the herd should be culled; the superintendent argued that the park could support 3,000 bison, while Ottawa officials set

the figure at 1,500. C.B. Blyth and R.J. Hudson, *Elk Island National Park: A Plan for the Management of Vegetation and Ungulates* (Elk Island 1987), 181-84; See also G. A. MacDonald, "Science and History at Elk Island National Park: Conservation and its Contradictions," unpublished paper presented before Canadian Historical Association, Calgary 1994.

55 See De Brou and Waiser, eds., *Documenting Canada*, 299-302.

56 Lamont *Tribune*, 1 October 1931; 29 October 1931; 17 December 1931.

57 *NAC*, RG 84, v. 218, f. W60, J.M. Wardle to R.A. Gibson, 4 November 1930. For an examination of the link between the Great Northern Railway and Glacier National Park, see M.G. Schene, "The Crown of the Continent: Private Enterprise and Public Interest in the Early Development of Glacier National Park, 1910-17," *Forest and Conservation History*, April 1990, 69-75.

58 Calgary *Herald*, 6 December 1929.

59 Frank Goble interview, 28 June 1993.

60 F. Goble to B. Waiser, 25 November 1993.

61 Quoted from interview in possession of Frank Goble, F. Goble to B. Waiser, 25 November 1993.

62 Goble, "The 20-Cent Men," 61.

63 *CPS*, Webster Collection, J.M. Wardle to H. Knight, 13 January 1932.

64 *Ibid.*, J.M. Wardle to J.B. Harkin, 4 April 1932; J.M. Wardle to J.B. Harkin, 24 March 1932.

65 For a summary of these projects see *NAC*, RG 84, v. 212, f. J121-3, v. 2, J.B. Snape to R.H. Knight, 30 March 1931.

66 Edmonton *Journal*, 21 November 1931.

67 *Ibid.*, 8 December 1930.

68 *Ibid.*, 3 December 1931.

69 *NAC*, RG 84, v. 213, f. J121-3, v. 3, A. Bury to T.G. Murphy, 18 November 1931.

70 Reverend Edwards surveyed 213 men in six of eight Jasper camps and found 197 without proper underwear, 195 without thick socks, 120 without outer coats, 125 without proper footwear, 117 without woollen shirts, 105 without work mitts, 90 without winter caps, 130 without cloth pants, and 120 without sweaters or wind breakers. The daily temperatures were -20°F. Edmonton *Journal*, 20 November 1931.

71 *NAC*, RG 84, v. 213, f. J121-3, v. 3, J.M. Wardle to J.B. Harkin, 23 November 1931.

72 *Ibid.*, J.B. Harkin to H.H. Rowatt, 30 November 1931.

73 *Edmonton Federal Records Centre [EFRC]*, Parks Canada, 85-86/147, v. 20, f. R12-3, Banff Advisory Council to T.G. Murphy, 8 August 1931.

74 *NAC*, RG 22, v. 582, f. B121-3, v. 2, J.B. Harkin to H.H. Rowatt, 16 September 1931.

75 *EFRC*, 85-86/147, v. 20, f. R12-3, memorandum for file, P.J. Jennings, 31 October 1931.

76 See, for example, Calgary *Daily Herald*, 5 November 1931.

77 *EFRC*, 85-86/147, v. 20, f. R12-3, P.J. Jennings to J.M. Wardle, 27 November 1931.

78 *Ibid.*, J.M. Wardle to P.J. Jennings, 2 December 1931.

79 *NAC*, RG 2, PC 3056, 10 December 1931; PC 117, 20 January 1932.

80 In early 1932, for example, Wardle contacted the prime minister's office when additional funds were needed to keep the Banff relief operations going until the end of February. *NAC*, Manuscript Division, R.B. Bennett Papers, p. 490665, J.M. Wardle to A.W. Merriam, 11 January 1932.

81 *Provincial Archives of Alberta [PAA]*, National Parks Branch, Engineering and Construction Service, 69.218, v. 12, f. B60–23 (120b), J.M. Wardle to J.B. Harkin, 6 October 1931.

82 Calgary *Daily Herald*, 10 December 1931.

83 Edmonton *Journal*, 21 September 1931.

84 *Ibid.*, 29 September 1931.

85 *Ibid.*, 3 December 1931.

86 *PAA*, 69.218, v. 12, f. B60–23 (120a), J.B. Harkin to H.H. Rowatt, 19 February 1932.

87 Confidential interview with former Riding Mountain relief worker, 14 April 1994.

88 Calgary *Daily Herald*, 24 December 1931; 31 December 1931.

89 *Ibid.*, 10 December 1931.

90 *NAC*, RG 22, v. 586, f. K121-3, J.M. Wardle to J.B. Harkin, 3 November 1931.

91 *Ibid.*, J.B. Harkin to H.H. Rowatt, 12 March 1932.

92 For a review of federal-provincial co-operative highway building, see D.W. Monaghan, "A Capital Idea: Federal-Provincial Relations and the Construction of the Trans-Canada Highway, 1949–1956," unpublished paper presented before Canadian Historical Association, Ottawa, 1993.

93 In an effort to circumvent the avalanche problem, the Canadian Pacific Railway built the Connaught Tunnel below Rogers Pass in 1916. The story of the railway's struggle with the environment is told in J.G. Woods, *Snow War: An Illustrated History of Rogers Pass, Glacier National Park, BC* (Toronto 1985). The Trans-Canada Highway opened in the pass area in 1962.

94 *NAC*, RG 84, v. 210, f. GR60, J.M. Wardle to J.B. Harkin, 2 April 1931.

95 *Golden Star*, 8 August 1930.

96 No relief work was undertaken in nearby Mount Revelstoke and Glacier National Parks in favour of providing local employment on the Golden-Revelstoke project.

97 *CPS*, Webster Collection, A.G. Wilkins to J.M. Wardle, 15 November 1931.

98 Ben Fisher interview, 22 March 1994.

99 *CPS*, Webster Collection, J.M. Wardle to A.G. Wilkins, 16 November 1931.

100 *NAC*, RG 22, v. 584, f. GR1, J.M. Wardle to J.B. Harkin, 30 November 1931.

101 *Ibid.*, J.B. Harkin to H.H. Rowatt, 30 November 1931.

102 In late February 1932, for example, Premier Brownlee of Alberta complained that the scheduled closure of the camps would create a dangerous situation in the already overburdened cities. See Bennett Papers, pp. 477972–74, J. Brownlee to R.B. Bennett, 24 February 1932.

103 Construction of the bathhouse continued through the spring, well beyond

the life of the 1931 relief act; it was officially opened on 27 June 1932.

104 Struthers, *No Fault of Their Own*, 59-60, 76; Thompson and Seager, *Canada 1922-1939*, 216.

105 Between 15 September 1931 and 31 March 1932, 4,354 people were given employment on one of the many parks projects. Canada, *Annual Report of the Department of the Interior*, 1932, pt. iii, "National Parks of Canada," 91.

106 Ben Fisher interview, 22 March 1994.

107 Confidential interview with former Riding Mountain relief worker, 14 March 1994; 14 April 1994.

108 *Debates*, 13 April 1932, 1999.

109 Struthers, *No Fault of Their Own*, 60, 92; Thompson and Seager, *Canada 1922-1939*, 218-19.

110 *Ibid.*

111 *PAA*, 69.218, v. 12, f. B60-23 (120a), J.M. Wardle to J.B. Harkin, 22 April 1932.

112 *Statutes of Canada*, 22-23 George V, chap. 36, "The Relief Act, 1932," assented to 13 May 1932.

113 *Debates*, 28 April 1932, 2446; 11 May 1932, 2839.

114 Bennett Papers, p. 493667, R.C. Rathbone to R. Armitage, 1 June 1932; see also Calgary *Herald*, 19 May 1932.

115 *PAA*, 69.218, v. 12, f. B60-23 (120a), J.M. Wardle to J.B. Harkin, 23 April 1932.

116 Calgary *Herald*, 27 May 1932.

117 *PAA*, 69.218, v. 12, f. B60-23 (120a), J.M. Wardle to J.B. Harkin, 2 June 1932.

118 *Ibid.*, J.E. Brownlee to T.G. Murphy, 17 June 1932; T.G. Murphy to J.E. Brownlee, 23 June 1932. These heavy-handed tactics worked until the end of July, when Calgary and Edmonton stopped providing relief for the single unemployed. Local men could no longer be intimidated into going to the highway camps, and relief officers had to turn to transients to fill any vacancies.

119 Edmonton *Journal*, 3 July 1932; 4 July 1932.

120 *PAA*, 69.218, v. 13, f. B60-23 (121c), G. Hoadley to T.G. Murphy, 16 July 1932.

121 *Ibid.*, f. B60-23 (121b), J.M. Wardle to J.B. Harkin, 4 August 1932.

122 Calgary *Daily Herald*, 10 September 1932.

123 Banff *Crag and Canyon*, 16 September 1932.

124 Edmonton *Journal*, 7 June 1933.

Transients *(pages 85-128)*

1 For a contemporary assessment of the single transient and unemployed youth problems during the 1930s, see L. Richter, ed., *Canada's Unemployment Problem* (Toronto 1939), 111-221.

2 A. Roddan, *Canada's Untouchables* (Vancouver 1932), 14. See also I. Baird, *Waste Heritage* (Toronto 1939).

3 *National Archives of Canada* [*NAC*], Manuscript Division, R.B. Bennett

Papers, pp. 49366–72, W.A. Gordon to R.B Bennett, 14 June 1932.

4 B. Roberts, *Whence They Came: Deportation from Canada, 1900–1935* (Ottawa 1988), 171. There were 17,229 public charge deportations between 1929–30 and 1934–35.

5 H. Palmer, *Patterns of Prejudice: A History of Nativism in Alberta* (Toronto 1982), 127–32.

6 Quoted in F. Goble to B. Waiser, 25 November 1993. See also H.M. Cassidy, "Relief and Other Services for Transients," in Richter, ed., *Canada's Unemployment Problem*, 178–80.

7 *NAC*, Bennett Papers, pp. 49366–72 , W.A. Gordon to R.B. Bennett, 14 June 1932.

8 L. Brown, *When Freedom Was Lost: The Unemployed, the Agitator, and the State* (Montreal 1987), 31–45.

9 L-R. Betcherman, *The Little Band: The Clashes between the Communists and the Political and Legal Establishment in Canada, 1928–1932* (Ottawa 1985), 93, 105.

10 G.S. Kealey and R. Whitaker, eds., *RCMP Security Bulletins: The Depression Years, Part I, 1933–34* (St. John's 1993).

11 Betcherman, *The Little Band*, 142.

12 *Public Archives of Alberta [PAA]*, National Parks Branch, Engineering and Construction Service, acc. no. 69.218, v. 13, f. B60-23 (120c), J.M. Wardle to J.B. Harkin, 14 September 1932.

13 *NAC*, Government Archives Division, Indian and Northern Affairs, RG 22, v. 583, f. G–1, J.B. Harkin to H.H. Rowatt, 28 October 1928.

14 Relief work at Point Pelee was included in the October 1932 order-in-council that provided funds for transient camps in national parks (*NAC*, Government Archives Division, Privy Council, RG 2, PC 2358, 21 October 1932). A later order-in-council (PC 2581) that dealt specifically with Point Pelee was never approved.

15 In late November 1932, the Bennett government approved two grants (totalling $50,000) to provide relief work for national park residents who were otherwise disqualified from the transient camps.

16 F. Goble, "The 20-Cent Men," unpublished manuscript, 312.

17 F. Goble to B. Waiser, 25 November 1993.

18 Confidential interview with former Riding Mountain relief worker, 14 April 1994.

19 C. Neville interview, 25 March 1994; L. Burkett interview, 13 July 1994.

20 *Canadian Parks Service [CPS]*, Western Regional Office, Webster Collection, J.M. Wardle to H. Knight, 20 February 1933. Frank Goble, who was in the Waterton camps during the winter of 1932–33, heard nothing about written complaints.

21 *Ibid.*, J.M. Wardle to J.B. Harkin, 18 March 1933.

22 Lamont *Tribune*, 10 November 1932.

23 *NAC*, RG 22, v. 583, f. E2, J.M. Wardle to J.B. Harkin, 11 February 1933.

24 This latter work was probably done in part to appease the Prince Albert Board of Trade, which had unsuccessfully lobbied the Parks Branch to use

the relief workers to build several rows of small, cheap cottages, for rent or purchase, along the waterfront. *Ibid.*, Parks Canada, RG 84, v. 1734, f. PA21, pt. 3, v. 2, J. Curror to T.G. Murphy, 20 April 1932.

25 Prince Albert *Daily Herald*, 13 January 1933.

26 *Ibid.*, 2 May 1933.

27 *NAC*, RG 22, v. 588, f. RM2, "List of Occupations."

28 Confidential interview with former Riding Mountain relief worker, 14 April 1994.

29 Canada, House of Commons, *Debates*, 22 November 1932, 1450.

30 The letter was subsequently reproduced in the 1 December 1932 issue of the Winnipeg-based *Jack Canuck*.

31 *Debates*, 22 November 1932, 1450.

32 *Ibid.*, 23 November 1932, 1484.

33 *NAC*, RG 22, v. 588, f. RM2, J.B. Harkin to S.M. Rogers, 17 December 1932; S.M. Rogers to J.B. Harkin, 27 December 1932.

34 *Ibid.*, J. Smart to J.B. Harkin, 10 December 1932.

35 This bath schedule was confirmed by Ed Turner during a May 1991 interview.

36 *NAC*, RG 22, v. 588, f. RM2, J. Smart to J.B. Harkin, 10 December 1932.

37 *Ibid.*, J.M. Wardle to J.B. Harkin, 29 March 1932.

38 *Ibid.*, J. Smart to J.B. Harkin, 10 December 1932.

39 Minnedosa *Tribune*, 30 March 1933.

40 Walter Crossman interview, 24 April 1994.

41 The Minnedosa *Tribune* carried regular weekly reports on the various activities in the park camps, including reviews of the Saturday evening programme.

42 *NAC*, RG 22, v. 588, f. RM2, J. Smart to J.B. Harkin, 10 December 1932.

43 Ed Turner interview, August 1991.

44 Lorne Burkett interview, 13 July 1994; see also Minnedosa *Tribune*, 30 March 1933.

45 Quoted in *NAC*, RG 84, v. 218, f. U316, J.B. Harkin to H.H. Rowatt, 23 December 1931.

46 *NAC*, RG 22, v. 588, f. RM2, J. Smart to J.B. Harkin, 11 April 1933.

47 *Ibid.*, H.H. Rowatt to J.B. Harkin, 28 December 1932.

48 *Ibid.*, J. Smart to J.B. Harkin, 25 January 1933; Frank Goble to B. Waiser, 25 November 1993; F. Goble to B. Waiser, 10 August 1994.

49 Prince Albert *Daily Herald*, 2 February 1933.

50 For the month of December 1932, there were 2,958 men housed in the national park camps, who provided 60,924 man-days of work for the month. The DND camps employed 1,982 men in January 1933, and the man-days of work for the month were 41,127. *Debates,* 24 February 1933, 2460, 2462.

51 Dauphin *Herald and Press*, 16 March 1933.

52 Prince Albert *Daily Herald*, 22 May 1933.

53 Edmonton *Journal*, 7 June 1933.

54 *NAC*, RG 84, v. 212, f. B60–23, v. 2, J.B. Harkin to H.H. Rowatt, 16 May 1933.

55 *Ibid.*, memorandum of meeting, 31 May 1933. To please the Defence

Department, it was subsequently agreed to call the park camp food allowance a "ration list."

56 *Ibid.*, J.B. Harkin to H.H. Rowatt, 2 June 1933.

57 *NAC*, RG 2, PC 730, 20 April 1933.

58 *Golden Star*, 7 July 1933.

59 Banff *Crag and Canyon*, 19 May 1933.

60 *NAC*, RG 84, v. 219, f. W60-4, J.M. Wardle to J.B. Harkin, 8 January 1934.

61 Lorne Burkett interview, 13 July 1994.

62 Ben Fisher interview, 22 March 1994.

63 *NAC*, RG 84, v. 219, f. W60-4, J.M. Wardle to J.B. Harkin, 4 July 1933.

64 *Ibid.*, 9 September 1933.

65 *Waterton Lakes National Park* [*WLNP*], Historical Files, J.K. Mulloy to C.K. LeCapelin, 23 December 1933.

66 This figure was arrived at by dividing the total July expenses (wages, groceries, clothing, materials, etc.) by the total number of man-days worked that month. *NAC*, RG 84, v. 212, f. B60-23, v. 2, J.M. Wardle to J.B. Harkin, 9 September 1933.

67 *Ibid.*, v. 218, f. U316, J.B. Harkin to H.H. Rowatt, 6 November 1931.

68 *Ibid.*, v. 420, f. B60-23, v. 12, J.M. Wardle to J.B. Harkin, 2 February 1934.

69 B. Broadfoot, *Ten Lost Years 1929-1939: Memories of Canadians Who Survived the Depression* (Toronto 1973), 96.

70 *NAC*, RG 84, v. 212, f. B60-23, v. 2, J.M. Wardle to J.B. Harkin, 15 July 1933.

71 Prince Albert *Daily Herald*, 25 April 1933.

72 Financed through private donations, Frontier College hired university students or graduates to conduct classes in the camps in elementary subjects. The instructors would work a regular shift alongside the other men and then teach in the evening. Because of the scattered nature of the park camp operations, classes were offered only at Riding Mountain.

73 The cook and his flunkies put in long days, and these mealtime provisions were necessary if they were to keep on schedule. F. Goble to B. Waiser, 25 November 1993.

74 Ben Fisher interview, 25 March 1994.

75 Quoted in *NAC*, RG 22, v. 588, f. RM2, H.H. Rowatt to J.B. Harkin, 28 December 1932.

76 Confidential interview with former Riding Mountain relief worker, 14 April 1994.

77 *Prince Albert National Park* [*PANP*], Historical Files, J.A. Wood to A. Ross, 25 November 1932.

78 *NAC*, RG 84, v. 213, f. B60-23, v. 12, H.H. Rowatt to J.B. Harkin, 15 November 1933.

79 *Ibid.*, 30 November 1933.

80 *NAC*, Government Archives Division, Labour, RG 24, v. 2966, f. Unemployment Relief Meeting, 12 December 1933.

81 *NAC*, RG 84, v. 73, f. E313, H.A. White to T. Murphy, 30 September 1933.

82 Quoted in *Ibid.*, v. 212, f. B60-23, v. 2, J.B. Harkin to J.M. Wardle, 29 September 1933.

83 *Ibid.*, A.G. Wilkins to J.M. Wardle, 23 November 1933.

84 *NAC*, RG 22, v. 581, F. B1-1, P.J. Jennings to J.B. Harkin, 16 April 1934.

85 *Ibid.*, P.J. Jennings to J.B. Harkin, 24 April 1934.

86 *NAC*, RG 84, v. 213, f. B60-23, v. 12, J.B. Harkin to H.H. Rowatt, 3 January 1934.

87 Wardle calculated that the average cost per meal for all national park relief operations for the period April to December 1933 was 11.17 cents; the average cost per man per day for the same period was 33.51 cents. *Ibid.*, J.M. Wardle to J.B. Harkin, 2 February 1934.

88 *Ibid.*, J.B. Harkin to H.H. Rowatt, 16 February 1934.

89 *Ibid.*, "Unemployment Relief in National Parks," 12 March 1934. This document provides a detailed account of relief work in the various national parks for the period 1 April 1932 to 31 January 1934. *Debates*, 10 April 1934, 2017-23.

90 *Ibid.*, v. 213, f. B60-23, v. 12, J.M. Wardle to J.B. Harkin, 24 February 1934.

91 *NAC*, RG 22, v. 581, f. B1-1, J.M. Wardle to J.B. Harkin, 10 May 1934.

92 A. Finkel, *Business and Social Reform in the Thirties* (Toronto 1979), 100, 104, 113.

93 L. Glassford, *Reaction and Reform: The Politics of the Conservative Party under R.B. Bennett 1927-1938* (Toronto 1992), 127.

94 *NAC*, Bennett Papers, pp. 497287-88, T.G. Murphy to R.B. Bennett, 24 January 1934.

95 Glassford, *Reaction and Reform*, 127-28; *Debates*, 10 April 1934, 2122-23.

96 J. Struthers, *No Fault of Their Own: Unemployment and the Canadian Welfare State, 1914-1941* (Toronto 1983), 119-20.

97 Doug Owram, *Building for Canadians: A History of the Department of Public Works* (Ottawa 1979), 237-43; Janet Wright, "Building in the Bureaucracy: Architecture of the Department of Public Works," unpublished M.A. thesis (History), Queen's University, 1988, 80-83.

98 *Statutes of Canada*, 24-25 George V, chap. 59, "The Public Works Construction Act," assented to 3 July 1934.

99 Owram, *Building for Canadians*, 239; Wright, "Building in the Bureaucracy," 83-85.

100 *NAC*, Bennett Papers, pp. 497514-16, T.G. Murphy to R.B. Bennett, 28 March 1934.

101 *NAC*, RG 22, v. 581, f. B1-1, Memorandum of Meeting, 1 August 1934.

102 *Ibid.*, J.B. Harkin to R.A. Gibson, 29 December 1934.

103 *Ibid.*, T.G. Murphy to A.G. McNaughton, 1 August 1934.

104 *Ibid.*, J.M. Wardle to J.B. Harkin, 2 August 1934.

105 *PAA*, acc. no. 69.218, v. 9, f. B56-34 (92b), "East Entrance Buildings, 1930-41"; S. Coutts, "East Gate, Banff National Park, Banff, Alberta," Federal Heritage Buildings Review Office, Building Report 84-55.

106 J. Harris, "Administration Building, Banff National Park, Banff, Alberta," Federal Heritage Buildings Review Office, Building Report 85-53.

107 *Edmonton Federal Records Centre [EFRC]*, Parks Canada, acc. 85–86/147, v. 47, f. PW1, "Return of Men Employed," 7 September 1935.

108 Banff *Crag and Canyon*, 19 October 1934; Calgary *Albertan*, 23 November 1934. Prior to starting work on the Cascades, Parks officials contacted England's Crystal Palace about its collection of antediluvian animals.

109 *NAC*, RG 84, v. 66, f. B28–1, v. 2, H.C. Beckett to J.B. Harkin, 24 July 1935.

110 E. Mills, "Bathhouse, Miette Hot Springs, Jasper National Park, Alberta," Federal Heritage Buildings Review Office, Building Report 83–66.

111 E. Mills, "Administration Building, Waterton Lakes National Park, Alberta," Federal Heritage Buildings Review Office, Building Report 84–23.

112 E. Mills, "Registration Building, Waterton Lakes National Park, Alberta," Federal Heritage Buildings Review Office, Building Report 84–03.

113 F. Goble to B. Waiser, 25 November 1993.

114 *PAA*, acc. no. 69.218, v. 13, f. B60–23 (122b), J.B. Harkin to R.A. Gibson, 13 November 1934.

115 Edmonton *Journal*, 18 October 1934.

116 Edson *Leader*, 11 October 1934.

117 Edmonton *Journal*, 15 June 1939.

118 *NAC*, RG 84, v. 209, f. GR60, v. 4, J.M. Wardle to J.B. Harkin, 29 November 1934.

119 *Ibid.*, A.G. McNaughton to R.A. Gibson, 1 March 1935.

120 *Ibid.*, "Memorandum: Big Bend Highway," 5 December 1934.

121 *Ibid.*, "Memorandum," 29 April 1935.

122 Court Neville interview, 25 March 1994.

123 J.B.S., "The Big Bend Road." A copy of the ballad was kindly provided to the author by James Sime of Golden, British Columbia.

124 Court Neville interview, 25 March 1994.

125 T. Parkin, "Mysterious Big Bend highway in Rockies challenged travellers," Victoria *Times-Colonist*, 3 October 1993.

126 Owram, *Building for Canadians*, 244; see, for example, *EFRC*, acc. 85–86/147, v. 48, f. U324, C.M. Walker to T.S. Mills, 1 June 1936.

127 L. Brown, "Unemployment Relief Camps in Saskatchewan 1933–36," *Saskatchewan History*, v. 23, autumn 1970, 101–2.

128 In June 1935, Premier Bracken of Manitoba wanted the Riding Mountain camps reopened to accommodate the mass of unemployed gathering in Winnipeg in anticipation of the On-to-Ottawa trekkers. S.R. Hewitt, "We Are Sitting on the Edge of a Volcano: Winnipeg During the On-to-Ottawa Trek," *Prairie Forum*, v. 19, n. 1, spring 1994, 51–64.

129 *NAC*, RG 84, v. 59, f. U56–3, C.M. Walker to T.S. Mills, 12 November 1937; 16 December 1937.

130 Canada, *Annual Report of the Department of the Interior*, 1936, pt. iii, "National Parks of Canada," 88.

131 *NAC*, RG 27, v. 2245, "Report on the Department of National Defence Unemployment Relief Scheme for Single, Homeless Men (8 October 1932 to 31 March 1936)," 60, 62–63. It is not possible to provide an exact tally of the number of men who passed through the national park camps. The

annual reports for 1933 and 1934 provide only the number of man-days of relief work.

132 Canada, *Annual Report of the Department of the Interior*, 1932, pt. iii, "National Parks of Canada," 70; *Annual Report of the Department of the Interior*, 1934, pt. iii, "National Parks of Canada," 84.

133 Their efforts were comparable to those of the heralded Civilian Conservation Corps in the United States. See J.A. Salmond, *The Civilian Conservation Corps, 1933–42* (Durham, N.C. 1967).

134 See, for example, L.S. MacDowell, "Canada's 'Gulag': Project #51 Lac Seul (A Tale from the Great Depression)," *Journal of Canadian Studies*, v. 28, n. 2, summer 1993, 130–58.

135 F. Goble to B. Waiser, 25 November 1993.

136 Court Neville interview, 25 March 1994.

Conchies *(pages 129–74)*

1 In December 1936, the ministries of Immigration and Colonization, the Interior, Mines, and the superintendent-general of Indian Affairs were consolidated in the new Department of Mines and Resources. The National Parks Bureau now came under the Lands, Parks, and Forests Branch, and the commissioner's position was replaced by a branch director. Commissioner J.B. Harkin retired when these changes were implemented.

2 *National Archives of Canada* [*NAC*], Government Archives Division, Indian and Northern Affairs, RG 22, v. 734, f. U-1000, pt. 1, R.A. Gibson to L.R. LaFleche, 11 June 1941.

3 See D. De Brou and B. Waiser, eds., *Documenting Canada: A History of Modern Canada in Documents* (Saskatoon 1992), 368–69.

4 *Ibid.*, 379–85.

5 T. Socknat, *Witness Against War: Pacifism in Canada 1900–1945* (Toronto 1987), 227–30.

6 W. Janzen, *Limits on Liberty: The Experience of Mennonite, Hutterite, and Doukhobor Communities in Canada* (Toronto 1990), 207.

7 T.D. Regehr, "Mennonites in Canada, 1939–1970: A People Transformed," v. 3, ch. 1, draft manuscript.

8 See B. Waiser, *Saskatchewan's Playground: A History of Prince Albert National Park* (Saskatoon 1989).

9 See L. Bella, *Parks for Profit* (Montreal 1987), 93–94.

10 *NAC*, Government Archives Division, Parks Canada, RG 84, v. 110, f. U165-2, L.R. LaFleche to R.A. Gibson, 3 March 1941.

11 The first aid training was likely provided in the event that any of the men decided to join the ambulance service or some other medical unit.

12 *NAC*, RG 84, v. 110, f. U165-2, L.R. LaFleche to R.A. Gibson, 7 May 1941. Prince Albert, for example, initially expected to take in 150 men on the assumption that only 700 would be made available to the parks; according to LaFleche's May 1941 letter, however, 692 men (525 Mennonites and 167 Pacifists) from Saskatchewan alone—more than the combined total for all the other western provinces—were to be given alternative service work.

13 Gibson's revised scheme called for five summer camps: Banff, 150 men; Jasper, 180; Prince Albert, 200; Riding Mountain, 200; and Cape Breton Highlands, 14. There would also be two winter camps: Kootenay, 121; and Prince Albert, 142. *Ibid.*, R.A. Gibson to L.R. LaFleche, 13 May 1941.

14 *Ibid.*

15 *Ibid.*, L.R. LaFleche to R.A. Gibson, 19 May 1941.

16 Canada, House of Commons, *Debates*, 29 May 1941, 3528.

17 *NAC*, RG 84, v. 110, f. U165-2, J. Smart to R.A. Gibson, 29 May 1941.

18 *NAC*, RG 22, v. 734, f. U-1000, pt. 1, J.G. Gardiner to T.A. Crerar, 9 June 1941. It is not clear why formal approval of the programme was delayed so long. There was considerable pressure on the King government, especially from western Canada, to ensure that the conscientious objectors performed some kind of alternative service work. There may have been some question, however, about whether the men should have performed work of direct benefit to the national war effort.

19 *NAC*, RG 84, v. 110, f. U165-2, J. Smart to R.A. Gibson, 24 June 1941.

20 Henry Sawatzky interview, 5 April 1994; John C. Klassen interview, 26 April 1994; Anton Dyck interview, 6 June 1994.

21 *NAC*, RG 84, v. 194, f. RM165-2, O.E. Heaslip to C.D. McPherson, 16 June 1941.

22 A small number had married since the time of the National War Services Registration census.

23 John Klassen interview, 26 April 1994.

24 Henry Sawatzky interview, 5 April 1994.

25 Anton Dyck interview, 6 June 1994.

26 Jacob Unrau interview, 17 March 1994; George Kroeker interview, 7 April 1994.

27 *NAC*, RG 84, v. 194, f. RM165-2, O.E. Heaslip to J. Smart, 1 April 1941. As of June 1941, physically fit men of military age (18-45) were prohibited from working in the government service.

28 John Eidse interview, 21 March 1994.

29 George Kroeker interview, 7 April 1994.

30 Quoted in *NAC*, RG 84, v. 194, f. RM165-2, J.D.B. MacFarlane to J.Smart, 13 August 1941.

31 *Ibid.*, G.D. McPherson to L.R. LaFleche, 29 August 1941.

32 Anton Dyck interview, 6 June 1994.

33 John Klassen interview, 26 April 1994.

34 George Kroeker interview, 7 April 1994.

35 John Klassen interview, 26 April 1994.

36 Anton Dyck interview, 6 June 1994.

37 John Klassen interview, 26 April 1994.

38 Henry Sawatzky interview, 5 April 1994.

39 Jacob Unrau interview, 17 March 1994.

40 *NAC*, RG 84, v. 110, f. U165-2, pt. 2, J.G. Rattray to J. Smart, 14 July 1941.

41 Henry Sawatzky interview, 5 April 1994; Anton Dyck interview, 6 June 1994.

42 *NAC*, RG 84, v. 110, f. U165-2, pt. 2, R.A. Gibson to J. Smart, 12 July 1941.

43 *Prince Albert National Park* [*PANP*], Historical Files, f. PA165-2, S.T. Wood to L.R. LaFleche, 11 July 1941.

44 Jacob Unrau interview, 24 March 1994.

45 *PANP*, Historical Files, f. PA165-2, H. Knight to J.G. Rempel, n.d.

46 *Ibid.*, A.S. Redford to secretary, Department of National Defence, 23 August 1941; *NAC*, RG 84, v. 110, f. U165-2, pt. 2, R.A. Gibson to J. Smart, 12 July 1941. Some of the men who volunteered failed their medical examination and were thereupon ordered back to the park to complete their term at alternative service work. Upon investigation of the matter at the urging of the superintendent, these men were discharged.

47 J.W. Driedger interview, 8 March 1994; J.M. Penner interview, 8 March 1994; P.K. Fehr interview, 15 March 1994; A.W. Dueck interview, 16 March 1994.

48 *PANP*, Historical Files, f. PA165-2, H. Knight to A.S. Redford, 9 September 1941.

49 A.W. Dueck interview, 16 March 1994.

50 J.W. Driedger interview, 8 March 1994.

51 P.K. Fehr interview, 15 March 1994.

52 J.M. Penner interview, 8 March 1994.

53 *PANP*, Historical Files, f. PA165-2, George Tunstell, "Memorandum re Work Camps for Mennonite and Conscientious Objectors, Prince Albert National Park," 11 July 1941.

54 P.K. Fehr interview, 15 March 1994.

55 A.W. Dueck interview, 4 March 1994.

56 P.K. Fehr interview, 15 March 1994.

57 A.W. Dueck interview, 4 March 1994.

58 P.K. Fehr interview, 15 March 1994.

59 Prince Albert *Daily Herald*, 2 September 1941.

60 A.W. Dueck interview, 4 March 1994.

61 Quoted in Edmonton *Journal*, 21 August 1941.

62 Paul Poetker interview, 15 March 1994.

63 Peter Unger interview, 21 April 1994.

64 Janzen, *Limits on Liberty*, 210-12, 228.

65 Nick Thiessen interview, 21 March 1994.

66 *NAC*, Government Archives Division, Forestry, RG 39, v. 41, f. 49855, pt. 1, G. Tunstell, "Inspection of Alternative Service Work Camps in Jasper National Park during the period September 25th to 29th," 20 October 1941.

67 Nick Thiessen interview, 21 March 1994.

68 Peter Unger interview, 21 April 1994.

69 *Ibid.*

70 Paul Poetker interview, 15 March 1994.

71 *Ibid.*

72 As of 15 November 1941, only 263 of the 742 men ordered to report to the parks were still in camp. *NAC*, RG 39, v. 41, f. 49855, pt. 1, G. Tunstell, "Alternative Service Work Camps Summer Operations 1941," 16 December 1941.

73 John Eidse interview, 21 March 1994.

74 *NAC*, RG 39, v. 41, f. 49855, pt. 1, "Alternative Service Work Camps," table viii.

75 *Ibid.*

76 *NAC*, RG 84, v. 110, f. U165-2, pt. 3, H. Knight to J. Smart, 24 September 1941.

77 *Ibid.*, "Circular Memorandum No. 381," 9 November 1941.

78 *Ibid.*

79 *NAC*, RG 39, v. 41, f. 49810, pts. 1-2, O.E. Heaslip to J. Smart, 12 November 1941.

80 *Ibid.*, f. 49855, pt. 1, G. Tunstell to J. Smart, 17 March 1942.

81 *Ibid.*

82 *Ibid.*, G. Tunstell to J. Smart, 12 March 1942.

83 Calgary *Herald*, 23 February 1942.

84 *Winnipeg Federal Records Centre [WFRC]*, Parks Canada, W84-85/407, Box 15, f. PA165-2, H. Knight to J. Smart, 16 March 1942.

85 *NAC*, RG 39, v. 41, f. 49810, pts. 1-2, G. Tunstell to J. Smart, 13 March 1942.

86 *NAC*, RG 84, v. 110, f. U165-2, pt. 3, R.A. Gibson to L.R. LaFleche, 6 December 1941. This last point was endorsed by Colonel J.G. Rattray, who served as programme liaison officer. In November 1941 he had suggested that volunteers found to be physically unfit should be put to work in national parks in order to bring them up to fighting form. *Ibid.*, f. U165, J.G. Rattray to J. Smart, 21 November 1941.

87 Anton Dyck interview, 6 June 1994.

88 *Ibid.*

89 A.W. Dueck interview, 4 March 1994.

90 Peter Unger interview, 21 April 1994.

91 Henry Sawatzky interview, 5 April 1994.

92 *NAC*, RG 84, v. 111, f. U165-2, pt. 4, J. Smart to R.A. Gibson, 14 January 1942.

93 *NAC*, RG 39, v. 41, f. 49810, pts. 1-2, Circular Memorandum No. 476, 14 March 1942.

94 Minnedosa *Tribune*, 22 January 1942.

95 *Debates*, 17 February 1942, 671.

96 *NAC*, RG 39, v. 41, f. 49810, pts. 1-2, B. Sinclair to J. Smart, 25 July 1942.

97 *NAC*, RG 84, v. 110, f. U165-2, pt. 3, R.A. Gibson to J. Smart, 30 June 1942.

98 *Ibid.*, J. Smart to R.A. Gibson, 18 July 1942.

99 *NAC*, RG 39, v. 41, f. 49810, pts. 1-2, H.L. Holman to D.A. Macdonald, 8 June 1942.

100 Prince Albert *Daily Herald*, 19 August 1942.

101 *Ibid.*, 9 July 1942.

102 For a listing of individual cases by park camp, see *NAC*, RG 84, v. 110, f. U165-2, pt. 6, "Men 'Absent Without Leave' From Alternative Service Work Camps As From April 1st, 1942."

103 *Debates*, 18 May 1942, 2529-30. See also S. Hanson and D. Kerr, "Pacifism, Dissent and the University of Saskatchewan, 1938-1944," *Saskatchewan History*, v. 45, n. 2, fall 1993, 3-14.

104 See, for example, *NAC*, RG 84, v. 111, f. U165-2, pt. 5, P.J. Jennings to Regina Divisional Registrar, 6 August 1942.

105 The speed with which the police proceeded in some of these cases did not always please Parks officials. The cost of apprehending the men was to be absorbed by the police, and they did not want to spend vast sums of money chasing down defaulters. Some of the men consequently remained "at large" for months. *Ibid.*, v. 111, f. U165-2, pt. 6, J.G. Rattray to G.R. Benoit, 19 September 1942.

106 *PANP*, Historical Files, f. PA165-2, F.G. Wilson to H. Knight, 21 August 1942; H. Knight to A.S. Redford, 4 May 1943.

107 During the period from 1 April 1942 to 30 March 1943, there were thirty-five cases of men deserting or failing to report. *NAC*, RG 84, v. 111, f. U165-2, pt. 7, "Operation of Alternative Service Work Camps in National Parks and Forest Experiment Stations, April 1st, 1942, to March 31st, 1943."

108 *PANP*, Historical Files, f. PA165-2, C. Camsell to L.R. LaFleche, 1 September 1942; *NAC*, RG 39, v. 41, f. 49810, pts. 1-2, B. Sinclair to J. Smart, 25 July 1942.

109 *NAC*, RG 84, v. 111, f. U165-2, pt. 6, J. Smart to R.A. Gibson, 30 September 1942.

110 A.J. Dick interview, 25 April 1994.

111 *NAC*, RG 84, v. 111, f. U165-2, pt. 6, translation of 23 September 1942 article.

112 *NAC*, RG 39, v. 41, f. 49810, pts. 1-2, D.A. Macdonald to Jackson, 5 December 1942.

113 *Ibid.*, D.A. Macdonald to file, 29 December 1942.

114 *NAC*, RG 84, v. 112, f. U165-2, pt. 7, "Operation of Alternative Service Work Camps."

115 "Habbakuk" is a misspelling of "Habakkuk," a book in the Old Testament.

116 It is also likely that some of the Banff internees provided assistance with the pressure testing of pykrete beams by the National Research Council at Lake Louise in the late winter of 1943. A.J. Dick interview, 25 April 1994; F.J. McEvoy, "Professor Pyke's Secret Weapon: Putting the Sea War on Ice," *The Beaver*, April/May 1994, 32-39; Andreas Schroeder, "Project Habbakuk," unpublished article.

117 *NAC*, RG 84, v. 111, f. U165-2, pt. 6, C.H.E. Powell to J. Smart, 29 January 1943.

118 Prince Albert *Daily Herald*, 25 January 1943.

119 These "donations" eventually exceeded $2 million.

120 *NAC*, RG 84, v. 111, f. U165-2, pt. 6, R.A. Gibson to J. Smart, 2 April 1943.

121 *Ibid.*, "Alternative Service Work Camps, Statement of Discussions on the 28th of April, 1943."

122 *Debates*, 16 July 1943, 4961; see also 31 May 1943, 3198.

123 *PANP*, Historical Files, f. PA165-2, O. Regier to R.S. Hinchey, 30 June 1943.

124 Prince Albert *Daily Herald*, 14 July 1943.

125 *Public Archives of Alberta* [*PAA*], National Parks Branch, Engineering and

Construction Service, acc. no. 69.354, box 7, f. B200(81a), J. Smart to P.J. Jennings, 1 September 1943.

126 *Ibid.*, 10 September 1943.

127 Canada, *Report of the Department of Mines and Resources*, 1944, "National Parks Bureau," 86.

128 A.J. Dick interview, 25 April 1994.

129 *NAC*, RG 84, v. 112, f. U165-2, pt. 7, L.E. Westman to R.A. Gibson, 27 October 1943.

130 *Ibid.*, H. Mitchell to T.A. Crerar, 6 November 1943.

131 *Ibid.*, A. MacNamara to C. Camsell, 27 December 1943. The other two proposed detention centres were Kananaskis Park (Seebe, Alberta) and Petawawa Forest Experiment Station (Chalk River, Ontario).

132 *PAA*, acc. no. 69.354, box 7, f. B200(81a), J. Smart to J.N. Jennings, 15 January 1993.

133 *NAC*, RG 39, v. 41, f. 49810, pts. 1-2, G. Tunstell to Dominion Forester, 23 May 1944. Some conscientious objectors were denied the opportunity to do alternative service work and sent to military prison. See W. Janzen and F. Greaser, *Sam Martin Went To Prison: The Story of Conscientious Objection and Canadian Military Service* (Winnipeg 1990).

134 See, for example, Edmonton *Journal*, 3 February 1943. "Unless Alberta is to be a mere dumping ground for the turbulent and unwanted sects of Europe, we cannot permit these groups to be in Canada and yet not of it. There cannot be two kinds of citizenship in this country . . . The time has come when exceptions to this rule must be regarded as an intolerable deadweight on the shoulders of the rest of the community."

135 Janzen, *Limits on Liberty*, 229-30.

136 W. Kaplan, *State and Salvation: The Jehovah's Witnesses and Their Fight for Civil Rights* (Toronto 1989), xi.

137 *Ibid.*, 174-85.

138 For the period 1 April 1943 to 31 March 1944, 565 men spent time in national park camps: Mennonites, 348; Hutterites, 37; and Jehovah's Witnesses, 7. For the following year, 1944-45, 595 men passed through the camps: Mennonites, 206; Hutterites, 101; Jehovah's Witnesses, 218. During the 1944-45 reporting period, 284 men were transferred to agriculture or industry. *NAC*, RG 84, v. 112, f. U165-2, pt. 8.

139 The camps at Prince Albert were not reopened because the park was selected by the Department of National Defence as a test site for military equipment under extremely cold temperatures (code-named "Project Eskimo"). The park was consequently invaded by several hundred men and their vehicles and artillery during the winter of 1944-45. One can only wonder what trouble might have erupted if the alternative service camps were still in operation at the time.

140 *NAC*, RG 39, v. 41, f. 49810, pts. 1-2, L.E. Westman to R.A. Gibson, 25 August 1944.

141 *NAC*, RG 84, v. 112, f. U165-2, pt. 8, 19 September 1944 memorandum.

142 Banff *Crag and Canyon*, 20 October 1944.

143 *NAC*, RG 39, v. 41, f. 49810, pts. 1–2, H. Mitchell to L.S. St. Laurent, 26 October 1944.

144 *Ibid.*, F.P. Varcoe to H. Mitchell, 8 November 1943.

145 *NAC*, RG 84, v. 112, f. U165-2, pt. 8, J.A. Wood to J. Smart, 8 January 1945.

146 *NAC*, RG 39, v. 41, f. 49810, pts. 1–2, C.K. LeCapelain to J. Smart, 15 January 1945.

147 *Mount Revelstoke and Glacier National Parks* [*MRGNP*], Historical Files, f. G165-2, G.F. Horsey to R.H. Mann, 23 June 1944.

148 Kaplan, *State and Salvation*, 207–12.

149 For the period 1 April 1945 to 31 March 1946, 98 men reported to the park camps. *NAC*, RG 84, v. 112, f. U165-2, pt. 8, "Operation of Alternative Service Work Camps in the National Parks for the Period April 1st, 1945, to March 31st, 1946," table 1.

150 *Report of the Department of Mines and Resources*, 1946, "National Parks Bureau," 107.

151 *Debates*, 3 October 1945, 710.

152 *NAC*, RG 84, v. 112, f. U165-2, pt. 8, J. Smart to R.A. Gibson, 1 March 1946.

153 *Ibid.*, J.D.B. MacFarlane to J. Smart, 18 March 1946,

154 *Edmonton Federal Records Centre* [*EFRC*], Parks Canada, W85-86/148, v. 5, f. Y165-2, G.F. Horsey to C.S. Henley, 18 August 1945.

155 *PAA*, acc. no. 69.354, box 6, f. B165-2, pt. 77b, M.A. Widawski to J.A. Glen, 28 May 1946.

156 *Ibid.*, G.R. Carroll to J. Smart, 14 June 1946.

157 *Ibid.*, f. B165-2, pt. 77a.

158 Banff *Crag and Canyon*, 20 October 1944.

"Japs" (pages 175–216)

1 The Department of Mines and Resources had five branches or divisions: Mines and Geology; Lands, Parks, and Forests; Surveys and Engineering; Indian Affairs; and Immigration. The National Parks Bureau was part of the Lands, Parks, and Forests Branch. The Engineering and Construction Service of the Surveys and Engineering Branch acted as a general engineering agency for all divisions of the department.

2 For an analysis of anti-Orientalism in British Columbia, see P.E. Roy, *A White Man's Province: British Columbia Politicians and Chinese and Japanese Immigrants, 1858–1914* (Vancouver 1989), and W.P. Ward, *White Canada Forever: Popular Attitudes and Public Policy Towards Orientals in British Columbia* (Montreal 1990).

3 Ward, *White Canada Forever*, 148–50.

4 G.S. Kealey and R. Whitaker, eds., *RCMP Security Bulletins: The War Series, 1939–1941* (St. John's 1989), 416–18. All Japanese in Canada already had to carry identity cards.

5 W.P. Ward, "British Columbia and the Japanese Evacuation," *Canadian Historical Review*, v. 67, n. 3, September 1976, 296–301.

6 P. Roy et al, *Mutual Hostages: Canadians and Japanese During the Second World War* (Toronto 1990), 84–88.

7 The three-man commission consisted of Vancouver industrialist Austin Taylor (chairman), the assistant commissioner of the RCMP, F.J. Mead, and the assistant commissioner of the BC provincial police, John Shirras.

8 Roy, *Mutual Hostages*, 95-98. For a recent reassessment of the Japanese threat, see the controversial article, J. Granatstein, "The Enemy Within," *Saturday Night*, November 1986, 32-42.

9 Roy, *Mutual Hostages*, 95.

10 Ward, "British Columbia and the Japanese Evacuation," 305-8.

11 A.G. Sunahara, *The Politics of Racism: The Uprooting of Japanese Canadians During the Second World War* (Toronto 1981), 48-49.

12 E. Reid, "The Conscience of a Diplomat: A Personal Testament," *Queen's Quarterly*, v. 74, winter 1967, 587.

13 *National Archives of Canada* [*NAC*], Government Archives Division, External Affairs, RG 25, v. 3004, f. 3464-B-40-C, "Conference on the Japanese Problem in British Columbia," 10 January 1942; Roy, *Mutual Hostages*, 110.

14 *NAC*, Government Archives Division, Indian and Northern Affairs, RG 22, v. 716, f. EC5-1-18, C.M. Walker to J.M. Wardle, 22 January 1942.

15 *Public Archives of Alberta* [*PAA*], National Parks, Engineering and Construction Service, acc. no. 69.218, box 4, f. 131, 93-96.

16 Canada, House of Commons, *Debates*, 10 April 1934, 2018-23.

17 *NAC*, RG 22, v. 732, f. SE4-1-69, C. Camsell to E.H. Coleman, 21 August 1940. It was also suggested that internees could clear Indian reserve lands for agricultural purposes.

18 *Debates*, 6 August 1940, 2556-57; Edmonton *Journal*, 31 January 1942.

19 *NAC*, RG 22, v. 716, f. EC5-1-18, J.M. Wardle to C.M. Walker, 24 January 1942.

20 *NAC*, Government Archives Division, Parks Canada, RG 84, v. 210, f. EC7-27, J.M. Wardle memorandum for file, 24 January 1942.

21 *NAC*, RG 22, v. 723, f. EC7-24, H. Hereford to A. MacNamara, 21 January 1942.

22 *Ibid.*, v. 716, f. EC5-1-18, J.M. Wardle to C. Camsell, 29 January 1942

23 *NAC*, RG 84, v. 64, f. ENG-20-3, J.M. Wardle to A. Dixon, 30 January 1942.

24 *Ibid.*

25 *NAC*, RG 22, v. 740, f. U2700(1), J.H. Mitchell to C.M. Walker, 9 February 1942.

26 *NAC*, RG 84, v. 210, f. EC7-27, "Mileage Statement: Yellowhead–Blue River Highway," 11 February 1942.

27 *NAC*, RG 22, v. 716, f. EC5-1-18, J.M. Wardle to T.S. Mills, 12 February 1942.

28 *Ibid.*, R.A. Gibson to J.M. Wardle, 7 February 1942.

29 *Ibid.*, v. 740, f. U2700(1), J.M. Wardle memorandum for file, 14 February 1942.

30 *NAC*, Government Archives Division, Privy Council Office, RG 2, PC 1348, 19 February 1942.

31 *NAC*, RG 84, v. 211, f. EC7-27-1, T.S. Mills to J.H. Mitchell, 17 February 1942.

32 *NAC*, RG 22, v. 740, f. U2700(1), J.M. Wardle to T.S. Mills, 19 February 1942.

33 *Ibid.*, A. MacNamara to J.H. Mitchell, 19 February 1942.

34 T.U. Nakano with L. Nakano, *Within the Barbed Wire Fence: A Japanese Man's Account of His Internment in Canada* (Toronto 1980), 8–9.

35 George Funamoto interview, 7 October 1994; Kinzie Tanaka interview, 5 October 1994.

36 This term is from the title of one survivor's account of the war years: Y. Shimizu, *The Exiles: An Archival History of the World War II Japanese Road Camps in British Columbia and Ontario* (Wallaceburg 1993).

37 *NAC*, RG 22, v. 740, f. U2700(1), A. MacNamara to J.H. Mitchell, 19 February 1942.

38 Nakano, *Within the Barbed Wire Fence*, 9.

39 Quoted in R.H. Keyserlingk, "Allies or Subversives? The Canadian Government's Ambivalent Attitude towards German-Canadians in the Second World War" in P. Panayi, ed., *Minorities in Wartime: National and Racial Groupings in Europe, North America and Australia during the Two World Wars* (Oxford 1993), 239.

40 Shimizu, *The Exiles*, 59–78.

41 Roy, *Mutual Hostages*, 111.

42 *NAC*, RG 22, v. 740, f. U2700(3), F.J. Mead to C.M. Walker, 24 April 1942. The chairman of the British Columbia Security Commission later dismissed this claim, suggesting that it was just another Japanese excuse to avoid placement in a road camp.

43 *New Canadian*, 24 February 1942.

44 B. Broadfoot, *Years of Sorrow, Years of Shame: The Story of the Japanese Canadians in World War II* (Toronto 1977), 144.

45 *New Canadian*, 5 March 1942.

46 Lucerne was a former Canadian Northern divisional point that had been abandoned eighteen years earlier in favour of Jasper; the empty houses were occupied by project officials.

47 *New Canadian*, 25 February 1942; Edmonton *Journal*, 11 April 1942; *NAC*, RG 22, v. 740, f. U2700(5), Geikie camp petition, 15 June 1942; George Funamoto interview.

48 *NAC*, RG 22, v. 740, f. U2700(2), G. Upton, "Alien Enemies in Protected Areas, British Columbia," 3 March 1942.

49 Confidential interview with former Geikie evacuee, 28 September 1994.

50 Quoted in *NAC*, RG 22, v. 740, f. U2700(1), T.S. Mills to J.M. Wardle, 25 February 1942.

51 *NAC*, RG 84, v. 210, f. EC7–27, J.M. Wardle to Jackson, 25 February 1942; J.M. Wardle to T.S. Mills, 26 February 1942; Wardle was under the impression that the prime minister wanted a thousand Japanese moved every ten days. J.M. Wardle to A. Dixon, 26 February 1942.

52 George Funamoto interview.

53 Nakano, *Within the Barbed Wire Fence*, 14–22.

54 *Ibid.*, 23.

55 *Ibid.*, 22.

56 *New Canadian*, 14 March 1942.

57 *NAC*, RG 22, v. 740, f. U2700(2), R.A. Gibson to J.M. Wardle, 24 February 1942.

58 *NAC*, RG 84, v. 110, f. U165, R.A. Gibson to Jackson, 18 February 1942.

59 *Ibid.*, J.H. Mitchell to T.S. Mills, 12 March 1942.

60 Confidential interview with former Geikie evacuee; Edmonton *Journal*, 8 April 1942.

61 *New Canadian*, 23 May 1942.

62 *Ibid.*, 27 June 1942 (translated in Shimizu, *The Exiles*, 152).

63 *Ibid.*, 14 May 1942.

64 *NAC*, Government Archives Division, Royal Canadian Mounted Police, RG 18, v. 3563, f. C–11–19–2–9, pt. 1, R.C. Vaughan to P.J.A. Cardin, 17 February 1942.

65 *NAC*, RG 22, v. 579, f. U2760(1), J.M. Wardle to T.S. Mills, 11 March 1942. The opposition of the Parks Bureau and Canadian National to the presence of Japanese in Jasper was later given as a reason for turning down a proposal from the Brewster Transportation Company to use Japanese labourers to build a road to Lake O'Hara in Yoho National Park. *Ibid.*, v. 723, f. EC7–24(CN), R.A. Gibson to J.M. Wardle, 20 March 1942.

66 *Ibid.*, v. 740, f. U2700(2), J.A. Wood to J. Smart, 12 March 1942.

67 *Ibid.*, R.A. Gibson to J.M. Wardle, 17 March 1942.

68 *Ibid.*, J.M. Wardle to S.T. Wood, 17 March 1942.

69 *NAC*, RG 25, v. 3004, f. 3464–J–40, pt. 1, S.T. Wood to H. Keenleyside, 1 May 1942; Shimizu, *The Exiles*, 28–29.

70 *NAC*, RG 84, v. 211, f, EC7–27–1, S.T. Wood to J.M. Wardle, 18 March 1942.

71 Edmonton *Journal*, 7 April 1942.

72 Edmonton *Bulletin*, 3 April 1942.

73 *NAC*, RG 22, v. 716, f. EC5–1–18, C.M. Walker to G.W. McPherson, 18 March 1942.

74 Edmonton *Journal*, 11 April 1942.

75 *NAC*, RG 22, v. 740, f. U2700(2), J.H. Mitchell to J.H. McVety, 19 March 1942; f. U2700(3), J.H. MacDonald to T.A. Crerar, 27 April 1942.

76 Kinzie Tanaka interview.

77 *NAC*, RG 84, v. 211, f. EC7–27–1, J.H. Mitchell to J.M. Wardle, 3 April 1942; *New Canadian*, 30 May 1942.

78 Roy, *Mutual Hostages*, 114.

79 *NAC*, RG 84, v. 211, f. EC7–27–1, "RCMP Jasper Detachment Report," 7 May 1942. The story of the supposed Decoigne strike was thoroughly investigated by park and police authorities and was found to be based on a rumour picked up by a reporter at the Edmonton courthouse.

80 Edmonton *Journal*, 11 April 1942.

81 *Ibid.*

82 Confidential interview with former Geikie evacuee, 28 September 1994.

83 Because of censorship, the Japanese quickly learned to use only one side of the page. Shimizu, *The Exiles*, 72.

84 Edmonton *Journal*, 11 April 1942.

85 *Ibid.*, 7 April 1942.

86 *NAC*, RG 22, v. 740, f. U2700(2), J.H. Mitchell to C.M. Walker, 15 April 1942;

A.P. Ridley to Officer Commanding, E Division, RCMP, 15 April 1942.

87 Edmonton *Journal*, 7 April 1942.

88 *NAC*, RG 22, v. 740, f. U2700(3), C.M. Walker to E.C. Webster, 11 April 1942.

89 *Ibid.*, v. 716, f. EC5-1-18, A. Dixon to J.M. Wardle, 24 April 1942.

90 *Ibid.*, v. 724, f. EC7-24-1, pt. 1, J.M. Wardle to A. MacNamara, 30 April 1942.

91 *Ibid.*

92 The "Asahi" baseball club had been a passion for the Japanese living in the Vancouver area, and they transferred this love of the game to the camps. George Funamoto interview.

93 *NAC*, RG 22, v. 724, f. EC7-24-1, pt. 1, J.M. Wardle to T.S. Mills, 4 June 1942.

94 *Ibid.*, v. 740, f. U2700(4), A.P. Ridley, "Strike at Lucerne Camp B2," 23 April 1942.

95 *Ibid.*, v. 725, f. EC7-24-4, Canadian Postal Censorship, A. Takagi to Mrs. A. Takagi, 16 May 1942.

96 Of the 1,315 men on the project pay lists for May, the number of married (640) and single (675) workers was almost evenly divided. The breakdown for the Jasper camps was as follows: Geikie 1A: 28 married, 57 single; Decoigne 2A: 9 married, 20 single; Decoigne 3A: 50 married, 13 single. *Ibid.*, v. 740, f. U2700(6), "Yellowhead-Blue River, May Pay List 1942."

97 *New Canadian*, 25 April 1942; 9 May 1942.

98 *NAC*, RG 22, v. 740, f. U2700(4), J.H. Mitchell to T.S. Mills, 30 May 1942.

99 *Ibid.*, J.M. Wardle to A. MacNamara, 30 May 1942.

100 George Funamoto interview.

101 Confidential interview with former Geikie evacuee.

102 *New Canadian*, 29 April 1942.

103 *NAC*, RG 84, v. 211, f. EC7-27-1, J.M. Wardle to A.C. Taylor, 13 June 1942.

104 Shimizu, *The Exiles*, 59-71; Roy, *Mutual Hostages*, 115-17. The Nisei Mass Evacuation Group protest ultimately figured in the security commission decision to send families intact to interior housing projects.

105 *NAC*, Government Archives Division, Labour, RG 27, v. 650, f. 23-2-5-6, pt. 11, Kinzie Tanaka to British Columbia Security Commission, 26 May 1942.

106 *Ibid.*

107 Tanaka's work in the Red Pass engineer's office meant that he travelled up and down the line on a regular basis and could see firsthand how the situation was deteriorating in the camps. He consequently decided to write the security commission on his own initiative; he did not tell anyone about the letter, nor did he receive an official response. Tanaka interview.

108 *NAC*, RG 27, v. 650, f. 23-2-5-6, pt. 11, A.C. Taylor to A. MacNamara, 30 May 1942.

109 *NAC*, RG 22, v. 724, f. EC7-24-1, pt. 1, S.T. Wood to L. St. Laurent, 8 June 1942. Whereas Wood urged family reunification and the closure of the camps, Wardle suggested that the guard simply be increased.

110 Quoted in *Ibid.*, v. 740, f. U2700(5), T.S. Mills to J.M. Wardle, 8 June 1942.

111 *NAC*, RG 84, v. 211, f. EC7-27-1, J.M. Wardle to A. MacNamara, 10 June 1942.

112 *Ibid.*, J.M. Wardle to T.S. Mills, 11 June 1942.

113 *Ibid.*, J.M. Wardle to A.C. Taylor, 13 June 1942.

114 *NAC*, RG 22, v. 740, f. U2700(5), W.J. Wishart to J.H. Mitchell, 13 June 1942; W.J. Wishart to J.H. Mitchell, 15 June 1942.

115 *NAC*, RG 84, v. 211, f. EC7-27-1, J.H. Mitchell to T.S. Mills, 18 June 1942.

116 Kamloops *Sentinel*, 4 June 1942; see also Edmonton *Journal*, 9 June 1942.

117 *Debates*, 19 June 1942, 3480.

118 *NAC*, RG 22, v. 740, f. U2700(5), C.M. Walker to T.S. Mills, 16 June 1942.

119 *NAC*, RG 84, v. 211, f. EC7-27-2, "Yellowhead–Blue River Japanese Project, 1942-1946, General Report," 10 January 1947.

120 *NAC*, RG 84, v. 211, f. EC7-27-1, J.M. Wardle to C. Camsell, 20 June 1942.

121 *NAC*, RG 22, v. 740, f. U2700(5), J.H. Mitchell to T.S. Mills, 25 June 1942.

122 Quoted in *Ibid.*, v. 724, f. EC7-24-1, pt. 1, J.M. Wardle to T.S. Mills, 16 June 1942.

123 *Ibid.*, v. 740, f. U2700(5), T.S. Mills to C.M. Walker, 19 June 1942.

124 *Ibid.*, f. U2700(6), R.M. Corning to J.H. Mitchell, 22 June 1942.

125 *Ibid.*, f. U2700(5), C.M. Walker to T.S. Mills, 26 June 1942.

126 *NAC*, RG 84, v. 211, f. EC7-27-1, J.M. Wardle to C.W. Jackson, 25 June 1942.

127 *NAC*, RG 22, v. 740, f. U2700(5), B.E. Burpee to J.H. Mitchell, 11 June 1942.

128 *Ibid.*, Geikie camp petition, 15 June 1942; confidential interview with former Geikie evacuee, 28 September 1994.

129 *Ibid.*, f. U2700(5), S. Travers to J.H. Mitchell, 22 June 1942.

130 *Ibid.*, W.J. Wishart, "Report on Disturbance and Threatened Strike of Japanese at Camp 1A, Geikie, June 23, 1942," 26 June 1942. Inouye appeared before a magistrate the same day he was brought into Jasper and was found guilty of assault and sentenced to twenty dollars and costs or thirty days in gaol.

131 *Ibid.*, Work Camp 3A to J.H. Mitchell, 26 June 1942. The arrested men were no longer in the area; they had been sent, along with troublemakers from other camps, to detention facilities in Vancouver. Edmonton *Journal*, 26 June 1942.

132 *Ibid.*, J.H. Mitchell to Japanese Workers, 29 June 1942.

133 *NAC*, RG 84, v. 211, f. EC7-27-1, J.A. Wood to J. Smart, 24 June 1942; Jasper Women's Institute to Department of National Defence, 25 June 1942.

134 *NAC*, RG 22, v. 740, f. U2700(5), J.H. Mitchell to T.S. Mills, 20 June 1942; v. 714, f. EC1-1-10, pt. 1, "Summary of Camp Establishment and Operations, Japanese Construction Camps in Ontario and British Columbia, to June 30, 1942," 13 July 1942.

135 Quoted in *Ibid.*, v. 724, f. EC7-24-1, pt. 1, T.S. Mills to J.M. Wardle, 30 June 1942.

136 *Ibid.*, W.J. Woods to S.T. Wood, 29 June 1942.

137 Roy, *Mutual Hostages*, 99-101.

138 *Ibid.*, v. 724, f. EC7–24–2, E.G. Trueman, "Visits to Camps and Settlements of Japanese Evacuees," June 1942.

139 *Ibid.*, v. 740, f. U2700(5), J.M. Wardle to T.S. Mills, 3 July 1942.

140 *Ibid.*, J.H. Mitchell to R.L. Ralston, 3 July 1942. An earlier request that project engineers be empowered to intern troublesome workers had recently been turned down by the minister of Justice.

141 *NAC*, RG 84, v. 211, f. EC7–27–1, J.M. Wardle, "Memorandum for File," 10 July 1942.

142 *PAA*, Charles H. Grant Papers, acc. no. 77.22, box 8, f. 164, Jasper Park Chamber of Commerce et al to J.L. Ralston, 13 July 1942. The petition was signed by the Jasper Chamber of Commerce, Canadian Legion, Women's Institute, Junior Chamber of Commerce, Catholic Women's League, Daughters of England, Canadian Daughters, and the Volunteer Veterans Reserve.

143 *NAC*, RG 22, v. 740, f. U2700(6), A.H.L. Mellor to C.M. Walker, 6 July 1942.

144 *NAC*, RG 84, v. 210, f. EC7–27, C.M. Walker to T.S. Mills, 15 July 1942.

145 While at Red Pass, the consul general for Spain met with a delegation representing the camps in the area; their conversation dealt largely with general policy matters and not camp conditions. *New Canadian*, 29 July 1942. Walker dismissed the Geikie complaints on the grounds that the tent camps in the park had always been considered temporary and were soon to be closed anyway. *NAC*, RG 22, v. 740, f. U2700(6), C.M. Walker to T.S. Mills, 20 July 1942; f. U2700(7), J.M. Wardle to C. Camsell, 3 August 1942.

146 Quoted in Shimizu, *The Exiles*, 272.

147 *NAC*, RG 22, v. 740, f. U2700(6), C.M. Walker to T.S. Mills, 25 July 1942.

148 Ottawa *Citizen*, 28 July 1942; Edmonton *Journal*, 28 July 1942.

149 Edson-Jasper *Signal*, 30 July 1942.

150 *PAA*, C.H. Grant Papers, box 15, f. 164, E.T. Love to Jasper Park Development Committee, 28 July 1942.

151 *Ibid.*, E.T. Love to Jasper Park Development Committee, 3 June 1942.

152 *Ibid.*, J.M. Wardle to C.H. Grant, 1 June 1942; Edson-Jasper *Signal*, 30 July 1942. On 27 July, the day the government formally announced the removal of the Japanese from the Yellowhead project, the Golden Board of Trade asked the British Columbia minister of Public Works whether the Japanese could be put to work on the Big Bend Highway. *NAC*, RG 22, v. 724, f. EC7–24–2, E.C. Dobell to R. Bruhn, 27 July 1942. At a subsequent public meeting, the matter was unanimously overturned, forcing the board of trade to withdraw its request. *Golden Star,* 3 September 1942.

153 *NAC*, RG 27, v. 175, T.J. O'Neill to A. MacNamara, 31 July 1942.

154 *NAC*, RG 84, v. 210, f. EC7–27, C.M. Walker to T.S. Mills, 27 July 1942.

155 Nakano, *Within the Barbed Wire Fence*, 38–41.

156 *NAC*, RG 22, v. 740, f. U2700(7), C.M. Walker to T.S. Mills, 6 August 1942.

157 *NAC*, RG 84, v. 210, f. EC7–27, J.M. Wardle to A.C. Taylor, 9 September 1942.

158 *NAC*, RG 22, v. 740, f. U2700(7), T.S. Mills to J.H. Mitchell, 15 September 1942.

159 *Ibid.*, J.H. Mitchell to T.S. Mills, 18 September 1942.

160 *PAA*, acc. no. 69.218/39, C.M. Walker to T.S. Mills, 25 September 1942.

161 *NAC*, RG 84, v. 210, f. EC7–27, J.M. Wardle to Secretary, Jasper Chamber of Commerce, 4 October 1942.

162 *Ibid.*, v. 211, f. EC7–27–2, J.M. Wardle to C.H. Grant, 5 July 1944; C.M. Walker to T.S. Mills, 20 September 1944; "Status of Yellowhead–Blue River Highway Project as at May 31st, 1946." Although the highway was technically not open to the public, it was used on a regular basis.

163 *NAC*, RG 22, v. 724, f. EC7–24–1, J.M. Wardle to T.S. Mills, 18 December 1944.

164 *Ibid.*, "Yellowhead–Blue River Project, List of Japanese on Above Project, with Brief Statement of Activities," 3 February 1945.

165 *Ibid.*, C.M. Walker to T.S. Mills, 17 January 1946.

166 *NAC*, Government Archives Division, British Columbia Security Commission, RG 36/ 27, v. 1, f. 17, "Memorandum Covering Japanese Movement Pacific Coast," 18 July 1942.

Nazis *(pages 217–50)*

1 *Riding Mountain National Park* [*RMNP*], Historical Files, G. Foerster interview, April 1985. The prisoners were first taken to Uruguay because they were originally destined for Australia. In his memoirs, Churchill suggested that the African victory marked the turning of the "Hinge of Fate"; he also claimed that he was accompanied by five thousand German prisoners on his Atlantic crossing. W.S. Churchill, *The Hinge of Fate* (Boston 1950), 603, 784.

2 Proclaimed by the Liberal government one week before Canada officially entered the war against Germany, the sixty-four Defence of Canada Regulations gave the King administration sweeping powers more in keeping with a totalitarian state. See D. De Brou and B. Waiser, eds., *Documenting Canada: A History of Modern Canada in Documents* (Saskatoon 1992), 360–63.

3 *Ibid.*, 364–68

4 See L. Hannant, "Fifth-Column Crisis," *The Beaver*, December 1993/January 1994, 24–28.

5 The procedure for the treatment of prisoners of war was outlined in the 1929 Geneva Convention. Canada was not only a signatory of the convention, but used the articles as a basis for its own prisoner-of-war policy at the beginning of the war. See *National Archives of Canada* [*NAC*], Government Archives Division, Privy Council Office, RG 2, PC 4121, 13 December 1939.

6 R.W. Stotz, "Camp 132: A German Prisoner of War Camp in a Canadian Prairie Community During World War Two," unpublished M.A. thesis (History), University of Saskatchewan, 1992, 11–28, 30–39. For a history of internment activities in Canada, see D.J. Carter, *Behind Canadian Barbed Wire* (Calgary 1980), and J. Melady, *Escape From Canada! The Untold Story of German POWs in Canada 1939–45* (Toronto 1981).

7 *NAC*, Government Archives Division, Indian and Northern Affairs, RG 22, v. 732, f. SE4-1-69, T.S. Mills to J.M. Wardle, 2 July 1940.

8 *NAC*, Government Archives Division, Forestry, RG 39, v. 33, f. 49638, Macdonald to R.A. Gibson, 18 July 1940.

9 *Ibid.*, R.A. Gibson to J. Smart, 23 January 1942.

10 *NAC*, RG 2, PC 36/500, 22 January 1943.

11 Canada also held a few hundred Italian merchant seamen, but no Italian or Japanese combatant prisoners.

12 *NAC*, RG 2, PC 2326, 10 May 1943.

13 *NAC*, Government Archives Division, Labour, RG 27, v. 965, f. 24, "History of Labour Projects PW," 2.

14 J. de N. Kennedy, *History of the Department of Munitions and Supply*, v. II, *Controls, Service and Finance Branches, and Units Associated with the Department* (Ottawa 1950), 256-57.

15 *NAC*, RG 2, PC 4326, 28 May 1943.

16 The Department of Labour also raised the question of using Japanese on fuelwood operations. Mines and Resources retorted that there was little chance of them doing better work cutting wood than they had done building roads. *NAC*, Government Archives Division, Parks Canada, RG 84, v. 64, f. ENG20-3, J.M. Wardle to J.N. Stinson, 21 June 1943.

17 *Ibid.*, v. 165, f. U165-7, R.A. Gibson to A. MacNamara, 18 May 1943.

18 *Ibid.*, f. RM165-7, R.A. Gibson to J.E. Spero, 8 June 1943.

19 J. de N. Kennedy, *History of the Department of Munitions and Supply*, v. I, *Production Branches and Crown Companies* (Ottawa 1950), 480-89.

20 *NAC*, RG 84, v. 165, f. RM165-7, O.E. Heaslip to J. Smart, 21 June 1943; R.A. Gibson to J.S. Whalley, 28 June 1943; Heaslip to Smart, 29 June 1943; Heaslip to Smart, 30 June 1943.

21 *Ibid.*, R.A. Gibson to J.S. Whalley, 24 July 1943.

22 *Ibid.*, 21 August 1943.

23 *NAC*, RG 2, PC 6180, 3 August 1943.

24 *Ibid.*, PC 1286, 24 February 1941.

25 *NAC*, RG 84, v. 165, f. RM165-7, R.A. Gibson to O.E. Heaslip, 27 August 1943.

26 *NAC*, Government Archives Division, National Defence, RG 24, microfilm C-5382, f. HQS 7236-34-3-9, R.S.W. Fordham to H.N. Streight, 6 August 1943.

27 Article 43 of the Geneva Convention permitted prisoners to elect their own representative or spokesman. This individual was designated the camp leader.

28 *NAC*, RG 24, C-5382, f. HQS 7236-34-3-9, R.C. Bull to H.N. Streight, 23 September 1943; *RMNP*, George Foerster interview, April 1985; Josef Gabski interview, 11 September 1994.

29 Stotz, "Camp 132," 48, 105-7.

30 J.J. Kelly, "Intelligence and Counter-Intelligence in German Prisoner of War Camps in Canada During World War II," *Dalhousie Review*, v. 58, n. 2, summer 1978, 285-94.

31 The Department of Labour hired civilian guards to supervise prisoners at the various worksites. When combatant prisoners were involved in a project, it was also necessary to have a detail of Veterans Guards at the site. *NAC*, RG 2, PC 28/5267, 30 June 1943.

32 For a list of the original Riding Mountain prisoners, including their rank, serial number, and signatures, see *NAC,* Government Archives Division, Labour, RG 27, v. 958, f. 8, "Department of Labour Pay List, October 1943."

33 *NAC*, RG 84, v. 165, f. RM165-7, J. Smart to R.A. Gibson, 13 October 1943.

34 *NAC*, RG 24, C-5382, f. HQS 7236-34-3-9, Director, Prisoners of War to Adjutant General, 13 March 1944.

35 Stotz, "Camp 132," 58-59.

36 *RMNP*, T. Tabulenas, "Whitewater Lake Prisoner of War Camp, RMNP, Supplement Report," 1978.

37 Minnedosa *Tribune*, 4 November 1943.

38 *NAC*, RG 24, C-5382, f. HQS 7236-34-3-9, Bebb, "RCMP Security Report," 3 November 1943.

39 *NAC*, RG 27, v. 965, f. 18, "Riding Mountain Camp," n.d.

40 *NAC*, RG 84, v. 165, f. RM165-7, O.E. Heaslip to J. Smart, 26 October 1943; J. Smart to O.E. Heaslip, 4 November 1943.

41 *Ibid.*, O.E. Heaslip to J. Smart, 9 November 1943.

42 There was no shortage of advice as to how to get the prisoners to work harder. National Parks Director Gibson suggested that the men receive an incremental bonus depending on how much wood they cut, while the commandant at Medicine Hat recommended that the daily quota simply be increased.

43 Quoted in *NAC*, RG 24, C-5382, f. HQS 7236-34-3-9, Officer in Charge of Veterans Guard to R.C. Bull, 22 November 1943.

44 *Ibid.*, "RCMP Security Report," 20 December 1943.

45 *Ibid.*

46 *Ibid.*, R.S.W. Fordham to H.N. Streight, 10 January 1944. The camp leader used the visit of the Swiss Consul to send word to Germany that the four prisoners had deserted. L. Manuel to R. Eistermann, 11 January 1944 (translated and typed 31 January 1944).

47 *Ibid.*, "RCMP Security Report," 23 December 1943; H.N. Streight to R.H. Mann, 12 January 1944.

48 *Ibid.*, L. Manuel to Swiss Consul General, 24 February 1944.

49 *Ibid.*, 14 January 1944.

50 *Ibid.*, W.C.H. Pinkham to H.N. Streight, 21 July 1945.

51 *Ibid.*, "RCMP Security Report," 17 December 1943; Adjutant-General to District Officers Commanding Military Districts No. 10 and 13, 21 January 1944.

52 Josef Gabski interview, 11 September 1994.

53 Howard Kelly interview, 14 August 1991.

54 Stotz, "Camp 132," 109-11, 116-18. This was the largest mass hanging in Canada since the 1885 North-West Rebellion.

55 Josef Gabski interview, 11 September 1994.

56 *Ibid.*

57 *Ibid.*

58 *RMNP*, George Foerster interview, April 1985.

59 *NAC*, RG 84, v. 165, f. RM165-7, R.H. James to K.W. Bash, 23 March 1944.

60 Josef Gabski interview, 11 September 1994; Howard Kelly interview, 14 August 1991.

61 *RMNP*, Josef Gabski interview, 11 September 1991.

62 Josef Gabski interview, September 1994.

63 This phrase is taken from M. Duliani, *The City Without Women: A Chronicle of Internment Life in Canada During World War II* (Oakville 1994), translated by A. Mazza.

64 *RMNP*, George Foerster interview, April 1985; Josef Gabski interview, 11 September 1994.

65 Josef Gabski interview, September 1994.

66 *Ibid.*

67 *RMNP*, George Foerster interview, April 1985.

68 *NAC*, RG 24, C-5382, HQS 7236-34-3-9, "RCMP Security Report," 7 January 1944.

69 Dauphin *Herald and Press*, 3 February 1944. The camp medical officer had visited the Flight Training School with another prisoner who needed emergency dental treatment.

70 *NAC*, RG 24, C-5382, HQS 7236-34-3-9, "RCMP Security Report," 15 January 1944. Interviews in the Riding Mountain area in 1991 indicate that stories are still being told about the wandering ways of the prisoners. Howard Kelly interview, 14 August 1991; Tony Ewasiuk interview, 13 August 1991.

71 *Ibid.*, RG 24, P.E. Tucker to S.T. Wood, 19 February 1944; P.A.K. Kirk to H.N. Sleight, 25 February 1944.

72 *Ibid.*, R.H. James, "Report on the Traffic of Prisoners of War with Ukrainian Civilians," 21 February 1944.

73 *NAC*, RG 27, v. 965, f. 5, "Meeting of Thunder Bay District Woods Operators Employing Prisoners of War," 7 February 1944.

74 *NAC*, RG 84, v. 165, f. RM165-7, R.H. Candy, "Report on Riding Mountain Prisoner of War Camp, Manitoba," 29 February 1944.

75 *Ibid.*, O.E. Heaslip to J. Smart, 13 March 1944; J. Smart to R.A. Gibson, 20 March 1944. Heaslip estimated that there could be as many as forty thousand cords of wood from the project in local depots by October 1944.

76 *NAC*, RG 24, C-5382, f. HQS 7236-34-3-9, L. Manuel to Swiss Consul, 3 March 1944.

77 *NAC*, RG 27, v. 965, f. 5, "Meeting of Thunder Bay District Woods Operators Employing Prisoners of War," 7 February 1944.

78 *NAC*, RG 24, C-5382, f. HQS 7236-34-3-9, R.S.W. Fordham to H.N. Streight, 11 April 1944.

79 *Ibid.*, L. Manuel to Swiss Consul, 16 March 1944. Camp records indicate that the prisoner died in hospital. *NAC*, RG 27, v. 959, f. 3, "POW Payroll, Rations

and Strength Statements for the month of March 1944." Howard Kelly, on the other hand, claims that the soldier was already dead when he was retrieved from the bush. Howard Kelly interview, 14 August 1991. The circumstances surrounding Neugebauer's death eventually landed on the desk of Norman Robertson, the Canadian undersecretary of state for External Affairs; in response to a formal complaint from the Swiss Consul, Robertson demanded a report on the weather conditions that day and whether the prisoners should have been ordered to work. *NAC*, RG 24, C-5382, f. HQS 7236-34-3-9, N. Robertson to Department of National Defence, 10 May 1944. Neugebauer was buried in Riverside Cemetery, Dauphin (lot B, section 45, block 4).

80 *NAC*, RG 84, v. 165, f. RM165-7, R.H. Candy, "Report on Riding Mountain Prisoner of War Camp," 29 February 1944.

81 *NAC*, RG 24, C-5382, f. HQS 7236-34-3-9, "RCMP Report," 7 March 1944; P.H. Tucker to S.T. Wood, 13 March 1944.

82 *Ibid.*, L.W. Smith to J.L. Ralston, 10 March 1944.

83 *NAC*, RG 84, v. 165, f. RM165-7, T.A. Crerar to J.H. Mitchell, 27 March 1944.

84 *NAC*, RG 24, C-5382, f. HQS 7236-34-3-9, RCMP Report, "Escaped Prisoners from Whitewater Camp," 18 April 1944.

85 This was the second time that Lopens had been picked up away from camp. He had been found at the Marco dance in mid-February.

86 *NAC*, RG 24, C-5382, f. HQS 7236-34-3-9, RCMP Report, C. Mann to H.P. Rocke, 27 April 1944.

87 *Ibid.*, R.S.W. Fordham to H.N. Streight, 15 May 1944.

88 *Ibid.*, G. Treiber to Swiss Consul General, 12 May 1944.

89 *Ibid.*, H.N. Streight to R.S.W. Fordham, 18 May 1944.

90 *NAC*, RG 2, PC 4428, 9 June 1944.

91 Karl Karg, one of the Riding Mountain prisoners transferred to northern Ontario, drowned within a few days of his arrival in the Sioux Lookout district. A second former Riding Mountain internee, Richard Becker, also drowned while canoeing in May 1945. Carter, *Behind Canadian Barbed Wire*, 317, 321.

92 *NAC*, RG 24, C-5382, f. HQS 7236-34-3-9, R.H. James and J.H. Keane, "Report on Prisoners of War Absent from Riding Mountain Camp," 16 June 1944.

93 *NAC*, RG 84, v. 165, f. RM165-7, G. Tunstell to Dominion Forester, 29 June 1944.

94 *NAC*, RG 24, C-5382, f. HQS 7236-34-3-9, "Schwarz Diary," R.C. Bull to H.N. Sleight, 16 June 1944.

95 *Ibid.*

96 *Ibid.*, J.M. Bella to Officer Commanding D Division, RCMP, 17 July 1944.

97 *Ibid.*, T.L. Reid, "Investigation re Report of Cameras and Developing Equipment in Riding Mountain Park Labour Project," n.d.

98 Keane was subsequently criticized for failing to purchase the eyeglasses through the International Committee of the Red Cross. He was also censured for the bear cub photograph and was evidently forced to resign over

the matter when internment authorities learned about it. *Ibid.*, H.N. Streight to R.S.W. Fordham, 3 March 1945; R.O.G. Morton to Secretary, Department of National Defence, 31 March 1945.

99 *Ibid.*, R.S.W. Fordham to H.N. Streight, 5 September 1944.

100 *Ibid.*, R.A. Macfarlane to Secretary, Department of National Defence, 5 October 1944. The prisoner with the camera was one of the camp thugs identified by the legionnaires in December 1943.

101 *NAC*, RG 84, v. 165, f. RM165-7, J.H. Keane to O.E. Heaslip, 28 October 1944.

102 *NAC*, RG 27, v. 661, f. 23-5-3, R.H. Davidson to A. MacNamara, 14 February 1945.

103 *NAC*, RG 24, C-5382, f. HQS 7236-34-3-9, R.H. Davidson to H.N. Streight, 25 November 1944; A.E. Walford to Officer Commanding Military District No. 10, 28 November 1944.

104 *Ibid.*, "RCMP Security Report," 6 November 1944; J. Leopold to H.N. Streight, 3 January 1945.

105 *Ibid.*, A.E. Walford to Officer Commanding Military District No. 10, 11 December 1944.

106 *Ibid.*, Director, Criminal Investigation Branch, RCMP, to Director, Prisoners of War, 14 December 1944.

107 *Ibid.*, "RCMP Security Report," 12 January 1945.

108 *Ibid.*, "RCMP Report," 5 January 1945; "RCMP Report," 8 January 1945.

109 *Ibid.*, E. Davidson, "Report on Visit to Riding Mountain Camp, Manitoba," 15 February 1945.

110 *Ibid.*, H.N. Streight to Director of Labour Projects, 17 January 1945; F.H. Wilkes to H.N. Streight, 16 January 1945.

111 Canadian military intelligence used a programme called PHERUDA to classify German prisoners of war: *P*olitical leanings; *A*ttitude towards *H*itler; *E*ducation; *R*eligion; *U*sefulness; *D*ependability; and *A*ttitude towards war effort. PHERUDA was used in conjunction with a separate interrogation report (dealing with personal details of the man's life) to classify a prisoner as black, grey, or white. Kelly, "Intelligence and Counter-Intelligence," 293.

112 *NAC*, RG 24, C-5382, f. HQS 7236-34-3-9, Davidson, "Report on Visit to Riding Mountain Camp, Manitoba," 15 February 1945. Davidson took issue with the recommendation in the intelligence report that only seventy-one men could be considered for private employment; he believed that the number of "white" Nazis was actually much higher. *NAC*, RG 27, v. 661, f. 23-5-3, R.H. Davidson to A. MacNamara, 15 March 1945.

113 *Ibid.*, Davidson to MacNamara, 14 April 1945.

114 The Parks Bureau was actually looking into the possibility of securing fifty German prisoners of war for Jasper National Park in June 1944, but decided against the idea when Tunstell's negative report on the Riding Mountain operation was received. *NAC*, RG 84, v. 147, f. J165-7, J. Smart to R.A. Gibson, 5 July 1944.

115 *Ibid.*, v. 165, f. RM165-7, J. Smart to O.E. Heaslip, 5 April 1945.

116 Reviewing the various work projects in mid-June 1945, Director Davidson

reported, "An interesting point, which is not for publication, is the number of 'accidental deaths' at the various lumber projects has increased markedly since V-Day and leads one to believe that some well earned justice is being given to the members of the Gestapo, who have so long ruled the various internment camps in the country. . . . However, this does not concern us and apparently is giving no one any great concern." *NAC*, RG 27, v. 661, f. 23–5–6–1, R.H. Davidson to A. MacNamara, 16 June 1945.

117 *Ibid.*, v. 965, f. 21, C.R. McCord to A.H. Brown, 27 June 1945.

118 *NAC*, RG 84, v. 165, f. RM165–7, O.E. Heaslip to J. Smart, 4 September 1945; J. Smart to R.A. Gibson, 29 November 1945.

Epilogue (pages 251–52)

1 Canada, House of Commons, *Debates*, 29 June 1984, 5308.

2 Canada, *Annual Report of the Department of the Interior*, 1934, pt. iii, "National Parks of Canada," 82.